THEATRES OF ACHIEVEMENT

John Higgins
Adrian Eggleston

Best regards,
John Higgins

Adrian Eggleston .

April 2006

**ENTERTAINMENT
TECHNOLOGY PRESS**

Historical Series

This book is dedicated to the late Betty Johnson

cover image: Leeds Grand Theatre and Opera House

THEATRES OF ACHIEVEMENT

John Higgins

Original illustrations by the Author

Photography by Adrian Eggleston

Entertainment Technology Press

Theatres of Achievement

© John Higgins
Original illustrations by the Author

© Photography by Adrian Eggleston

First edition Published March 2006 by
Entertainment Technology Press Ltd
The Studio, High Green, Great Shelford, Cambridge CB2 5EG
Internet: www.etnow.com

ISBN 1 904031 37 4

A title within the
Entertainment Technology Press Historical Series
Series editor: John Offord

CONTENTS

Some of the theatres above fall into more than one category, but have been classified as shown either from their current perspective, or to demonstrate a particular theme for the purposes of this book.

ACKNOWLEDGEMENTS

A debt of gratitude is owed to so many people such that without their help, interest and assistance this project would not have reached its happy fruition. It is impossible to individually name them all but I hope that, at least in spirit, my 'big thank you' will reach everyone involved.

Overwhelming thanks are extended to all of the theatre managements, their administrators and technicians, who have allowed and arranged for our visits, opened theatres, switched on lights, raised and lowered house curtains, etc. and provided, in many cases, an absolute wealth of information about their venues. This project would have been impossible without their co-operation, knowledge and invaluable help.

To Adrian Eggleston who has photographed the subjects of this book so superbly, taking great pains to achieve all of the shots that I requested: not just for his technical prowess but also for his faithful devotion and dedication to duty – not least, for example, for leaving his bed at 3am on more than one occasion to arrive at some far-flung stage door by the following 9.30am!

Special thanks are extended to John Offord and his partner Ken Sewell of Entertainment Technology Press Ltd. for taking on the risk of such ambitious project from a first-time author, and to Jackie Staines the technical editor who has dealt with all of its complexities so superbly ... for their faith in me and their invaluable guidance.

To the many libraries, reference, information and local studies services who have arranged for, and looked after me on my visits, and provided a colossal amount of information; in particular to the Wakefield Libraries & Information Services and Music and Drama Library at Balne Lane, Wakefield and the Barnsley MBC Central Library ... I seem never to have been away from their doorsteps!

To my wife, Carol, for her support, and for her patience endured during the endless hours that I dedicated to this project.

To the *Yorkshire Post*, Sheffield Newspapers Ltd., and *Blackpool Gazette* for permission to quote from various newspaper reports relating to the theatres in Leeds, Sheffield and Blackpool respectively.

To Janet and Steve Anderson of Piglet Printers, Barnsley, for sample illustration reproductions and electronic mail and IT processing assistance.

John Higgins, 2005

Symbolic ... Some Theatres of Achievement.

8 Theatres of Achievement

INTRODUCTION

When I was ten, something happened one January Saturday afternoon that was to have an affect upon the rest of my life. I was taken to the pantomime! The pantomime was *Little Miss Muffet* starring Charlie Cairoli – the famous circus-clown act of the day, and the venue was the Sheffield Empire Palace Theatre (known locally simply as 'the Empire').

Little did I realise at the time (the late 'fifties) – indeed, not until many years later – how very fortunate I was that my first visit to a professional theatre should have coincided with one which was created by one of the most successful and prolific theatre builders of all time, Frank Matcham. Fortunate, because that visit set a spark alive within me that was to glow so strongly that it has never since been extinguished, and my consequent association with theatre over the years, in its varying forms, has provided me with an enormous amount of pleasure. Although I remember vividly the 'fare' that was on offer that day – a wonderful children's pantomime incorporating all of the most important ingredients – I also remember that it was presented in absolutely brilliant surroundings: the sumptuous, warm, colourful riot of Matcham architecture and decoration at its best complementing the afternoon's entertainment to a T.

The following year was to prove equally fortunate, with another visit to the pantomime. This time, the same city – but a different theatre – the Sheffield Lyceum! The pantomime was *Goldilocks and the Three Bears* with comedian Peter Butterworth as dame and vocalist Ronnie Carroll, and again how very fortunate I was that my second visit to a professional theatre should occur in one created by another of the 'kings' of the Victorian theatre building age, W. G. R. Sprague. He, like Matcham, had the knack of creating the perfect setting for performance, not only achieving good sight-lines and acoustics, but executing with a flair and ingenuity so great that his audiences could not fail to be transported into a world of make-believe, encompassed by his ebullient and astonishing grandeur, with its ubiquitous gilt plaster-work, fine marbles and handsome draperies.

My third stroke of theatrical fortune as a child was that my annual weekly holidays tended to take place in Blackpool in Lancashire which, in the 'fifties, had many fine theatres – and we used to sample them all! The one that particularly made my childhood initiation complete was, again, designed by Frank Matcham – the Blackpool Grand – although at the time I could obviously have no idea that it was born of the very same creator as my Sheffield Empire Palace. Refurbished, it remains today as one of his finest achievements. In those days, during the summer seasons, the Grand would present a comedy play, often with the radio or television stars in vogue taking the leading parts. These were perfectly complemented by the uninhibited, but elegant, Matcham surroundings in turquoise, cream and old gold.

And so my childhood 'fortunes' were concluded – setting me a standard and expectation for life: whether the spark would have ever been ignited had my early theatrical experiences taken place in surroundings of any lesser grandeur than a Matcham or a Sprague I do not know. As it is, they led to a great appreciation of superlative theatrical architecture; architecture where the creators had "got it exactly right!" – where they had succeeded admirably in creating the perfect mood for the show; where they had succeeded admirably in stirring some spirit within!

The book that follows is therefore a celebration of the wealth and excellence of the theatrical venues that exist in our country today – which are able to stand shoulder to shoulder alongside the most famous theatres anywhere in the world. It features a selection of the most beautiful, historical, new or unusual by telling their story and show-casing their remarkable interiors, while illustrating how they may have shaped the development of theatre in Britain, generally.

They are, in my opinion, all achievers! Achievers in a variety of ways – some for their life-work contribution in a particular field; some for their technical prowess (both today and prior to the invention of modern technology); some for surviving the odds in an ephemeral world of make-believe; all architecturally; all for providing countless hours of pleasure to countless numbers of people.

The content is purposely restricted to examples situated in the regions – not because I view those to be found in the capital (which have, anyway, always received a good literary airing) to be any less significant but, rather, in order to highlight the many differing aspects of British theatrical activity.

And so from my early and continuing experiences began to spring curious observations and questions, in considering exactly how some of these wonderful 'palaces of delight' had come to be. Why, for example, did I one day hear someone refer to the upper-most balcony as the 'gods'? Why, when I eventually had my first taste of the 'gods', did I have to wind my way up a long and inferior stone stairwell via a separate entrance in a nearby back yard

– as opposed to the expected customary grand staircase in the main foyer – to find that my 'seat' was, in fact, not a 'seat' at all, but a backless leather bench? Why, on occasions, did I find that a most opulent and extravagant auditorium was not matched by an equally impressive street frontage – the facades in many cases being squashed tightly between neighbouring buildings? Why, when I began to study the situation of theatre in this country, did I discover that a large proportion of them were called 'Theatre Royal'?

There are, of course, reasons for all of these contemplations, and many more which come to mind. These things did not happen by chance – they were the result of the political, social and economic pressures prevailing at the time – and to find the answers we must look into history, not just of theatres in particular, but of life generally.

The first theatres were those built by the Greeks and then the Romans, and normally consisted of rows of seats set in an arc, raised one above the other opposite a stage where the acting would take place, behind which evolved simple scenery (the 'skene') and in front of which a large circular, later to become semi-circular, area (the 'orchestra' - place for dance) where the chorus would perform. The 'fare' that was presented sprang to a great extent from religion – and was performed at times of momentous festivals. Religion, in fact, was to have an important influence upon the life and development of the theatre in one way or another from these Greek times almost to the present day, sometimes utilising it in a didactic way, on other occasions shunning it as wicked, blasphemous or sinful, and curtailing theatrical activity altogether.

When the Roman Empire began to take precedence the 'fare' was, in many respects, reproduced from that formerly given by the Greeks, though sometimes not of the same calibre, if not without an increased spectacle, and with an emphasis on large-scale visual productions (such as chariot races and the like), and moving away from religion towards more popular entertainment. In Britain, open to the public and well worth a visit, Roman theatrical remains can still be seen at St Albans in Hertfordshire.

Following the collapse of the Roman Empire when theatres generally were to disappear acting, although perhaps continuing unofficially, was not to see a revival until around the 10th century, when much of the content was of a religious nature, and 'miracle' and 'mystery' cycles and 'morality' plays evolved. During the development process the presentations eventually moved out of the churches to the churchyards; then to market places, and to pageants – covered wagons which could be trundled around the towns. Plays were also given in inns where spectators could gather in the courtyards around three sides of a raised stage and it was this format, not unlike the bull and bear-bating pits which featured at the time, that would eventually be transposed into the early purpose-built theatres, the first of which was opened in England in 1576.

It should be noted that the subject matter of drama was not entirely confined to religious topics and, additionally, that the Royal Court and the nobility in their manor houses were also partial to a spot of entertainment, presenting plays, interludes and masques with some extravagance.

In 1642, however, the Puritan government, which did not like what it was seeing, closed down all theatres (by Act of Parliament) and there was a total ban on all productions for a period of eighteen years. Drama did continue unofficially – because the people obviously wanted it – and after 1660 when the monarchy was restored under the reign of Charles II, drama continued. What also was to continue, and which would have a significant effect upon all theatrical presentation from that day to this – and consequently upon theatrical building – was the control: the various rules, regulations, laws and acts of parliament. Some of these are considered below and may now seem curious to us.

When Charles II came to the throne he permitted only two companies in all of the county to open theatres to present straight drama. The Theatre Licensing Act 1737 endorsed this situation and the two theatres in question – (by now) Drury Lane and Covent Garden – both in London and known as the 'Patent Houses' as they operated by Royal Charter after being granted Letters Patent, were thus to hold a monopoly over all other managements.

Several circumstances were to emerge as a result. Where the other, 'minor' theatres wished to present drama, they could only do so by resorting to its disguise. A common ruse (others are discussed later) was to accompany it with music (a format to become known as *burletta*). At the outset, the music was much more prominent than later on since its inclusion gradually diminished, but it was one way of getting around the law. They were able to present other forms of entertainment such as music and dance and in the end the patent theatres might even have considered them to have been a threat as their increasingly spectacular productions became so popular. Another purpose of the 1737 Act was to implement censorship upon the works performed (a regulation that would last until its abolition in 1968!).

As the 18th century progressed, however, licences were eventually granted to theatre companies in other parts of the country (see examples of the 'Royals' in parts 1 and 2) and the number of theatres in the provinces grew – possibly aided by the 1788 Act which allowed JPs outside the metropolis to license theatrical interests – and following the turn of the century a 'Theatre Royal' could be found in every principal municipality.

Another form of entertainment growing in popularity alongside the more 'dramatic' fare was the 'music hall'. Originally starting out as 'turns' and concerts presented in the taverns, eventually many of the establishments were to provide separate halls specifically for the purpose of giving performances. Some of the entertainment was not unlike that on offer at the 'minor' theatres, with a mixture of music and drama and dance, but much of it was of a bawdier nature, attracting the lower classes, and one of the overriding features was the serving of food and alcoholic beverage.

Then came one of the most notable and important changes – eventually brought about by the passing of the Theatre Regulation Act 1843 – which was to affect the world of theatrical presentation and administration to a very great extent. As we have seen, up to now the 'minors' were not allowed to present straight drama. The 1843 Act changed all that and gave them the freedom to do so – alongside the 'majors' – launching many long awaited opportunities although, curiously, without any instantaneous impact. It did not allow, however, the sale and consumption of food or drink during the performance (when a music hall licence would be required) and it also, paradoxically, limited the patent houses to straight drama.

When thinking about music hall, the picture conjured up in the minds of most people is that of a boisterous audience (generally comprising the lower classes) in a smoke-filled room, possibly eating and drinking, dressed in Victorian garb, observing equally rumbustious artistes, with the whole scene presided over by a chairman of no less enthusiasm. The picture is probably not very far from the truth, and such music hall, with roots put down fairly early in the nineteenth century, was at its height of popularity from its last couple of decades through to the early decades of the twentieth. By now, though, the Metropolis Management & Building Acts Amendment Act of 1878 had brought about significant changes and begun to 'clean up the act' because it insisted upon certain standards of safety etc., so that many of the more dubious establishments simply fell by the wayside, to be replaced by buildings of ever increasing grandeur.

The number of music halls in the country at this time was growing quickly: initially mostly owned privately, later on (after 1862) more often by limited liability companies, some of the proprietors, combines and syndicates acquiring further halls and so establishing chains, or circuits. A few of the most notable names include Charles Thornton, whose 'City Varieties' (1865) in Leeds is the oldest survivor (see the fine example in part 3); Tom Barrasford and his Hippodromes (see Birmingham chapter); Richard Thornton (see Sunderland Empire chapter); Sir Oswald Stoll of London Coliseum fame (see Bristol Hippodrome chapter); and Sir Edward Moss of Moss' Empires fame. The paths of the latter three gentlemen would also eventually meet via the greatest tour of them all (that of Moss' Empires) and Frank Matcham, incidentally, was engaged to execute much of their building.

As music hall continued to become more respectable, with shows progressively lavish, audience expectation constantly advancing, and with competition from rival managements, then the buildings in which it was housed had likewise to meet new heights of impressiveness. This resulted in a great number of superbly designed music halls and variety houses, some of them extravagantly and opulently contrived – ornate and eclectic in style, drawing upon every imaginable scenario although chiefly theatrical – and simply the absolute word in luxury and appointment. Sadly many are no longer with us, but fortunately there are still a number of notable examples which have survived and are flourishing today, and a selection of them of them is included in later chapters. As the twentieth century moved on the traditional, early style, of music hall developed into what became known as variety, and this eventually completely lost popularity in the late 1950s.

So how did the buildings which housed the 'theatre' – the playhouses – progress from the time of Charles II? One notable point is that they had by now moved completely inside, so that the entire proceedings were under cover and free from the vicissitudes of the elements. Certain features were prominent above all others – there was a deep forestage where most of the acting occurred and, upon either side, were proscenium doors where the actors would make their entrances and exits. At the back was the scenic stage where all of the scenery was placed (much of it in the form of wings and shutters that could slide in and out in grooves) and it would have been rather unusual to have found actors 'playing' in this area, all of the action happening in front. As far as the audience was concerned, they were accommodated in the pit, galleries and boxes, with the well-to-do tenanting the boxes and being kept entirely separated from the lower classes, who occupied the galleries and pit.

Although it was considered that this type of theatre had certain advantages to its layout – for example the intimacy between actors and audiences – one of the most significant developments through the years was the gradually diminishing apron/forestage and eventual removal of the proscenium doors. This meant that the actors and scenery had now combined, to occupy the same stage, and the picture-frame stage as we know it – the proscenium – had been born.

Improved materials and expertise in building throughout the eighteen-hundreds also contributed to changes in theatrical layout, which allowed balconies to be supported upon columns so that the pit could expand beneath them, and eventually, with the introduction of the cantilever system, the total removal of any visible support. This obviously had a great impact upon sightlines but, as the new balconies which had gradually replaced the former galleries had become much deeper, larger proportions of the audience were by now to find themselves in seats further removed from the stage, and overshadowed by the overhang above.

Another changing feature was the overall shape of the auditoria, which hitherto had been rectangular and fan-shaped, and was now taking on a more rounded form, and in many cases that of a horseshoe, a fact that possibly may have aided the relationship between players and spectators, establishing a more intimate atmosphere. Gradually, also, the pit area was generally decreasing, the benches being replaced by stalls seats at the front, these being obviously more luxurious – and more costly (which pleased the managers as takings increased) – as were the seats in the dress circles that were emerging in place of the obsolete galleries.

The upper-most balconies remained one of the cheapest areas of the house and, being invariably positioned high above the heads of all others, became known colloquially as the 'gods', not least due to their close proximity with the firmament, but also with the cherubs, angelic and other heavenly embellishments which traditionally began to adorn the ceilings and upper reaches of all theatres of any decorative merit.

But 'theatre' was also improving its image and in the better areas of the house (stalls, dress circle and boxes) which by now were becoming increasingly sumptuous, it became customary for audiences to 'dress the part' – in a manner that would match their surroundings. Perhaps even the 'theatre' and its 'patrons' mutually affected each other, so that the ameliorating theatrical conditions were reflected in the presentation of the patrons, whose rising expectations further encouraged managements to make improvements in an attempt to attract more business and a better class of customers. Possibly, also, the interest shown in the theatre by Queen Victoria during her reign (1837-1901) aided the progressive improvements in its concept, for this had an effect upon how it was viewed not only by society, but also the church.

At this point in time – indeed, until well after the Second World War – class distinction formed a dominant feature of society's social make-up and it was for this reason that, as mentioned earlier, the different parts of the house were separated. The way that the divergent classes conducted themselves, thought, had differing priorities, dressed, even smelled, varied greatly, especially in the earlier decades, and so it was necessary to keep them separated in every sense of the word. Naturally, the wealth of the social class to which they belonged would dictate which parts of the house they could afford to occupy, and each area would be provided with totally separate facilities – from the entrance and the paybox, to the bars and toilets, etc. This explains why, even today, in some of the older theatres separate entrances still remain – as a remnant of a past tradition.

During the Victorian epoch, then, the entertainment business was to develop in leaps and bounds. Many changes were to take place outside the theatre which, collectively, were to have a pronounced effect upon it. Not only was the population gradually increasing, but also the industrial revolution had generated a migration of it, thus spawning large industrial regions and new cities and towns. Although conditions may have initially curtailed the working classes' leisure activities, as the century unfolded these were reformed via various factory and public health acts, leading to a reduction generally in working hours, and with better pay, an increasing accessibility to recreational pursuits. Thus, together with a flourishing national economy, a ready-made supply of prospective theatrical customers was eventually to hand.

Another very significant factor in the theatre's successful evolution was the introduction of the railways – indeed the improvement in transport-related factors generally – which obviously provided many more opportunities for patrons to visit the theatres and music halls and, together with new gas lighting in the streets and a reduction in crimes, made theatre-going altogether much easier.

And so the theatre and music hall's reaction to the situation described was to expand to meet new demands. From around the 1860s onwards, countless venues of entertainment sprang up all over the country – culminating with the most prolific building period, towards the end of the century spilling into the first decade of the new century – and producing some of the finest examples of theatrical architecture, some of which feature in later pages. Frequently they were built with a view to accommodating as many of these enthusiastic patrons as possible and so some of their seating capacities were far in excess of those that would be allowed by today's standards. It is also interesting to note that a great deal of them were situated on awkward plots between existing buildings, thus eliminating the expense associated with elaborate facades placed along busy main streets.

I have already mentioned how chains of music halls developed due to their immense popularity and that these would establish 'circuits' (some of them extremely famous, such as the 'Moss' Empires') upon which the various acts would work and travel. One final point to consider is the effect of working policy in relation to the progression of the playhouses.

The provincial theatres 'Royal', those so-called, and others that were appearing each presented regional circuit and stock companies to perform the entertainment. However, following the middle of the nineteenth century this practice was to greatly change, and one of the most significant reasons was the establishment and growth of the railways. The regional groups diminished – chiefly because it was now possible to set up touring companies, most of them coming from London and, with their greater prestige, these were more popular with the audiences. Managements also found advantages as just a couple of examples will demonstrate: on the production side they could plough resources into a specific show, come up with better standards than the locals could provide, keep it running for a longer period and even send out more than one company at once – all making for higher profits. Similarly, many theatres discovered that it was more lucrative to simply hire the place out as opposed to running their own companies, with all the expense and speculation associated with them. The result: many of the local companies were to disappear, 'pushed out' by the touring companies and a great number of the theatres became, or were purpose-built, touring houses.

We can only imagine, now, what theatre-going must have been like in these earlier times. Even when we visit one of the grand old ladies today, the atmosphere cannot resemble that at the time of building. One of the major advances, of course, has to be the lighting – no longer provided by candle-power, oil lamps or gas – and to sit, as we do, taking for granted all of the marvels of modern electricity, both from the functional front-of-house point of view to the wondrous effects produced on stage, it is hard to visualise the scene in bygone days. Several reports survive, for example, in which audience members complain about the wax from the candles dripping down onto their heads below, or spoiling the ladies' dresses. And when gas was in its infancy during the early 1800s, not only did it produce foul smelling odours which must have been extremely uncomfortable for audiences, it also put them at great risk – both from fire and from the possibility of explosion.

Imagine the smoke filled scene! Of course improvements were made as time progressed, and gas was much more successful than the former oil lamps, providing better illumination for the scenery and costumes and being a lot easier to control. It was also possible to dim the house lights during the performance – something that had not been practicable before – although it did take some time, even after the introduction of gas, for this to become the custom. Maybe it was because those who, hitherto, had gone to the theatre not only to see but also to be seen, could no longer show off their finery in the better class areas of the auditorium!

Stage houses also became very sophisticated, eventually being equipped with countless ideas for dealing with scenery. Traps cut into the floor through which the scenery (and people) could magically rise. The area above the stage developed into the present day fly tower from which scenery could be lowered and raised. The stage itself on occasions incorporated hand-winched or hydraulically controlled sections which could rise and fall so that it was possible to transport whole scenes from the cellar, or simulate ship-wrecks. In short, such contrivances became the expectation of the Victorian (see the Newcastle Journal Tyne Theatre in part 2 for a surviving 'living' example of hand-powered sub-stage machinery).

During Victoria's reign the safety aspect of working life grew in prominence – with the introduction of various factory acts, etc. Consequently, conditions in theatres on both sides of the footlights were also to improve when, eventually, greater attention began to be given to such issues as fire prevention, overcrowding and seating capacities, ventilation and sanitation, by committees and boards set up for the purpose.

But not everyone was happy with what they were seeing on the stage and by the turn into the twentieth century came moves to provide alternatives to the touring companies that currently ruled. Local companies resulted, and so developed the 'repertory movement' (a return to the old stock companies of previous times?) whose principles would provide opportunities for artistic stimulus and not simply profit. Out of a few early pioneering companies (the most notable, possibly, Miss Horniman's at the Gaiety in Manchester) came the momentum for many more. What was to become known as 'weekly rep' ensued as countless numbers of companies, much loved by their local communities, followed – all over the country – and with them the provincial theatres in which they would be housed. These ranged from converted halls to much grander establishments and as the maturing century, encompassing the many facets of change – for example, in tastes, ideas, operation and funding – progressed, the second half of it, albeit by now supporting fewer companies, brought some new and exciting enterprises. My selection, generally contained in parts 5, 6 and 7, ranges from the 'pioneers' through to esteemed newer and heterogeneous formats.

So what *of* theatre in the twentieth century? The two most significant factors to (adversely) affect its progression were the cinema from the 'twenties and television in the 'fifties. They were both to take their toll. Firstly the cinemas – people flocked to these new-found innovations in droves, initially to the silents, and then to the 'talkies'. Ironically the silents, in their infancy, had sometimes featured on 'cine-variety' bills in the music halls. But as cinema matured it became big business with glamorous film stars, unbelievable effects, and an ability to transport the cinema-goer to far away places. With it was also the emergence of a new breed of 'pleasure palace' – indeed, the 'picture palace' – and these were to spring up around the country in countless numbers with names like 'Ritz', 'Savoy', 'Regal', 'Regent', 'Gaumont', 'Electra', 'Plaza', 'Futurist' and 'Odeon'.

Many theatres would turn to films in an attempt to survive but there was also an abundance of purpose-built picture houses – some put up by the big film conglomerates to glorious effect, like nothing that had ever been seen before, and positively the last word in style, luxury and comfort. They had to meet the new expectations of a changing world, and their modernistic approach would, ironically, have some effect upon the architecture of subsequent theatre building.

How did theatre, then, survive in these times? With great difficulty, is probably the best answer. The 'fare' that was on offer largely comprised touring and weekly repertory which now may not always have seemed as glamorous or exciting as that which the film industry could provide although, curiously enough, there are many reports showing that local repertory theatres went on to do exceedingly well throughout the nineteen-forties, and into the 'fifties. However, with the advent of television – the box in the corner which, from the nineteen-fifties grew rapidly in popularity – came new opportunities for entertainment that had never before been thought of and these in their turn would adversely affect the cinema too! No longer did people have to go out on cold wet nights for their amusement and recreation – they could relax in the comfort of their own front rooms and watch a whole variety of presentations from armchair theatre to wild-life programmes, to the up-to-date news, to concerts and spectacle.

And so interest in theatre (and then cinema) declined, with the result that countless irreplaceable 'palaces of delight' were lost to the bulldozer from the late 'fifties onwards, gone forever. During such an economic climate some losses were obviously justifiable, but in an age of post-war architectural idealism many disappeared in what seemed to be a wholesale tearing-down of buildings in general. But every cloud has its silver lining – for although some very good theatres may have been unnecessarily lost, other excellent and innovative projects materialised in the decades after the Second World War (including new formats which even dispensed with the ubiquitous proscenium arch!), to which part 5 (Coventry), and the examples included in parts 6, 7 and 8, testify.

Today, at the time of writing, early in the twenty-first century, we have a mixed bag of theatrical stock ranging from a few survivors (in whole or part) from the Georgian period; substantially more from the Victorian and Edwardian era; those built during the remainder of the 1900s including the revolutionary models emerging from the post-mid-century new-build spurt; to those of more recent years, and you will find within these pages living examples from most. Much of the older stock has now been (and is being) splendidly refurbished to magnificent effect, with auditoriums sympathetically restored to that of their former glories but with modern-day comforts, and utilising materials and colours that blend perfectly with today's lighting. These auditoriums capture the original delight and mood splendidly while the 'practical' areas of many of the theatres – foyers, bars, cloakrooms and even entire backstage areas – have been completely revamped to newfangled standards. This not only provides the patron with the height of comfort and ideal conditions for viewing performances, but also allows the productions to be presented to the best possible effect. In some cases original stages have been enlarged, fly-towers heightened and all of the latest technology installed (e.g. sound and lighting, etc.), not to mention improvements in conditions for actors (new dressing rooms, etc.) and stage and administrative staff.

It is also worth noting how the philosophy of theatre management has changed since the Second World War. Where once the theatre would exist solely for, and open some half-an-hour before productions, it is not now unusual to find the buildings in use for much of the day, encouraging people to visit at times other than those of performances and thus, perhaps, cultivating habits that might stimulate greater interest in the theatre itself. Many theatres are equipped with good restaurants, bars, coffee bars and shops; provide lunchtime concerts and promotions; have exhibition spaces and art galleries, and studios where experimental theatre or small productions can take place. Educational projects also feature prominently in many managements' programmes involving creative partnerships, schools and other external agencies – not only utilising the buildings but outreaching local communities – in initiatives which extensively promote the arts and theatre-related activity. Truly a community spirit and one which will hopefully ensure yet another century of histrionic potency!

One further topic that should not go unmentioned, substantially embodied in the community and responsible for providing entertainment for well over a century, is the amateur movement. Arising out of the increasing leisure time of the late eighteen-hundreds alongside other growing recreational pursuits such as brass bands and choirs, etc., came the early operatic and dramatic societies. Often proudly representing a parent organisation such as a local church or employer, or simply their local town or city, they were to become a prominent feature of the British theatrical scene. While many have supplied live entertainment to areas of the country not fortunate enough to have their own professional theatres, others have regularly played the major professional venues to great effect, such as some of those portrayed within these pages. Their participants have, additionally, patronised British theatre avidly, and sometimes fed into the professional system where members have 'turned professional'. In 1899 NODA (the National Operatic and Dramatic Association) was formed to look after their combined interests, and is still fulfilling that valuable role today.

I began this chapter by mentioning two specific subjects – (a) pantomime, and (b) the effect of outstanding theatrical architecture, and conclude upon the same themes. Firstly, I would make the point that the Christmas pantomime – this truly British and marvellous institution – has emerged from my researches as a critical feature in the country's theatrical story. Even today it occupies a prominent position in the annual calendars of most major theatres because of its enormous popularity with the public: a popularity that has remained since it became established in the eighteenth century and widely developed, especially at Christmas, in the nineteenth. At one time it was not unusual for a production to run until Easter or longer, thus covering a high proportion of the entertainment year. Not least, therefore, the economics of many theatres owe a debt of gratitude spanning umpteen generations to this wondrous attraction.

Secondly, after speaking of my early childhood theatrical fortunes, which highlighted the brilliance of leading architects' work, I close by finishing the story. My Sheffield Empire Palace was demolished the year after that first experience and, within a few years the Sheffield Lyceum closed its doors and stood dark and decaying for many more (see part 2). However, there is a happy ending. Twenty-one years and £12 million later, the Lyceum was saved!

No doubt this is a story that can be repeated by other people in other cities who have grasped an opportunity, and have taken the initiative to save an important part of another heritage. In Sheffield I was present at a Lyceum gala reopening and, as musical director for one the city's large and leading city operatic societies which was appearing in the event, was honoured to be invited to compose and conduct the opening fanfare! To play such a wonderful venue, on such an auspicious occasion was, indeed for me, another good fortune and I couldn't help wondering, as I raised the baton towards the orchestra on that brilliant Grand Gala Opening Night, whether Mr Sprague was looking on!

Sheffield Empire Palace, 1895-1959.

1 EARLY BEGINNINGS

Britain has several very fine working examples of early theatres, some of which survive (either largely in whole, or in part) from as long ago as the eighteenth century. Here are a few of them...

- *Bristol Theatre Royal (1766)*
- *Richmond Georgian Theatre Royal (1788)*
- *Bath Theatre Royal (1805)*
- *York Theatre Royal (1765/1902)*
- *Lincoln Theatre Royal (1806/1893)*
- *Newcastle Theatre Royal (1837/1901)*
- *Northampton Royal (1884)*

Bristol Theatre Royal

As the oldest (*almost* continuously) working theatre in the country today, having opened its doors on Friday 30ᵗʰ May 1766, this Georgian gem of a provincial city theatre is aptly qualified to stand as the example with which to begin our story. Of course the years have brought with them alterations, redecorations and improvements in order to provide modern day audiences with the comforts to which they have become accustomed, not to mention reconstructed backstage facilities, but the chief area of importance – the auditorium – remains to a great extent a faithful and splendid reminder of the past.

Major alterations took place in 1972 and these allowed for the happy marriage of two adjacent buildings – the Theatre Royal and the redundant Hall of the Guild of Coopers, also of eighteenth century origin, which now provides the theatre with a splendid entrance with fine classical facade on cobbled King Street, compared with its previous meagre theatre frontage. Advantage was also taken at this time to incorporate, in the space given over by the original entrance, a small modern studio theatre (the 'New Vic'), thus forming an exciting conglomeration of buildings worthy of the important company (the Bristol Old Vic) which, since 1946, has been in occupation.

Back in the 1760s the original occupiers were the London companies, i.e. the stock companies from Drury Lane and Covent Garden, which toured here in the summer when their own venues were closed. Happily, this coincided with the popular local Hotwells season which no doubt helped to boost their trade, and the remainder of the year at Bristol would have been dark. By 1779, however, Bristol and Bath Theatres Royal had begun working in tandem, the stock company playing between the two. This proved very successful: indeed companies in other parts of the country around this time more often played *several* different locations, arranged upon a circuit, usually with the main town – containing the principal theatre – as the headquarters. Not all of the theatres would be open all of the time, either because of a lack of customers (particularly in more rural areas) or, later on, because they may only have been granted a licence to perform at certain times of the year. Generally periods of opening would coincide with other established, popular events such as a races week, assizes, or a fair which, as with the Hotwells season at Bristol, might augment the audience numbers.

So what did the audiences come to see? Bristol at this time just as elsewhere in the country came under jurisdiction of the 1737 Act and, as a 'minor' house, therefore, was forbidden from presenting straight drama, and offenders could be committed as "rogues and vagabonds". (It did not have Letters Patent!) Early performances were therefore camouflaged as being concerts at which a play and afterpiece would be presented gratis during the interval – a ploy which, just as elsewhere in the country, seemed to be their saving grace. Another trick practised by many companies was to present their plays free, but to charge for the refreshments. In 1778, however, it did achieve a Royal Licence under George III from which time it has legitimately been entitled to be called a 'Theatre Royal'! This was the second attempt to obtain a Royal Licence, and the Royal Arms can be seen at the centre-front of the upper circle today, and also on the facade in King Street.

Many famous players have trodden the boards here. The original London visitors included names such as William Powell, James Dodd, John Quick, Robert Baddely and Mrs Barry. The stock company also brought eminences in Sarah Siddons, Julia Betterton and William Charles Macready, and in the mid-nineteenth century the Theatre Royal was noted as one of England's most important training grounds – those emerging to go on to stardom including Kate and Ellen Terry, Marie Wilton (Mrs Bancroft) and Madge Robertson

(Mrs Kendal). In those days nearly all of the country's famed played here! Other notables include Jenny Lind and Henry Irving.

Now to venture into the auditorium: truly a walk into another era. The architect was local – Thomas Paty – and many similarities have been drawn with Wren's Drury Lane playhouse of 1674. Construction follows a plan provided by the carpenter at Drury Lane, although a notable difference is the fact that the Bristol house has the shape of a horseshoe. This horseshoe (as opposed to the customary rectangular or fan) was to become more prominent in theatre building, but the feature was unusual for the time and may possibly have been the first of its kind in Britain.

Today can be seen a house of four levels – but this was not always the case

Bristol Theatre Royal: Truly a remarkable achievement – that a house from such a distant era remains, so superbly, to tell us the tale today.

– in 1800 the auditorium ceiling was raised and the present gallery installed. Originally the first tier was divided entirely into dress boxes (each entitled after a renowned dramatist), the second tier forming a gallery with side boxes – later fully boxed – but of course today the house has been almost wholly opened up, to comply with modern standards and requirements. An interesting point is the fact that the eighteenth century saw ladies and gentlemen sending their servants ahead to keep places for them in the posh seats (i.e. the boxes), but as things progressed these became bookable in advance – via the *box* office!

The remainder of the house – the pit – is presently covered with comfortable stalls seating which years ago replaced the former benches, but a few wooden benches do remain up in the gallery, as a reminder of bygone days! Two of the most notable features of the period, of course, are proscenium doors and forestage and Bristol was not

Two forces meet: technologies old and new.

deprived – the original stage extending over the existing orchestra pit and in front of the present stage boxes. The original colour scheme was predominantly green and gold and the house was lit by candlelight – not forgetting that they were never dimmed for the performance! Oil was introduced around 1800, gas installed in 1820, and electricity in 1905.

Although today the stage is well equipped, with modern

In the gallery an example of original 18th century seating has been thoroughly preserved to demonstrate conditions long-gone.

fly-tower, etc. to present expectations, the major alterations in 1972 unfortunately swept away some historically important stage machinery – a fact that has not gone uncriticised.

Probably dating back to the Victorian era were below-stage contraptions such as corner traps and a grave trap and, above the gridiron, drums, barrels, spindle and rope apparatus for the raising and lowering of cloths, borders and curtains. One feature that did survive is the 'thunder run' – contained above the auditorium ceiling, this is a timber duct through which cannon-balls can be rolled, the effect producing a commotion and rumbling equal to the most violent of storms!

And so Bristol's story unfolds: in the early years doing very well but by the nineteenth century with more varied fortunes, and as that century progressed eventually came a gradual decline – albeit punctuated by moments of glory. Some of the problems of nineteenth century provincial theatres were common – such as the increasing menace of touring companies upon local stock companies. But local issues often didn't help: in Bristol a major hiccup being urban change (the area in which the Theatre Royal was situated

becoming no longer popularly residential). And with dilemmas in trade, local economy, port facilities, etc., they would all lead to lack of support, a lowering of standards, and a consequent deterioration in the condition of the theatre. Moving into the next century, through the First World War, into the Second World War, eventually in 1942 the theatre would close and become subject to auction. Fortunately the tide did finally turn. Recognising the historic importance of the Theatre Royal, the Council for the Preservation of Ancient Bristol started the ball rolling, closely followed by CEMA (the Council for the Encouragement of Music and Arts) and, subsequently the Arts Council. Their actions, together with some private individuals, led to the theatre's reopening on the 11ᵗʰ May 1943 when *She Stoops to Conquer* was presented with Dame Sybil Thorndike.

The theatre was now on a steady course and during the next ten years or so much was spent on repairs, improvements and decorations, etc. In 1946 the Bristol 'Old Vic' was formed from the 'Old Vic' in London, and the company took up residence (was this a return to the Theatre Royal's old stock days?). The Bristol 'Old Vic' enjoyed immediate success and was soon to become one of the most notable companies in the country. Its continued success – even internationally – and association with such an important building, coupled with the deplorably sub-standard staging facilities that prevailed, contributed in 1972 to the planning of a programme of major works. This would include new dressing rooms, workshops, etc. and a much larger stage and fly tower, bringing it into line with up-to-date standards.

The present policy provides Bristol audiences with repertory and visiting companies. Although many productions have transferred from Bristol to the West End, one notable show in 1954 – the musical *Salad Days* by Julian Slade and Dorothy Reynolds – went into the Vaudeville Theatre where its run of 2,329 performances broke records. Another important area is the Bristol Old Vic Theatre School, opened by Laurence Olivier in 1946, which is still preparing its students in all aspects of theatre work – acting, stage management, electrics, design, directing, sound, etc. And there is also a thriving education department. Performances, workshops and events take place in the Theatre Royal and the New Vic, while others go out directly into the community via schools, churches, village halls and other venues, etc. Notable actors to have been produced include June Barrie, Stephanie Cole, Ian Lavender, Peter O'Toole and Patricia Routledge. And in line with modern day thinking many of the spaces which today make up this marvellous complex are available for private hire – for functions ranging from conferences and meetings to weddings!

The Bristol story is really quite remarkable – considering the passage of time that has elapsed since its inauguration, and the periods where it has hung on by the skin of its teeth! – and owes its present, unique, situation to the foresight and caring of many individuals and organisations.

The seeds were originally sown in 1764 by some local business and professional men and the near £5,000 sum that was raised was made up of £50 each from 50 shareholders, £30 each from 47 shareholders, with the remainder from other shareholders and sources. The £50 contributors were allowed a complimentary viewing (not a seat) at each performance, and were allocated a silver ticket allowing right of entry.

Today the house is owned by a trust (the Theatre Royal Trustees) and leased to the Bristol Old Vic Trust Ltd. What an onerous and responsible task they have in ensuring the continuation and preservation of such an unparalleled and successful history!

The Royal Arms is prominently displayed upon the upper circle, confirming this house to be truly, a 'Theatre Royal'.

Richmond, Georgian Theatre Royal

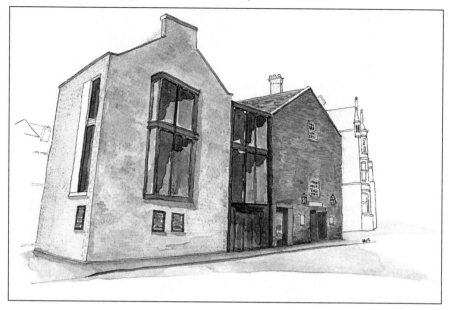

Richmond is a grand old Yorkshire town, complete with history-laden castle, museums, quaint shops and inns, all surrounding the market square atop a hillside looking down to the river – one could say that the idyllic scene is complete. Except that there is another attraction here … just around the corner, a fine example of a theatre dating back to Georgian times – actually the second oldest working theatre in England – only to be beaten by the Theatre Royal in Bristol by some twenty-two years (although the Georgian may well argue to being Britain's oldest most complete working theatre!). And an attraction it is: not only in that it *is* a working – professional and community – theatre presenting lively seasons of plays, concerts, poetry, opera, one-night stands, pantomime, talks, children's shows, and so on – it also has its own museum adjoining the very building which, with regular tours of the theatre itself, provides a truly visual and 'living' account of provincial Georgian theatrical life.

And so 'official' theatrical activity, characteristic of that occurring in the many other rural towns of this country, began in Richmond with the opening night of its Theatre Royal on 2nd September 1788. With notable restoration and refurbishment schemes taking place in the 1960s and in 2003, together with a continual programme of general improvement, the venue must now surely be at its peak in providing maximum authenticity within a framework of mod-cons and current standards and regulations.

The original part of the building which actually houses the theatre is considered to be typical of many a small-town playhouse of its time, both externally (it looks like a stone barn) and internally (the layout), and in its overall size and almost rectangular shape. Both front and back of house take up approximately equal proportions, and although a foyer has given patrons access to all parts of the house via a door at the front of the building for a number of years now, initially this was through a door in Friars Wynd to the side. Here the tiny old, single, paybox is cleverly retained for its historical significance, once considered to be cost-effective in dispensing with the need for staff covering further doors. Originally seat prices were: box 3/-; pit 2/-; gallery 1/-.

Today audience comfort has come full turn – from a computerised 'paybox', to the provision of a new extension block (thanks to the 2003 redevelopment) linked to the existing fabric via an attractive glass intersection, which provides much improved access and delightful foyer, bar and meeting space. And moving into the small auditorium, where even small portions of original artwork survive – once seating over 400, but now only about half of that – brings a truly amazing experience and step-back in time.

It has a rectangular pit, well raked and furnished with benches, surrounded by a single range of boxes to the sides and rear, with a gallery running all the way around up above which, likewise, has bench seating. Of particular interest – a feature already considered in the introductory chapter – are the proscenium doors, and each is surmounted by a 'Juliet' box. The names of prominent playwrights are inscribed above each of the other boxes – Collman, Goldsmith, Farquhar, Congreve, Otway, Shakespere [sic], Jonson, Vanburgh, Rowe, Dryden, Sheridan. The current decoration, again resulting from the latest refurbishment, and following much new research, sets out to replicate the auditorium of

Paybox, pre-computerisation!

Richmond, Georgian Theatre Royal: of special mention are the period features: a sky-painted ceiling, candlelight, proscenium doors and a deep forestage and, just visible to the wing on the right of the picture, an example of the groove method of dealing with scenery.

A view from the posh seats, the boxes where the gentry would have paraded, features period lighting, proscenium doors and forestage. The typical period scenery comprising wings and borders, etc. is a reproduction by artist Peter Crombie.

1816 and of tremendous value towards achieving this are the new lighting candelabras and chandeliers with their simulated flickering candles. In 1816 these were never dimmed during a performance – imagine the scene with a full house of four hundred: the elite of the town in the boxes, the exuberant lower classes in the pit and gallery in full flow, the actors entering and exiting through the doors onto the forestage, and the intimacy of this small house stimulating the whole exciting atmosphere!

Under the stage, towards the rear, can be found two dressing rooms: nowadays equipped with large mirrors and, of course, electric light bulbs, and sporting traditional open fireplaces, and steps leading up to the stage. The front area contains the machine room where traps have recently been reinstated so that *dramatis personae* can once again rise and fall through the stage in full theatrical fashion. Another interesting mechanism is the hand-winched footlights contrivance which could help to lighten or darken a stage by hauling the whole set of lamps upwards or downwards through an opening in the stage – it also assisted in the maintenance of the lamps – as required.

The theatre was built by an actor-manager called Samuel Butler, who in 1788 had written to the Mayor and Corporation of Richmond that he "wished to accommodate the town and county in a more commodious manner and he will with their approval and assistance erect a proper theatre". The museum contains some of Butler's original letters of application for licences. It was also in 1788 that the Act was passed which now allowed local magistrates to license theatrical activities outside of London – and this encouraged and stimulated theatrical building in local provincial towns. An abundance of these, as in Richmond, became known as 'Theatre Royal' but not having been granted Royal Patents they were not Theatres Royal at all, therefore acquiring their names by somewhat false pretences! However, this burgeoning of new

Dressing room showing open fireplace and steps leading up to stage.

'Theatres Royal' in many of the towns of importance put theatrical concerns on a more stable footing, gradually making the previously adapted inns and barns redundant for such purposes.

From early on some of the towns in a locality would become theatrically linked (even though many, initially, did not have a purpose-built playhouse), and thus circuits were formed – often bearing the name of its most important town or the county, or name of the company. Richmond was on a circuit and this included Ripon (1792), Harrogate (1788), Kendal (1789), Northallerton (1800), Beverley (1805), Ulverston and Whitby. Samuel Butler built theatres in all of these but Richmond is the only survivor. Theatrical 'circuit' companies would therefore tour these circuits, sometimes staying in a town for several months. Towns, however, would by no means have non-stop theatre – the company being resident on only a number of occasions throughout a year, the frequency depending upon the size of the town with calls often coinciding with local events, such as fairs and race-weeks, etc.

Samuel Butler died in 1812 (aged 62) and his family – who were part of the company – continued to run it and the theatre until 1830, by which time there had been apparently a decline in popularity, a loss of some of the towns from the circuit and, finally, the expiration of their lease. (It is generally accepted that between about 1820 and 1860 a lull in theatrical interest was prevalent throughout the country, and this is mentioned more fully in other chapters.) There were no further performances after 1848 but in its quite brief history the Theatre Royal could boast appearances by some of the most accomplished and acclaimed actors of the day, notably Edmund Kean and Macready.

Now was to follow a span of approximately one hundred inglorious years – when the building was adapted to other uses – prior to its amazing reawakening! Its pit was boarded over allowing not only for the storage below

Below the front of the stage, these footlights are ready to be winched into place.

of grain, furniture and wine, with usage of the upper parts as an auction room, but also with the passage of time for the lower reaches, or their purposes, to become completely forgotten about! Then in the 1930s a renewal of interest – from a local schoolteacher – sparked off further interests, research and realisation of the building's worth and prominence. Indeed in 1943 came the revival of the theatre – albeit without refurbishment, and upon the existing false floor – when the 850th anniversary of the enfranchisement of the borough of Richmond was celebrated. Eventually, however, the lower reaches (wine cellars!) were rediscovered, the importance of the building realised, and in 1960 a Trust formed with a programme of restoration and refurbishment. As usual in these cases a small number of people were prominent in orchestrating this marvellous 'renaissance' and, together with the many more who have since contributed towards its continued growth and amazing development, in making it what it has become today, they should be applauded.

A wealth of information can be gleaned from this 'living' theatre – not least aided by its excellent conducted tours and museum, which contains many original items. Its collection includes the usual letters, maps, engravings and photographs etc. that one would expect from a museum, in addition to special items, such as a brass snuff box which actually belonged to Edmund Kean, and autographs of royalty who have visited the theatre/museum. Of particular interest is the oldest (early 19th century) complete set of painted scenery surviving in Great Britain, and there are many displays, including working and movable examples of Georgian scenery, and costumes from the Georgian period which visitors may actually try on. Naturally, original handbills and playbills abound.

The grand reopening as a theatre, with a gala performance, was in 1963 and the museum opened in 1979. Since that time many famous and eminent people have trodden its boards, as they still continue to do. A further grand reopening was held in 2003 to mark the latest, £1.5 million, redevelopment and refurbishment which is truly inspirational: maximising the theatre-going experience and opportunity to gaze into the authentic theatrical past, while providing all of the expected modern-day surround amenities such as facilities for conferences, private parties, catering, gift-shop, etc., and even weddings. Moreover, the Georgian has also recently welcomed its new Royal Patrons TRHs The Prince of Wales and The Duchess of Cornwall.

A visit to this award-winning theatre and/or museum is a must! – and will provide far more information than has been possible to include in the space of the single chapter available here.

Bath Theatre Royal

One of the most significant dates in the history of Bath's theatrical activities occurred in 1768 when its Orchard Street theatre was successful in acquiring a Royal Patent. This was especially notable as it was the first provincial house in the country to achieve such status, the only others in the whole of the land at that time being the London venues of Drury Lane and Covent Garden (and, in the summer months only, the Haymarket). It was a great feather in the cap for both the city and the theatre or, rather, the Theatre *Royal* as it was now legitimately entitled to be called, which a continuing success would bear out. A success that would eventually lead to the building of a more prestigious Theatre Royal in Beaufort Square, opening on the present site on the 12th October 1805, with a performance of Shakespeare's *King Richard III*, sporting "entire new Scenery, Machinery, and other Decorations".

By this time Bath seems to have already accommodated its fair share of theatricals for there is talk of miracle plays in the fourteenth century, then evidence later of strolling players and the use of inn-yards and public houses for performances, and from the mid-1620s, the Guildhall. But when the city became spa-conscious later on in the seventeenth century, increasingly attracting fashionable visitors, the impetus came for a more permanent solution in a purpose-built house. This first arrived in 1705, lasting until 1738 when it was demolished, and performances took place at Simpson's Rooms; there was also The New Theatre from 1723 until that, likewise, was reduced to rubble in 1751. But all these ventures are said to have been less than adequate in their objectives. In 1750, however, this would be resolved with the opening of the Orchard Street venue!

The brain-child of John Hippisley who, from 1729 already had experience in entertaining the influx of high-class summer spa visitors to Bristol's Hotwells, with his little theatre there, Orchard Street opened its doors on the 27th October 1750 with Shakespeare's *Henry IV - part II*. Sadly, Mr Hippisley, however, was not in that first-night audience, having unfortunately died shortly after inaugurating the venture, which was then swiftly carried forth by one John Palmer, a successful brewer and chandler. Funding was achieved via subscriptions and shares – and a silver ticket (similar to that described in the previous chapter at Bristol) would entitle subscribers to view performances (except on benefit nights) free. Admission prices were: boxes 3/-; pit 2/-; 1st gallery 1/6; upper gallery 1/- – quite expensive!

John Palmer had a very enterprising son of the same name, also to become involved in the theatre and ultimately succeeding to the lease, and they worked hard to promote its success. Not least of their achievements was the aforementioned acquisition of the first provincial Royal Patent, and in the years that followed developed a very healthy reputation on both sides of the footlights. The acting was of the highest standard, not only attracting London 'stars' but also, indeed, nurturing new ones and, with continual improvements to the house, audiences eventually flocked to see them. One of the most famous was Sarah Siddons, and the popularity of Bath with the London managements was also reciprocated in the latest of the London products playing Bath not long afterwards.

In 1779 Palmer had, additionally, taken on the lease at the Bristol Theatre Royal and so from then on the company would play the two houses – on differing nights of the week, or to suit a particular round of local social activities when potential customers were at a premium. This amalgamation also led to lower costs in production, when some of the boosted funds were then spent on stage, thus further enhancing quality. (The association lasted until 1817 with Bath taking the title role, although in subsequent collaboration it was Bristol that would assume the lead.)

Nothing succeeds like success and by the early years of the new century the auditorium of the Orchard Street venue was proving too small for its customers who – both visitors to the city and locals alike – were patronising it wholeheartedly. And what with the fashionable areas of the city migrating to other quarters, a plan was hatched to build a new 'state-of-the-art' theatre – the chosen site being the present one, in Beaufort Square. The plans were drawn up by George Dance the younger, an architect of note for his many contributions to the architectural landscape of the country – including the façade of the London Guildhall – together with John Palmer who, by now, had become the City Architect.

I shall not attempt to describe the resultant theatre, which opened in October 1805, since it unfortunately burned to the ground on Good Friday 1862. Suffice to say that it was quickly replaced upon the existing site – much of the shell of the old building being retained in the new – indeed one remaining feature that can still be seen today is Dance's original grand frontage to Beaufort Square, although the entrance was moved to Sawclose during the rebuild.

Bath Theatre Royal: a first from the architect Charles John Phipps, who would go on to make his name in the world of theatre design.

The architect for the new theatre was chosen from the judging of six candidates whose designs were entered into a competition. The winner, notably with his first theatre design, was Charles John Phipps, about whom you will hear much in following chapters. A limited company was formed with capital raised from shares and the new 'Theatre Royal' (the present) opened to ovation on the 3rd March 1863 with a tremendously sumptuous *A Midsummer Night's Dream* – the cast including a sixteen year old Ellen Terry! Phipps' splendid auditorium has been described as "richly decorated" and structurally is more or less what you can see today. But the next two decades did not reflect these immediate glories.

Indeed, the path had been a stony one for some forty years – resulting from local matters, such as the fading of the city's glamour as a fashionable watering hole and, perhaps, frequent changes in management – against a background of national issues adversely affecting the histrionics generally. These included controversies ranging from simple changes in social habits, such as the tendency for later dining which then conflicted with customary performance times, the effects of the industrial revolution, the ever present religious attitudes purporting the evils of drama, to competition from rival entertainments (circus, menagerie, musical, etc.).

And although the early years at Bath and Bristol had undoubtedly been enhanced by the interest of the London players – who saw the circuit as an extremely fashionable and important extension to their London engagements – this situation would eventually backfire upon the provincial management as audiences were to become more discriminatory. Even nationwide they were beginning to support the London product, often spurning the work of local stock companies. Who could blame them? Their long runs permitted more polished performances and scenery and costumes were much grander than that of most stock companies who had to haul out tired material play after play to fit a wide range of productions.

The London 'star' – who could command higher payment also came at a price to local economies, and as the transport revolution furthered touring possibilities, the situation would lead to the eventual demise of the stock company altogether. A good contemporary description of the day concerning a touring company heading for the provinces was given by one of Henry Irving's biographers, Percy Fitzgerald, who sets the scene: "A huge theatrical train containing one of the travelling companies with all their baggage, comes up and thunders through. Here is the Pullman car in which the performers are seen playing cards, chatting or lunching. They have their pets with them, parrots, dogs, etc. It suggests luxury and prosperity, but this ease is dearly purchased".

Not until the last fifteen years of the century did the situation begin to turn around at Bath. By now the product on offer was changing – the ubiquitous farce and melodrama being overtaken by a new wave of writing – satisfying the more modern demands for realism. And Britain generally had moved into a new age, with an increasing optimism stemming from at least as far back as the Great Exhibition of 1851, accompanied by great headways in prosperity, leisure-time, mobility, and culture. Better standards came – and better audiences – and a golden era for the theatres.

And at the Theatre Royal the early new century had its notable events. In 1902 the Royal Patent, up for renewal, was granted only after the completion of substantial safety-related works (e.g. upgrade of exits, new asbestos fire-curtain etc.), and the opportunity was taken to improve the house generally with the installation of electricity, hot water radiators, etc., together with redecoration and refurbishment. Thus the theatre, with its new safety aspects

Bath Theatre Royal: a sumptuous foyer, leading to delights beyond, initially sets the scene.

and aesthetics, must surely have been one of the finest in the country. In 1905 came the Theatre Royal's centenary – plus the bi-centenary of Bath's first theatre. Henry Irving – the master of melodrama – also made his farewell appearance, his first in Bath having been in 1867.

Now a word about the players and productions. I have not yet even mentioned those prominent in the very early days: John Henderson, Sarah Siddons, Robert William Elliston, John Philip Kemble, William Charles Macready and Edmund Kean are among them. The twentieth century went on to satisfy the great demand for musical comedy – its popularity continuing from the 'nineties, as the round of *Maids of the Mountains, Quaker Girls and Belles of New York* and other pieces of the time gathered momentum. And there was the ever-present Gilbert and Sullivan contribution, often from D'Oyly Carte, some grand opera and even ballet – indeed the stage was graced by Anna Pavlova in 1920. Drama still featured prominently – the famous Frank Benson

Shakespearean Company played upon several occasions, now interspersed with more modern plays from newer authors such as Oscar Wilde and George Bernard Shaw through to Noel Coward and Agatha Christie. A sprinkling of famous names would include Sarah Bernhardt, Mrs Patrick Campbell, Dame Irene Vanbrugh, Sybil Thorndike, Donald Wolfit and John Gielgud. And pantomime often saved the day!

Drawing even closer to modern times, the roll of honour is equally distinguished. The Theatre Royal can boast more pre-West End productions than practically any other theatre, and still features the best players and companies available. Regular visitors include the Royal National Theatre, the Royal Shakespeare Company, the Northern Ballet Theatre and the Carl Rosa Company and top stars on a name-dropping list would include (at random) Charlton Heston, Anthony Quayle, Honor Blackman, Joan Collins, Paul Schofield, Anthony Hopkins, Steven Berkoff, Glenda Jackson, Peter O'Toole, Donald Sinden, Felicity Kendal, Derek Jacobi, Julie Walters, Tim Piggott-Smith, Maureen Lipman, Stephanie Cole, Wendy Craig, Josephine Tewson, Frank Middlemass, Anton Rogers, Alan Bates, Frank Finlay, Derek Nimmo, Bella Emberg, Postman Pat, The Grumbleweeds, Little and Large, Cannon and Ball, Tom Conti, Adam Faith, Rik Mayall, Lesley Joseph, Una Stubbs, Penelope Keith, Nicholas Lyndhurst, and David Tennant.

Picking up the story by mid-twentieth century is one that can be repeated by most theatres following the effects of the onslaught of cinema and television – resulting in poor audience attendances and consequential financial worries, despite some enterprising presentations. There were several changes in ownership and many endeavours to build success, and in 1974 although the house underwent a splendid and much needed refurbishment, difficulties still persisted. In 1979, however, there was a turning point.

The theatre was purchased by a charitable trust with non-profit making motives/principles and a second non-profit making trust would then run it. Thus the regeneration wheels were put into motion: appeals were launched, grants and subscriptions and generous support received, funds raised, and collaborations secured – most notably that with the National Theatre when, in September 1980 Sir Peter Hall, its director, announced that Bath would become the National base for middle-scale productions!

One of the most interesting aspects, of course, has to be the theatre itself – which closed in 1981 for its makeover. Firstly came very urgent structural work to the backstage foundations, which had been deemed to be unsafe, and this permitted the installation of a higher and technically modern fly tower. Other backstage improvements were then made, including those which brought up the requirements and facilities to modern day standards. The auditorium is delightful – remember it was Phipps' first theatrical commission – and retaining much of the former Georgian

Bath Theatre Royal: The Ustinov Studio.

influence is extremely elegant, and today's decoration predominantly in a warm crimson and gold is superb. The gorgeous velvet house curtain was bestowed by the widow of Sir Charles Chaplin, and bears his initials. Externally the George Dance elevation was in need of attention and was suitably revived. It is so commendable that all of these restoration goodies were able to take place – even though throughout, the venture was dogged by continual financial pressures. It should be recognised that a great number of people and organisations worked hard and gave generously to ensure that this remarkable theatre was saved for future generations.

The completion of this wonderful restoration and renaissance was suitably marked by a gala performance before a packed house on 30th November 1982 and, indeed, with royalty – HRH The Princess Margaret, Countess of Snowdon – in attendance. The play? Well, repeating history, the same which opened the present building in March 1863 – *A Midsummer Night's Dream.*

Today the theatre not only remains as a charming reminder of a colourful history but also continues its life work in a modern society. Not only does it include the Ustinov Studio – a small modern space ideal for smaller shows and workshops – the theatre added a new house in October 2005 – the Egg – aimed specifically at young people, in an adjacent Grade II Heritage listed building. Additionally, the Theatre Royal often hosts special events, which extend above and beyond normal performance times, and incorporates a restaurant, a bar, a pub, and suites ideally suited to private entertaining. Hopefully the Theatre Royal is on course for a long and happy future and I am sure that its early pioneers would be proud!

York Theatre Royal

Within its city walls glorious York contains a cornucopia of historic building, some of which dates back almost 2000 years, and its medieval flavour can still be tasted by walking amongst its hotchpotch of streets, squares, religious establishments, inns and shops. In theatrical terms it is no less blessed, for the presence of a permanent theatre was recorded as long ago as 1734 and, indeed, the people of York have been treated to their entertainment continuously from the *same site* (that of the present Theatre Royal) since 1744. Additionally, rival entertainment was provided from 1902 when the Grand Opera House opened in New Clifford Street, and although that has not gone uninterrupted, this venue remains today as York's other significant theatrical house.

In fact, the Grand Opera House was partly responsible for the major building works that created the present stage and auditorium of the Theatre Royal which at the time – (Grand Reopening 24 February 1902) – was felt necessary in order that the Royal could adequately respond to the huge popularity expected of the New Clifford Street venture. The work was undertaken by architect Frank Tugwell of Scarborough and, basically, took the house into the twentieth century.

In addition to safety measures it included, in particular, the comfort of the audience – remember, at this time their expectations were ever advancing – and swept away unsightly pillars, now redundant in the light of improved technology and materials. The result provided a house on four levels with an almost uninterrupted view of the stage, whose circles and gallery curve in a most pleasing manner when viewed from the side-boxes or the front.

Today the stalls seating – replacing the long-gone pit accommodation – can be seen to follow an almost similar grand curve, and the whole gives the impression of capacious proportions, yet with circles of some half-dozen rows at most, retains that all important intimacy and relationship with the stage. The upholstery, hangings and house curtains are in warm crimson, contrastingly set against circle-fronts, boxes and proscenium of predominantly white, cream and gold, and a glittering chandelier of cut-glass tops the scene.

The auditorium has seen several redecorations since its 1902 inception – not the least following a serious fire in March 1917, when flames licked through the house to the tune of £2,000! But the next major works since Frank Tugwell's intervention were not to occur for another sixty-five years when, in 1967, a new main entrance and reception area, to include café and bars etc., was added to the side of the existing 1880 exterior. Designed by Patrick Gwynne this, largely glass, structure follows the route of complete contrast, rather than that of imitation of the existing, and is deemed to work very successfully. In addition to its catering facility it provides spaces for exhibitions and foyer-type entertainments, attractive views from both inside and out and of the warm stonework of the building itself and, especially important, gathers up the entrances to all parts of the house, utilising a modern and open internal staircase. Thus, the theatre is quite eclectic, showing off architecture from 1967, 1902, and the 1800s, as well as remnants of structures here and there from as far back as Georgian times.

Returning to those times, an interesting point to note, initially, is that York's first recorded theatre, built in the Minster Yard, was a reconstructed tennis court – as had been the case with some earlier continental, and even London, theatres. The next theatre was built ten years later upon the present site (formerly that of the old St. Leonard's Hospital) and, advertised as the New Theatre, it is this which was to begin the long history of links, both structurally and traditionally, to the building that stands here today.

In 1765 a larger, more elaborate, theatre replaced the original, and a Royal Patent was granted in 1769 from which time it became a 'Theatre Royal'! – only the third provincial house at that time to go legitimate, after Bath 1768 (see previous chapter) and Norwich 1768. It is known to have had, typically for the period, a square-shaped auditorium with a pit, a tier containing boxes, a gallery and an upper gallery. Changes came in a major refashioning in 1822, however, when the shape of the auditorium was altered towards the horseshoe, on the lines of more recently built venues (the provincial trend-setter may well have been Bristol as far back as 1766 - see earlier chapter), and it is said to have had separate entrances for the boxes and pit, and the gallery.

Gas lighting took over from the ubiquitous candles around 1824 and other important adaptations were made around 1836 when St. Leonard's Place had been created, principally necessitating re-orientation so that the front would face the new street. This also incorporated a further splitting of entrances (between boxes and pit) – the classes were now well segregated! – and refurbishment of the interior. Finally, 1875 saw the last major reconstruction of the era (note that in all of the above, lesser improvements were made from time to time which I have not mentioned), and this produced the building which Frank Tugwell subsequently utilised to create the present house. It also, unfortunately, almost severed the continuous link between the past and the present, excepting for certain small portions of structure which, it is generally

Even with well over 800 seats the York Theatre Royal auditorium remains remarkably intimate. Here, unfortunately, the proscenium arch is masked by the black drapes of the current touring production.

thought, remain intact today!

But a house of this standing does not reach its age on bricks and mortar alone, for these have literally been shaped by a history teaming with characters and events and customs. To be selective let me turn attention to a few of the more significant.

Until it received its Letters Patent, as with most other theatres in the land, it had to resort to the devious means discussed in previous chapters to escape prosecution under the 1737 Theatre Licensing Act. The York stock company worked on a circuit – recognised as one of the most important – and for around a hundred years played towns incorporating Newcastle, Beverley, Wakefield, Leeds, Pontefract, Doncaster and Hull at one time or

A stairway to the gods – preserved today to provide additional access and exit, but typical as the main access to the upper reaches of most theatres and music halls in bygone days, when social division was imperative.

another. With its base at York – considered to be *the* trendy centre of the era – visits were arranged between the Theatre Royal and the other towns so that, where possible, they coincided with relevant local events, for example the famous York races, when visitors were at a premium.

While this peripatetic existence provided a better chance for constant

employment as, individually, most towns did not have the resource to attract audiences on a more permanent basis, it also created difficulties inherent with the business. Not least was the travel itself – in this age not so easy considering road conditions and means of available transportation – coupled with the sheer volume of cartage which would include the players, stage staff and musicians etc., in addition to costumes, props and, in some cases scenery, as well. The stock company would also generally carry not just one production but a repertory of them – not only a logistical nightmare but a headache for the players, who had to remember all of the lines of all of the characters they portrayed in all of the plays!

Of the many managers who, with varying degrees of success or fortune, have striven to keep the Theatre Royal alive throughout the centuries, one of the most notorious, who must not go unmentioned, is a man named Tate Wilkinson – his managerial reign lasting from 1766 until his death in 1803. He lived in a house that still stands today towards the back of the theatre, now utilised to contain most of the administrative functions. His achievements, seemingly based upon a kindness and enthusiasm, with much experience brought from London and elsewhere, included that of making his company honourable (it is he who obtained Letters Patent), providing a solidarity to the stock company and the circuit, and tempting many of the great actors of the day to play in York.

A few of the luminaries to tread the Theatre Royal's boards during the first couple of hundred years or so would comprise the following (it is interesting to see how many (inevitably) crop up in other chapters in this book!): John Philip Kemble, Sarah Siddons, Edmund Kean, William Charles Macready, Ellen Terry, Henry Irving, Herbert Beerbohm Tree, Lillie Langtry, Sarah Bernhardt and Mrs Patrick Campbell.

Eventually the circuit (and stock company) would fold as the nineteenth century increasingly brought the London 'stars' to York, with their more sensational touring productions. And so the Theatre Royal continued as a touring house but was to become graded only as a No 2 date – the No 1 gradings reserved for those touring theatres with the largest stages and seating capacities, placed in the major towns which could fill them. Accordingly, the No.1 houses also tended to receive the more ambitious productions – although York does seem to have had its fair share of visiting stars!

The Theatre Royal, throughout periods of differing fortunes, remained open! It could not escape the eventual ravages of cinema, however – ironically introducing short films as a novelty into what had degenerated into 'variety' programmes a decade or so before – and the 'talkies' took hold of the country big-time. In 1922 a short season of repertory had been tried with some success and, from time to time, was repeated over the following years. It was in 1934, however, that a permanent company was formed (York Citizens' Theatre Ltd.) – 'legitimate' theatre returned to the Theatre Royal Stage – the policy had almost turned full circle, mirroring that of the old stock company! One of its notable features was the 'weekly rep' format and it also played 'twice-nightly' which must have been quite demanding – although in line with trends over the rest of the country, productions eventually ran for three or more weeks. During the Second World War years the Theatre Royal also took advantage of the availability of the many notable companies and famous names who, being evacuated from the London bombs, visited the provinces in abundance.

If wartime provided a measure of success and popularity, then provincial theatre was to pay for it not long afterwards. The advent of television dealt a bitter blow during the 1950s. Fortunately the York Theatre Royal managed to keep afloat – although many theatres did not – and today survives safely under the ownership of York City Council (the concept of local-authority ownership now a sign of the times) with its theatrical interest leased to the York Citizens' Theatre Trust. Here the policy of a resident repertory company whose work is interspersed with some touring productions continues to work successfully.

I mentioned earlier some of the old stagers who have played the Theatre Royal; let me now continue by naming a few of those *not-quite*-so-old, who appeared either as members of the repertory company or who came on tour: Sir John Gielgud, Michael Redgrave, Sir Donald Wolfit, Julia McKenzie, Dame Margot Fonteyn, Phyllis Calvert, Sir Ralph Richardson, John Barrie, Dame Judi Dench, Jean Alexander, Charlton Heston, Ian Carmichael, Pierce Brosnan, John Alderton, Sheila Hancock, Jean Fergusson, Zoe Wanamaker, Richard Harris, Evelyn Laye, Roy Dotrice, Stuart Grainger, Derek Jacobi, Matthew Kelly. The list is amply diverse and the productions equally so, ranging from comedy to tragedy, opera to ballet to pantomime, and variety – including "packs of performing poodles" and "educated horses".

In 1994, following on from a restoration appeal, the auditorium was totally refurbished, and a programme of improvement has continued. Not least was the introduction, in 2003, of a permanent Studio Theatre which, together with innovative schemes, collaborations, partnerships and projects encompassing young people, educational work, new writing and even world premiers, spectacularly brings the historic Theatre Royal into a new age – the twenty-first century!

Lincoln Theatre Royal

I have three stories of significance here – one concerning typically historical theatrical beginnings, another about a remarkable repertory company, and a further account which details the more recent situation: all intertwined, of course, around the destinies of a very special theatre!

Lincoln is an historic and very beautiful city, with red roofed buildings perched upon the sides of a steep hill topped by an imposing cathedral and fine castle. Theatrical tradition officially stretches back to 1732 from which date details of the first permanent theatre can be found, though it is doubtless that performances took place before this, customarily via strolling players who may also have banded together to provide theatricals in barns, inn-yards, and wherever they could. Known as 'The Playhouse', the theatre was situated in the castle grounds in Drury Lane and was built by one Erasmus Audley, a joiner who lived in The Bail, Lincoln. In 1764 the theatre was moved to the Kings Arm's Yard and eventually rebuilt here, reopening on 10th September 1806.

Management, at least from around 1750, was under William Herbert, indeed playbills in Lincoln Public Library that show the 'Herbert Company' or his 'Company of Comedians' abound, and by 1764 he had been joined by James Shaftoe Robertson. Eventually succeeded by his son Thomas, the theatre would remain in the Robertson family for more than 80 years and it became head of the Lincoln circuit (otherwise known as Robertson's circuit) which included the theatres in Boston, Grantham, Spalding, Peterborough, Huntingdon, Wisbech and Newark-on-Trent. Reports exist which show that the theatre was visited by The Duke of York – brother to George III and next in succession to the throne – who came to see a play called *Midas* on Monday, September 27th 1766.

Lincoln Theatre Royal: a delightfully warm, intimate and much loved old playhouse on three levels.

Disaster struck on 26th November 1892 when a great fire burnt the place to the ground and interestingly there are also allusions to explosion, recently installed gas lighting, a compressed gas tank and lime lighting equipment, all or any of which may have had notable contributions to the conflagration – perhaps a sign of the times? The final, substantially the present, theatre rose up on the same site, opening with a production of *Charley's Aunt* on December 18th 1893 performed by "the Company from the renowned Globe Theatre, London". The building was designed by "Messrs Crewe and Sprague, London" … "to seat 800 to 900, actual 840" … which, curiously, compares with a present capacity of 482. The street upon which it stands today became Clasketgate in 1957, formerly to be known as Butchery Street, and the present, and disappointing, main entrance is an invention from around the 1930/40s.

Since its position in the King's Arms Yard the theatre has had various spells when alternately entitled 'The New Theatre' or just simply 'The Theatre' – eventually, of course, becoming 'The Theatre Royal'. But, alas, as such the theatre is an impostor for it is not a 'true' Theatre Royal at all – it never having received Letters Patent from the Crown – actually, therefore, like numerous contemporaries all over the land who received their licences via local magistrates under the 1788 Act. One example still available shows that on July 6th 1803 Robertson applied to the 'sessions' in Lincoln for a licence "by virtue of an Act of Parliament passed in the 28th year of Reign of His Present Majesty [1788] entitled An Act to enable JPs to license Theatrical Representations occasionally under the restrictions therein contained" which was duly granted "of such Tragedies, Comedies, Interludes, Operas, Plays and Farces as now are or hereafter shall be acted, performed as represented either of the Patent or Licensed Theatres in the City of Westminster …"

And according to the many playbills such fare *was* presented: in the very early days predominantly of a music hall nature with singing, dancing, comic opera, ballad opera, melodrama, even acrobatics etc., then plays, including Shakespeare – always retaining the aforementioned extravaganzas sandwiched between the acts e.g. "Accompanying this Play will be several Entertainments of Singing and Dancing between the Acts" … or … "In the course of the evening the following Musical Acts will be presented" [listed]. Was such retention Lincoln's pre-licence days' attempts at subterfuge to prevent being committed as "rogues and vagabonds" under the 1737 Act, as discussed in other chapters? By the time we arrive in the twentieth century, however, the Royal seems to have become very much more of a straight drama house, now minus the fripperies, and visits by famous theatrical and West End companies of the time are recorded, for example those of Mr Osmond Tearle, Mr Frank Benson and Mr Henry Baynton. As the century progressed and moving with the times other productions, such as musicals and revues and variety, began to replace the dramas altogether.

My next story begins after the Second World War. In the early 'fifties the theatre was up for sale and, in the event, the lease was taken by "one of Britain's youngest theatrical managers" who, optimistically, proposed a complete change of policy – once-nightly rep. Local rags announced "ambitions to build Lincoln into one of Britain's leading theatrical cities … "to present plays immediately after, and in some cases before, West End runs … "the permanent company to be augmented from time to time by guest 'stars' ". However by 1955 dismal headlines such as "Curtain Falling on Repertory?" began to adorn the local newspapers and the company was under notice amid obvious financial difficulties.

In May 1955 a public meeting was held to decide the future of the theatre and, despite its evident plight, an overflowing response clearly demonstrated the deep feeling that locals held for their Theatre Royal. The outcome was the formation of the Lincoln Theatre Association – a non-profit making organisation that would provide once-nightly weekly repertory – and this

The OP fly floor, high up in the fly tower, confirms that the Theatre Royal is still a 'hemp-house'. These are the ropes that are used to raise and lower scenery – the full weight of which is taken up by the flymen. This is a typical scene to be found in many British theatres where counterweighting – i.e. weights to balance the load of the scenery – has not been installed.

Detail of the plaster-relief on the upper section of the proscenium arch, together with a painted house border.

was implemented and continued well supported and on a stable footing for some time to come. Eventually they managed to buy the theatre, quashing such horror stories as one prospective purchaser who had wished to turn it into a dance hall!

Now if weekly repertory wasn't gruelling enough for its participants (see part 5), imagine the effect of the next events. Away from Lincoln, the post-war years had initiated the Midlands Theatre Company which presented plays to theatres in Coventry, Nuneaton and Loughborough on a three-weekly cycle. With the opening of the new Coventry Belgrade Theatre (see part 5), however, the Midland Company was wound up, thus leaving the other towns without any professional theatre. Firstly Loughborough requested the Lincoln rep to provide them with a play every third week – a challenge that was accepted. Some time later a similar request came from Scunthorpe, which had just acquired a new civic theatre. The challenge, again, was duly accepted and finally, a further request in the early 'sixties then came from Rotherham, another town where a fine civic theatre had just been built and – you've guessed it – Rotherham joined the party! It was almost a return to the old circuit days! While a great deal of organisation obviously took place within the Lincoln Theatre Association, and eventually the rep was split into two separate companies so allowing more rehearsal time, etc. with a three-weekly cycle that was becoming the norm everywhere, the workload – including travel to the various towns by coach – must have been nigh impossible! This, the pinnacle of a superb achievement – the resuscitation of a failing old theatre, the inauguration of a permanent repertory company and its progression to two separate production units and a pioneering touring regime which provided other communities with live professional theatre – must surely be applauded. But the bubble would burst.

In 1969 the Lincoln company, for various reasons, terminated its regular touring policy. Reports generally throughout the 'sixties about the company or the theatre had been many and varied – while much good work was obviously produced, other notices proclaimed an "uphill battle to prevent 'Bingo Nightly' sign in place of 'Rep Season' " – and the overall theme was one of cash shortages. By the 'seventies a further worry for the Theatre Royal arrived as details were announced for a super new and modern theatre complex that was planned for the Brayford Pool. This is a whole subject in itself and posed a threat for several years, but as it failed to reach fruition (building was never even started) we need not be further concerned with it. Suffice to say there was much wrangling between those who wanted it and those who didn't and talk of "financial nightmares" and "millstones"; it also resulted in a "Save the Theatre Group" which, additionally, was concerned about the fate of the Royal. In the meantime, however, things unfortunately had become so bad at the Theatre Royal that the Lincoln Theatre Association sadly voted to go into liquidation. However, the day was saved (for the Royal, but regrettably not the company) when the council agreed to buy the ailing theatre "as a home for local amateur groups, an auditorium for public events and for other theatrical enterprises" – so it was once more reprieved!

My final story will bring us up to date. Having purchased the theatre in 1976, the city council then decided to lease it to a professional theatre management company. The opportunity was also taken to carry out some necessary structural work plus a substantial internal refurbishment. The policy, of course, changed from repertory to much more broad-based entertainment, with a plan to stage 36 weeks of professional productions plus a 4½ week pantomime and 10 weeks' potential amateur work, and within a short while came reports of top class shows, larger audiences and big names. Today the same situation applies – with council ownership still leasing out to private management. However, with subsidy continuing to play an important role the financial pressures unfortunately also remain. But a glance at the current *What's-on* list shows a healthy and varied programme of attractions.

The Theatre Royal is a little jewel and, having battled on for over a hundred years, its demise would prove a great loss to the City of Lincoln where its presence is considered by many to be both historically and culturally essential. Credit is due to the countless people who have striven endlessly over time to ensure its continued and successful existence. To conclude, here are just a handful of the famous players to have graced its stage – in no particular order

some who arrived as unknowns and learnt their skills here in repertory and went on to make their mark, others who came already as stars: John Hanson, Charlton Heston, Pat Phoenix, Penelope Keith, Anna Carteret, Jean Boht, John Savident, Jimmy Edwards, Richard Todd, Sir Michael Redgrave, Nyree Dawn Porter, Harry H. Corbett, Warren Mitchell, Charlie Drake, Kate O'Mara, Dora Bryan, and Hinge and Bracket.

Newcastle-upon-Tyne Theatre Royal

The magnificence of the 'house' that stands today in Newcastle's Grey Street arrived in several separate packages, each replacing some former damaged or redundant element from a previous era and all, finally, being subjected to a rigorous make-over in 1986/87. Thus the present building represents eclecticisms from a variety of periods and craftsmen and, having preserved its treasures and reworked the rest, happily unites to form one of the most aesthetically pleasing, and technologically advanced, theatres in the country.

The city's chronicle of entertainments naturally began some centuries earlier, likely evolving through the customary route from the liturgical dramas to strolling players, etc., and the first official reference to drama in the accounts of the Corporation has been traced back to July 1561.

Theatrically speaking, the city of Newcastle upon Tyne 'came of age' on 13th June 1787 when Letters Patent granted by King George III to a John Erasmus Blackett authorised the building of a playhouse. The move had followed petitions to the House of Commons for a licensed theatre in the city, and so the first Theatre Royal – designed by David Stephenson, who had already designed All Saints' Church – arose in Mosley Street (just around the corner from the present). With 1,350 seats it is said to have been extremely popular, presenting reputable stock companies and receiving new melodramas and London stars – those of note including Mrs Sarah Siddons and John Philip Kemble. Performances were generally limited to race weeks, assize times and the winter season. The productions here – the inaugural one being a comedy entitled *The Way to Keep Him* or *A School for Ladies* performed on the 21st January 1788 – were therefore free from the diversions known to have been adopted previously in the nearby Turks Head Long Room where, unlicensed, plays had been performed 'gratis' alongside musical concerts in an attempt to thwart the law.

The dramas were played out until the 25th June 1836 when the theatre closed due to 'city centre' redevelopment – a new theatre already having been included in the urban plans by Richard Grainger some two years earlier – and

Newcastle Theatre Royal: Matcham in French Renaissance style at the turn of the century (1901).

the exterior of this later building is the one that still remains today to remind us of its Regency roots, designed by John and Benjamin Green, a few streets away from the original. The opening production was *The Merchant of Venice* on the 20th February 1837 and business must have continued pretty successfully afterwards (despite competition from the fabulous Tyne Theatre and Opera House which opened on the 23rd September 1867 – see part 2), for well over half a century later, in 1895, came major internal works which increased the size of the auditorium and the seating capacity. These reconstructions were to the designs of architects W. Lister Newcombe and Walter Emden but, alas, were destined to be short-lived for following a performance of Frank Benson's company in *Macbeth* on Thursday 23rd November 1899, the place burned to the ground!

Actually, the stone exterior survived and, looking back, perhaps the entire situation was to the theatre's ultimate advantage. It allowed retention of the original exterior which, with its fine portico is noted as being exceptional

Grand, upper circle and gallery fronts are well complemented by an equally impressive ceiling, originally executed by De Jong of London.

among British theatre buildings, and simultaneously paved the way for the vastly improved auditorium that was to emerge – in fact another fine example from the drawing board of Frank Matcham. The reconstructed theatre went up pretty quickly too – work beginning in June 1901; opening night 31st December 1901 with the pantomime *The Forty Thieves!* – punctuality always being noted as another of Matcham's merits!

The opening night was greeted with amazement by a packed house: the extravagance of the auditorium with its De Jong of London plasterwork being admirably complemented by sumptuous draperies, positively glowing in the electric house lighting. In French Renaissance style, it could boast nearly 1,800 seats. Thus the new building would begin a distinguished career as a touring theatre, with every major company and performer of note destined to play. Many of the years were to become under the control of the famous Howard and Wyndham circuit who steered the Royal through the various highs and lows of the times, but in the early 1970s the City Council acquired the property, leasing it to an independent Trust to undertake the day-to-day management. By now, however, were emerging a number of serious deficiencies, predominantly in the backstage areas which no longer provided accommodation commensurate with that of modern-day expectation and technology, and which were causing major companies to consider removal of Newcastle from their touring circuits. And the once-exalted front of house, with tired upholstery and lacking comfort and facility, now found its glories much more thinly spread.

The remedy did not arrive until the mid-1980s, but when it did, it was wholesale! A massive improvement scheme was drawn up by the RHWL Partnership, a firm of architects with much experience in theatre regeneration, and a number of their projects feature in other chapters. As with many of them, the venture comprised the replacement of obsolete infrastructure and designs by those in keeping with today's requirements, alongside a careful restoration programme that, where possible, retained and breathed new life into original attributes.

Backstage areas were enlarged, equipped with more and better dressing rooms, shower and WC facilities, etc. together with rehearsal spaces, wig/wardrobe/laundry/band rooms etc., and generous improvements to the stage house itself. Front of house saw a total and much needed rehash of public circulation spaces – in particular the provision of a new grand marble staircase which, running the entire height of the building, now serves all patrons, from stalls to gallery, allowing everyone to enter via the principal foyer. Previously, in the fashion of our Victorian and Edwardian predecessors, the cheaper parts of the house were served by separate side doors with only the

grand circle and stalls customers enjoying the supremacy of the main entrance via the fine classical portico. In turn superb catering and function facilities were also created, including state-of-the-art bars, restaurant, coffee shop, wine bar, grand saloons and reception areas etc. These not only enhanced the audience experience, but allowed the Royal to extend its services into daytime activity.

But the jewel in the crown, of course, has to be the sumptuous auditorium. Following careful research this was restored as closely as possible to its original, with a colour scheme and upholstery faithful to Matcham's designs. Generally the elaborate plasterwork is in various shades of cream with gold highlights, set against a background of plum; the heavy house curtains and attendant draperies in original style are, likewise, in a deep plum, with seating in Victorian green. When lit, the effect is elegant and enchanting. The seating capacity, to modern standards, is 1,294 – compare this with the original!

The work was completed in 1987 which, notably, coincided with the 150th anniversary of the present Theatre Royal, Grey Street, building, and the 200th anniversary of the granting of Letters Patent – the Royal Licence. All was revealed on the evening of 11th January 1988 with a grand reopening performance of Robert Bolt's *A Man For All Seasons*, starring no less than Charlton Heston. This continued the Theatre Royal's reputation for high class drama and quality performance, for the house has played host to the most eminent actors, actresses, singers, dancers and companies in its day. Among the current luminaries are the Royal Shakespeare Company and Opera North but all of the major West End productions tour here, together with the top national and international dance and ballet companies.

The story, however, is unending – for as I write in early 2006 are promised further works of major improvement following the acquisition of adjacent building. This will allow additional enhancement of the stage, backstage and technical facilities, together with box office and visitor centre and education centre developments, etc. Here, most surely, is a theatre well worth visiting both by performers and audiences alike.

Northampton Royal

Here is a very important theatre since it provides first-hand evidence to support many of the facts and theories already considered in respect of theatres and theatrical habits of the late Victorian age. It opened on the 5th May 1884 and although a disastrous fire badly damaged the auditorium and adjacent parts in 1887, the whole was quickly restored so that what we have today largely represents the original work. Its creator was Charles John Phipps, one of the most eminent theatre builders of his time (see 'Act I Curtain'), and as such it is also high-ranking as one of his noted survivors.

In April 2005 the theatre closed, together with its next door neighbour the Derngate (theatre) (see chapter in part 6), for a proposed period of 14 months, for the extensive refurbishment and development of both houses. The theatres are now jointly managed by Northampton Theatres Trust Ltd. which was formed in 1999, but were previously run by separate charitable trusts. The merger and works will allow the two venues – built side by side but like chalk and cheese – to be physically connected, thus capable of sharing resources such as an all-mod-cons foyer and new creativity centre, whilst retaining their own unique individuality and style.

When it reopens, the Royal will have been restored to its former Phippsian glory and although sporting the aforementioned foyer, the Guildhall Road exterior (and note its original name above the entrances 'Royal Theatre and Opera House') will be retained. This will ensure that the playgoer is not deprived of the pre-theatre Victorian experience, the charming original foyer decked out in appropriate period style still available to offer a pleasing first impression. It also continues to demonstrate the small amount of space taken up by the façade along the main roadway – like so many theatres in England – the frontage typically having been crammed between neighbouring buildings.

The foyer leads the patron towards all parts of the house, situated at right-angles to Guildhall Road, and divided into stalls, dress circle and balcony, with seating for 583. In bygone days, of course, typically strict segregation of the classes was observed when benches, prior to the introduction of the stalls, would have accommodated the pitites and the balcony (which is still stepped), the galleryites, whilst the circle was divided into 'dress' and 'upper' with a balustrade in between, for the higher classes. Amazingly, the theatre in those days was said to have held around 1500 people, and up to 1700 when necessary, although this seems quite impossible when compared with today's figure and bearing in mind the actual area available.

The delightful and intimate auditorium in warm red demonstrates the characteristic theatrical style which had evolved since the Georgian period (with its tiered galleries), but prior to the overall introduction of the cantilever system (which allowed deeper, overhanging balconies without any visible support). The rounded arrangement, by now fully developed, shows horseshoe balconies supported upon slender columns, which meet richly ornamented single private boxes adjacent to the proscenium. There have been several house curtains during the life of the Royal, at least three of them in the form of a painted act drop – a feature of the Victorian era – the latest of these depicted a Venetian scene and this, in view of its (not surprisingly) frail condition and obvious rarity value, was put away for safe keeping some years ago and still remains intact. The present safety curtain, however, to some extent almost allows the tradition to continue, being painted with a superb tapestry of miscellaneous, yet relevant, notions – woven magically together to great effect – with a colour scheme highly complementary to the rest of the house. This is well worth seeing.

A mention must be made of the lighting, which for many years following the opening of the Royal Theatre and Opera House, was provided by gas. It is interesting to note that Phipps' designing of the theatre was immediately subsequent to his creation of the magnificent Savoy Theatre for R. D'Oyly Carte (1881), which was not only the first theatre in London to be lit by electricity but, indeed, the first *building*. This was not to be copied at the Royal, however, which – like its contemporaries and the rest of the country – had to wait several years until electricity became more widely available to theatres and to the provinces. In any case, it was not considered a foregone conclusion that electric lighting was entirely superior to its predecessor, gas, since some actors complained (for example, Henry Irving and Ellen Terry) that electricity was too harsh and that many of the subtle qualities made possible by gas were irretrievably lost.

But safety was another aspect for consideration and the eventual installation of electricity in theatres obviously reduced the threat of fire or explosion, which accompanied the unpredictable usage of gas with its naked flames and myriad taps and piping. The authorities were increasingly becoming concerned with such hazards, and the associated problem of foul air and ventilation, in addition to overcrowding and adequate exit facilities, although the Royal does seem, comparatively speaking, to have been well provided with the latter. This concern would gradually lead to health and safety improvements on both sides of the footlights as time went on.

The current policy of the Royal is generally that of a professional producing theatre with an amount of repertory and a traditional Christmas show. Along with its Derngate neighbour a large chunk of outreach, community and schools

Northampton Royal: another delightful house provided by Charles John Phipps.

Typical of the period, horseshoe balconies are supported upon slender columns.

work is also undertaken by the Trust as a whole. From 1927 and for many years afterwards the company in residence was the Northampton Repertory Players Ltd., which was hugely successful – having such prestigious names passing through its ranks as Errol Flynn, Freda Jackson and James Hayter. Prior to this the Royal was a touring theatre taking in many of the touring companies that were on the circuits and famous names from the golden days include Henry Irving, Ellen Terry, Wilson Barrett and Mrs Patrick Campbell – obviously names which you will see repeated throughout the chapters and venues of this book.

Opera was also well represented, including performances by the Carl Rosa Opera Company and the D'Oyly Carte, though it is difficult to imagine grand opera, including orchestra and all of the trimmings, being presented in such a small, yet admittedly, delightful house. In those days the theatre was actually known locally and, indeed, billed as 'The Opera House', until, eventually, the name 'Royal Theatre' began to be used almost exclusively. Other, lighter, musical offerings were also popularly received such as those of George Edwardes fame, and many glamorous nights featured shows like *The Maid of the Mountains* (which originally opened at Daly's Theatre, London in 1917 playing 1352 performances and touring continuously for ten years afterwards, being equally a favourite when it visited Northampton).

As with so many towns and the theatres in them, the success and growth of Northampton and its Royal owed much to the introduction and development of the railways. Here, the Royal Theatre and Opera House was dually catered for as in 1872 the Midland Railway had come to the town, providing services in addition to those already on offer from the London and North Western line. It is also notable that in the following years the Derngate bus terminus was to contribute by bringing in countless passengers from the outlying country areas and that after its closure, its final donation to the world of theatre was to bequeath the very land upon which it stood, to become the site of the Derngate (theatre) (see part 6) already mentioned.

In 1960 the Royal Theatre came under the ownership of the Northampton Corporation – thus providing it with a measure of protection and preservation. The town of Northampton must be one of the richest boroughs in the country in terms of theatre provision, where two such diverse, yet outstanding, venues (the Royal and the Derngate) stand side by side not in competition, but in providing complementary and quality works to the community in the world of drama, music, dance and art.

2 THE GREAT INDUSTRIAL CITIES AND TOURING

The growth of the great industrial towns and cities of the Midlands and North supplied an audience in situ with an insatiable appetite for entertainment – for many providing an escape from the rigours of their hard working lives. With continuously improving technology and expectation, the result was a proliferation of sumptuous 'Palaces of Delight'...

- *Nottingham Theatre Royal (1865)*
- *Newcastle, Journal Tyne Theatre (1867)*
- *Leeds Grand Theatre and Opera House (1878)*
- *Wakefield Theatre Royal & Opera House (1894)*
- *Wolverhampton Grand Theatre (1894)*
- *Sheffield Lyceum Theatre (1897)*
- *Sunderland Empire Theatre (1907)*
- *Bradford Alhambra Theatre (1914)*
- *Liverpool Empire Theatre (1866/1925)*
- *Birmingham Hippodrome Theatre (1899/1925)*
- *Birmingham Alexandra Theatre (1901/1935)*
- *Stoke-on-Trent Regent Theatre (1929)*

Nottingham Theatre Royal

If asked to describe the Theatre Royal, Nottingham in one single phrase, I should have to say that it is "a symphony in green and gold". And although that statement may well whet the appetite of the would-be theatre goer, it could not adequately prepare him/her for the delights to be encountered within. A first glimpse of the Theatre Royal will no doubt be one of the exterior, encompassing the majestic portico entrance, preserved from its day of opening on the 25th September 1865, and splendidly kept in brilliant cream and gold. But then upon entering, the carefully planned spacious foyers, cleverly combining the ambience of the old and the functionality of the new, serve as a prelude to the opulence that is about to follow.

The history of the present building, architecturally, can really be divided between three principal eras and two eminent theatre architects, Charles John Phipps and Frank Matcham – although the most recent reconstruction by Renton Howard Wood Levin should not be forgotten. In the first period the Theatre Royal stayed much as it was when built by Phipps.

In 1897, however, a further theatre, after much revamping of the Theatre Royal's ancillary and dressing room areas, was built alongside. This was the Empire Theatre, designed by Frank Matcham for the increasingly important Moss' Empires chain. It goes without saying that the Empire, extravagantly ornate, was an immediate success – and was to remain so for many years. It fitted in well with the *legitimate* policy of the Theatre Royal, for their presentations did not oppose, the Empire producing music hall and variety bills. At the time of the Empire's construction, part of Frank Matcham's remit was to carry out improvements to the Theatre Royal. Thus, the second period in the Theatre Royal's architectural life began, with changes not only to some of the dressing room areas provoked by the inauguration of the Empire, but also significant changes to Phipps' auditorium. Perhaps one of the most notable was the installation of the cantilever system – which allowed the supporting columns of the galleries and circles to be removed from sight, providing a much improved view of the stage.

The Empire's fortunes closely resemble those of its contemporaries presenting, originally, all of the old music hall greats, followed by the equally popular names of the Second World War and variety eras. Then, with the general trend and waning popularity, strip shows were tried in an, unfortunately in this case, unsuccessful survival attempt, and the Empire's curtain descended for the last time in 1958. It was demolished in 1969 and today much of the area released by the demolition has been cleverly utilised by the newly formed foyer and bar spaces.

The third (and present) period in the Theatre Royal's structural history began in 1978 following a decision by Nottingham City Council, having purchased the property saving it from closure in 1969, to enter into a programme of extensive refurbishment, thus regenerating it into one of the most impressive touring houses to be found in the country today.

The style of the 1978 alterations is synonymous with modern major refurbishment schemes undertaken in other Victorian or Edwardian theatres, which successfully provide for up-to-date needs, yet carefully retain the mood of the past. One of the most significant features is the sweeping away of previously cramped public areas and their replacement with fine spacious bar and buffet facilities at all levels, together with the provision of elegant connecting staircases. Thus, the modern-day playgoer – whatever the price of his/her seat, in stalls, dress circle, upper circle or gallery – will enter under Phipps' portico to the main grand salon, the old separate entrances to the cheaper parts of the house having been done away with. An added advantage is that the design and decoration of the bars and foyers, sympathetically in tune with the auditorium, allows an audience to be wooed in advance of the entertainment to follow. The spaces are also used in the daytime – not only providing food and drink, but permitting the theatre to become part of the community upon quite a different plane.

The auditorium is splendid and accommodates 1186 people upon four very comfortable levels, all with good sightlines. Even the gallery, now re-seated – having done away with the original benches – provides extremely favourable and theatrical conditions, charmingly retaining the 'birds-eye' viewing experienced by our Victorian counterparts. The original pit, in general with the changing times, was also transformed into stalls seating some years ago and the colour scheme of the whole, in green and gilt, with quite grandiose embellishment at every turn, makes a refreshing change from the ubiquitous maroons of so many other houses. An innovation which pleases me enormously is the heavy velvet house curtain which, in one configuration, will part in the centre and drape towards the uppermost corners of the proscenium arch, to fall again in similar manner, in truly old-fashioned style. (This arrangement was often used in theatres and music halls prior to the invention of fly-towers when it was impossible to raise curtains or pieces of scenery directly above the actors' heads.)

There has been a theatre in Nottingham since approximately 1760. The building that housed it prior to the current Theatre Royal was in St Mary's Gate, which then became a music hall for a few years but it did not possess the splendour of the present building. Its founder was a James Augustus Whitely who was an Irish actor-manager and who, at one time, along with his company, was committed by the authorities for performing without a licence. He was finally granted a licence but until then had to be mindful of the 1737 Theatre Licensing Act, adopting such ruse' as advertising concerts of music with "a play presented free during the interval"!

James Whitley's theatre in the early days formed part of the Midland Circuit

Nottingham Theatre Royal: several hues of green and gilt are used to great effect in this elegant house, and the beautiful ceiling completes the scene. The swagged house curtain, additionally, makes a pleasing innovation.

that incorporated other 'dates' such as Worcester, Wolverhampton, Derby, Retford and Stamford. When in town (which generally coincided only with special events such as race weeks, assizes, and the goose-fair) the stock

Heavily gilded cherubs show off plasterwork typical of box and dress circle fronts in a Matcham house.

The safety curtain sports a typically Victorian theatrical notion of cherubs engaging in music and dance, by Henry Bardon.

company would present all the shows – but as time progressed and many of the circuit and stock companies gave way to the popularity of visiting 'stars', the Theatre Royal in Nottingham was no exception. Indeed, by 1870 it had become, essentially, a touring house and the famous 'stars' from London appeared at the new, splendidly appointed, theatre, much as they had done in its predecessor's day. Brothers John and William Lambert, incidentally, were responsible for the building of the new (present) theatre.

The famous names and companies to have graced the stage of the Theatre Royal throughout the years are those who will mostly be seen to grace many of the other pages in this book, as they have toured and performed in all of the renowned houses in the land. The Carl Rosa Opera Company and D'Oyly Carte were among early visitors who have returned many times. The Royal Shakespeare Company, the Royal National Theatre, Opera North and the Northern Ballet Theatre have also brought major successes. The people of Nottingham have therefore been provided with a wide range of theatre often on its way to or from the West End, from the classical repertoire of drama, ballet and opera, to the lighter musicals such as *The Merry Widow* and *Lilac Time* and, more recently, the major blockbusters *Cats*, *Evita*, *Singing In The Rain*, *Buddy*, *Miss Saigon* and *Beauty and the Beast*. The earliest stars who began to demonstrate the theatres' important status – just a selection – include John Quick, Charles Kemble, Sarah Siddons, William Charles Macready, Lillie Langtry, Sarah Bernhardt, Henry Irving, Ellen Terry, Mrs Patrick Campbell and J. Forbes-Robertson. And around the turn of the century (1900) and its early decades typically appeared Anna Pavlova, Cicely Courtneidge and Jack Hulbert, Evelyn Laye, John Gielgud and the enormously popular Gracie Fields. Julie Andrews and Ken Dodd were later visitors, and the bill of fare, ever changing, continues to present equally popular personalities from the modern world of stage, screen and television.

Pantomime, as in many of England's theatrical circles, has always featured prominently at the Theatre Royal. The first to be presented following the opening of the Phipps building in 1865 was *The House That Jack Built* and in keeping with the Victorians' penchant for spectacular effects, utilised hazardous understage apparatus to make the house magically rise up through the floor as it was being built! Of course, Robin Hood has always been a particular favourite with Nottingham's panto audiences as I am sure he, along with his merry men, will continue to be for many years to come in this very, very prestigious house.

Newcastle, Journal Tyne Theatre

Under new management, sporting a new name and bursting into a new era, the Journal Tyne Theatre, after a short spell of closure, has recently made a spectacular comeback into the world of live theatre, reflecting its latest niche in presenting a lively mixture of shows, music, dance and concerts, etc. Formerly the Tyne Theatre and Opera House it has, over the years, experienced a somewhat chequered history including fierce competition from the city's other great house – the Theatre Royal (see part 1) – a cinematic period, a serious fire and complex management issues, etc., but now leaps forward into an enthusiastic and exciting future. In its time, the Opera House has played host to countless splendid theatrical and operatic successes and the most distinguished performers, and its brilliant, virtually original, auditorium is matched by unique Victorian stage machinery that remains intact and working, the likes of which cannot be found elsewhere in the country, and earning it Grade I listed status.

Walking along Westgate Street it is a shame that the predominantly brick exterior does not accentuate either the delights to be found within, or the importance that the building holds in the British theatrical story – a story that began on Monday 23rd September 1867 when the curtain rose on the first performance: *Arrah-Na-Pogue* by Dion Boucicault. An account in the *Newcastle Daily Chronicle* on Wednesday 18th September 1867 gives away much information, and credits the architect, a Mr W. Parnell, on the clever design of his apparently one-off theatrical project. Estimated to hold 3,000 persons (note today's capacity is 1,100) the house is described as having a "rich and cheerful aspect", no doubt induced by the colour scheme, seemingly a "brilliant scarlet".

Attention was drawn to the number and size of the entrances – strict segregation, of course, being observed in relation to the different parts of the house, in keeping with the order of the day. There are four levels, the three tiers forming a traditional horseshoe shape and thus confirming the typical mid-nineteenth century configuration, with slender columns, prior to the invention of the cantilever. Still in evidence is the rich plasterwork along the circle fronts, surrounding the eight private boxes – some of which are adorned by delightful caryatids, and around the impressive proscenium arch, and the present colour scheme is in royal blue. The house is said to have had excellent acoustics from the start – apparently aided by the fact that the walls are not plastered, but lined with wood, and the character of the charming ceiling whose shell-like properties are carried right to the back of the gallery, thus transporting sound to the extremities.

The attributes of the stage were also brought to attention in 1867 but the most amazing fact today is that some are still in existence. The gas arrangements, of course, are not, and were described as "having five gas battens" and "for the stage are of the most elaborate yet simple character, all parts of the theatre being regulated from a central point near the prompter's box. There will be 100 gas burners in the footlights". Now to the icing on the cake! The stage, originally described as having "all the modern improvements and appliances and will surpass, we understand, in completeness and extent, any stage in

Newcastle Journal Tyne Theatre: it now seats 1,100 but at its opening is reputed to have regularly entertained in excess of 3,000!

A feature of the auditorium – noted from its 1867 outset – is the fine ceiling which, shaped like a shell, covers the whole area from the proscenium to the gallery, transmitting the sound excellently to the upper reaches of the house.

the provinces", remarkably, still does! Not having been used for countless years, and having lain undisturbed and long forgotten, the Victorian wooden understage machinery was 'rediscovered' in the early 1970s and restored to working order. Considered to be inimitable, this puts the Tyne Opera House in an international class of its own!

There are four bridges, each 28' 2" in length by 3' 2" wide – which work like lifts, capable of transporting both people and scenery through the stage, to a depth of fourteen feet below, or four feet above it. Between each of these are two cuts 28' 2" long and 11" wide (eight in total) through which flats can rise and fall between the cellar and the stage. There are also two 'demon' traps, a grave trap, three object traps, two staircase traps and a carpet cut, thus comprising the most complete set of such machinery to be found in the

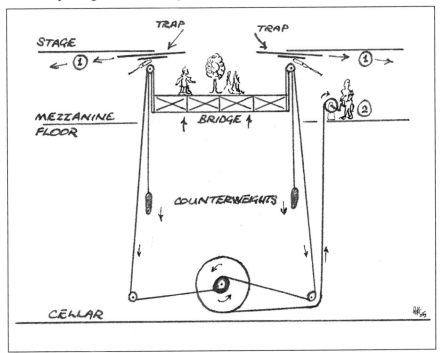

A very simple sketch (not to scale) to illustrate the layout of the stage cellar and, in principle, the basic workings of a bridge (stage-lift).
(1) the trap slides out to reveal the cut, through which the scenery and actors will be raised as the bridge (stage-lift) is winched into position by the stage hands (2) operating from the mezzanine floor.

Directly below the stage – the mezzanine floor. The roof in this picture is the underside of the stage, through which the scenery or actors will be raised. The traps (sliders), bridges (stage-lifts) and winches etc. are all operated from here.

Below the mezzanine – the lowest floor, containing drum and shaft mechanism. The ropes from the winches on the mezzanine floor above pass around the large circumference of these drums. Further ropes, in turn passing around their spindles (shafts) of much smaller diameter, are attached directly to the bridges (stage-lifts). Thus the ratio of the gearing, together with some counterweighting, assists the operator by easing the load.

country. A trip into the cellar is a revelation, where the traps, drums, ropes and winches can be clearly seen. They are operated from a mezzanine floor about 9 feet below the stage, with the master drums being on the cellar floor itself at a total depth of approximately 30 feet! Above the stage is the grid at about 70 feet serviced by modern-day counterweight sets, though still in existence are old 'Chinamen' drum and winch apparatus.

And so the Victorians, who wanted their spectacle, were certainly not disappointed with the well equipped Tyne Theatre and Opera House! There are accounts of the sinking of Spanish galleons, earthquakes, shipwrecks, transformation scenes in pantomimes, and even a scene showing the Grand National complete with real horses and water-jumps. Neither were they, or their successors, short-changed when it came to product – for all of the most eminent names and companies have played this famous stage. From dramatists Wilson Barrett, Henry Irving and Ellen Terry, Osmond Tearle, and Sarah Bernhardt to the musicians of the Covent Garden Opera Company, the Royal Italian Opera Company and Carl Rosa Opera Company (with Carl Rosa himself conducting on a visit in March 1877). Even Placido Domingo appeared in 1983! And on a lighter note, the George Edwarde's Company from London's Gaiety Theatre, and the music hall greats, such as Vesta Tilley (who starred in *Babes in the Wood* in 1888) and George Robey who played in Aladdin in 1895,

Harry Lauder, Little Tich, and Dan Leno featured prominently along with, of course, the year-after-year ubiquitous pantomime!

The first few years of operation, however, came from a stock company, prior to the touring system taking hold, and there have obviously been many changes in the manager and licensee department since that era. Three of the most notables were Augustus Harris, of London's Theatre Royal, Drury Lane management fame, taking the reigns in 1887 and who, as a master at providing spectacle, was no doubt at home at the Tyne. After his death in 1896, Messrs Howard & Wyndham (eventually renowned as the powerful booking agents) took over until 1917. The theatre then closed in 1919 and became The Stoll Picture Theatre, when Oswald Stoll (yes, the very man who had had the London Coliseum (Matcham) built in 1904, and who also ran a major chain of variety theatres – see Bristol Hippodrome Theatre in part 3) took control.

Mr Matcham – a figure not entirely unknown to Mr Stoll, of course – was contracted to oversee the alterations and the newfound occupation was to last for a period of no less than 55 years, still acknowledged externally

in the wording in the stained glass window above the main entrance! The conversion work saw a projection box installed to the rear of the upper circle plus attendant works but, fortunately, had not affected the sub-stage machinery or the brilliant plasterwork of the house. By 1974, however, the movies had lost their draw and, alas, degenerated into those of dubious content, casting a similarly degenerative shadow over the once acclaimed theatre and opera house, but even they failed and the building went 'dark'.

The theatre's next chapter saw new life breathed into the old place by an enthusiastic team of amateurs – the nucleus being from the Tyneside Operatic Society – who formed a trust and spent over three years of renovation and refurbishment work, hiring in professionals where specialists were needed, and utilising Community Industries and Job Creation Schemes. Of particular note was the restoration work carried out below stage under the direction of Dr David Wilmore, which reinstated to the Tyne something quite exclusive.

The 'New Tyne Theatre', as it became known, reopened in 1977. In 1985, however, disaster struck, for on Christmas Day fire broke out backstage, causing much damage to that area and part of the proscenium but, fortunately, not to the sub-stage machinery. Another beginning, amazingly less than eleven months later, saw Geraint Evans CBE reopening the (now, 'Tyne Theatre

and Opera House') yet again, this time following a £1.5 million refurbishment: to an even greater standard than before.

It has to be said that the Journal Tyne Theatre, to use its present name, has undergone more than its fair share of problems, but these are outside the scope of this book. With its current lively and varied programme of shows and events and a generous array of facilities, however, the future looks bright as Newcastle continues to reap the rewards of this most important and historically unusual theatre, which contributes greatly to the city's cultural heritage.

Leeds Grand Theatre and Opera House

Here we have a house so aptly named – truly of operatic proportion, and presented with all of the trappings of the grandiose – a showpiece executed in the splendid magnificence of its age, which even today remains unrivalled amongst its peers.

Built as a touring theatre, in a time when such venues provided some of the accoutrements of their guests' productions, the accommodation was so generously equipped (for example containing carpenters' shop, plumbers' shop, smiths' shop, armoury, wardrobe and sewing rooms, gasfitters' workshop, property workroom, modelling room, painting-room complete with four painting frames, etc., etc.) that it occupies a site of around three quarters of an acre! Included in that area, in addition to all of the other usual and important theatrical necessities, was an assembly room capable of accommodating 1,200 persons – with the attendant kitchen, supper and retiring rooms, cloakroom, lavatories etc., and six 'commodious' shops whose extra rental income would subsidise the building's chief concern. Its total cost exceeded £60,000.

The night of Monday the 18th of November 1878 must have been a thrilling one – the grand opening! The theatre was packed to capacity, many people having had to be turned away, but the lucky ones, eagerly awaiting the delights to follow, found the occasion quite breathtaking upon exchanging that dark November night for the gas-lit auditorium, brilliant in decoration and ornamentation, whose predominant colours of crimson and gold made the front of house look warm and cosy.

Excellent accounts of the evening appeared in both *The Yorkshire Post and Leeds Intelligencer,* and *The Leeds Mercury* the following day which, additionally, provide an insight to the state of theatre in Britain generally at the time. We are told that the house comprised "pit and pit stalls, dress circle, upper circle, amphitheatre circle, gallery, six stage boxes, eight family boxes, eight upper private boxes and six amphitheatre boxes: the whole giving seating accommodation for about 2,600 persons, in addition to which standing room is provided for 200 more". This obviously illustrates how times (and regulations) have changed as the same house today will accommodate 1,450 without, of course, the services of the gentlemen at one time employed to pack as many pittites and galleryites together on a row as was humanly possible.

"Shortly after the hour fixed for the commencement of the performance" (the *Leeds Mercury* tells us) "Mr Wilson Barrett, the lessee and manager, stepped in front of the drop scene – a beautiful work of art by Mr Telbin (see also part 5 for mention of his work at Liverpool) representing Kirkstall Abbey – and heartily welcomed the audience to that theatre, which he considered one of the finest in Europe. The burst of applause which had greeted his words made him, he said, feel rather like the naughty little boy who got the prize by mistake – (*a laugh*) – for this magnificent theatre, built by their own townspeople, did not owe its existence to him, but to the talent of the architects, Messrs Corson and Watson…"

"With regard to the building, he wished to point out its complete safety. (*Hear, hear.*)…" and went on to extol the virtues of the roominess of the exits (prompted by a disaster which had recently occurred at the Colosseum in Liverpool in which people were killed in a false alarm panic escape). He continued …"If the stage were one gulf of fire, every gentleman in the building would have time to light his cigar comfortably – (*a laugh*) – give his arm to his lady love, and saunter pleasantly out of the building. (*Laughter and hear, hear.*)"

Now the 'fashionable' audience of that evening obviously contained its fair share of dignitaries, the most important of whom occupied some of the proscenium boxes, from which they were invited to speak. These included the Chairman of the Directors, Sir Andrew Fairbairn, His Worship the Mayor, The Borough Engineer (Assistant Town Clerk), the Chief Constable, and Mr George

Corson and Mr J. R. Watson. The content of what was said clearly illustrates some of the issues of the day. Already the safety aspect of such buildings had been raised and was undoubtedly an apprehension – indeed Leeds audiences didn't have to look very far for evidence upon which to base their concerns. It was only in 1875 that the Theatre Royal in Hunslet Lane had burned to the ground, then less than a year later the Amphitheatre in King Charles's Croft followed suit! This left Leeds without any reputable theatre and, of course, paved way for the building of the Grand. Coincidentally, it was in the very year of the Grand's opening that the Metropolis Management & Building Acts Amendment Act was passed which specifically tackled the safety issues in London's public buildings – afterwards to be mirrored increasingly in the provinces.

Other observations compared the Grand Theatre and Opera House with such venues in other countries – for instance Europe and America – and general opinion seemed to have it that "few of them would compare with this splendid house". Notably, the parallel was also drawn between the funding of many continental establishments and those in England, whereby our foreign neighbours often erected and ran their extravagant edifices by way of municipal powers and public subscription, whereas we had to rely purely upon commercial success, carefully cutting our coats to the size of our cloth! This seemed to make the excellence of the Grand even more momentous!

His Worship the Mayor reflected upon the past correlation of drama and morals and the influence it had had on the manners, virtues and vices of the people. "The drama has either been a great teacher of and incentive to virtue, or it has been the minister of vice – (*cheers*)…"! He continued "…and now we can say of the English stage…it has attained to a dignity, grandeur, and purity…" and concluded by praising the "public-spirited" proprietors, the manager Mr Wilson Barrett and his actress-wife ("favoured by the appreciation of her Sovereign"), [and] "coupled with the large and influential assemblage now before us, pledges for the future success of this undertaking. (*Cheers*.)" Finally, he referred to "the architectural character of this noble temple of drama" and called upon the audience to recognise the architects.

"Mr Corson added a few words from another box, but was not audible at any long distance. His speech was followed by loud and repeated cries for Mr Watson, but that gentleman modestly refrained from adding to the speeches of the occasion." Clearly these were architects and not speech-makers!

The opening production was Shakespeare's comedy *Much Ado About Nothing* and the leading man was the English actor-manager Wilson Barrett

Leeds Grand Theatre and Opera House: with a full house the accommodation extends to five levels, the tiers rising like a wedding cake towards the upper slips and sumptuous ceiling.

– the very one and only who was now the first manager and lessee of the Leeds Grand Theatre and Opera House! When the performance was over he again addressed the audience, in flamboyant style! This time, the gist of many of his words showed his concern for the respectability of the theatre and its continued improvement and image, the type of people who attended, and the church's view and influence. Quite obviously up to recent times the theatre had been considered by respectable people as "not a proper place to go". The church had also had plenty to say on the subject but now "the most liberal and pure-minded men" … "were trying to make it what it should be – a means of educating, and not degrading the masses". Drama's image was gradually changing and no doubt the building of such fine theatres as the Grand, and the many other venues of extreme quality that were to join them over next few decades (the 'boom' was yet to come) were contributing greatly to the continuing amelioration.

Now at this time Leeds was at the hub of the Industrial Revolution: not only was the population increasing dramatically, but the resultant prosperity also brought with it a civic pride, and the birth of other fine Victorian building in the city. Not least was the Town Hall – a magnificent construction designed by Cuthbert Broderick and opened in 1858 by Queen Victoria and her Consort, Prince Albert. Word has it that a comment made by Prince Albert on that occasion may have prompted the idea of building a new theatre. The idea was not to come to fruition until 1876, however, when "a meeting of influential gentlemen" finally got it together, with a mind to building a first class theatre, "their primary object, the elevation of the drama in Leeds."

They certainly went to town and spared no expense, as you may already have gathered – a fact that you can even witness for yourself upon visiting the fine theatre today. The exterior of some 170 feet, decidedly Gothic in appearance, testifies to the era in which it was built, and the theme is carried forward to the auditorium – from the principal entrance a grand staircase will sweep you to the upper levels of the house, whilst a promenade encircles the rear stalls. (Originally, of course, access to the gallery was from a back street so that, in keeping with the tradition of the times, those patrons of a lesser standing – together with matching social skills – would be segregated from their 'betters' and, indeed, have their own payboxes.)

The auditorium remains essentially as it was on the opening night and, with its sweeping lines of horseshoe tiers, semicircular proscenium arch (32 feet wide and 42 feet high) and opulent draperies, is quite dazzling. The plaster-

A good view of the proscenium, showing its spectacular arrangement, curved arch and proliferation of decoration, which covers every imaginable surface.

88 Theatres of Achievement

work is extravagant: richly cut and covering every imaginable surface, yet with less frothiness than will be found in many of the Matcham concoctions, still to be invented. In no way does this diminish the final result, however. Messrs. Corson and Watson's (it is said, one-off) theatrical design, makes for a more sophisticated, classical, effect yet perfectly preserves that essential fantasy setting for opera, ballet and drama to this very day!

The backstage accommodation is equally extravagant, taking up as much space as the auditorium, and with a stage area approximately 72 feet wide and 75 feet deep. Originally incorporating sub-stage machinery consisting of extensive traps and bridges (removed in the 1970s), the total height from the cellar to the roof of the stage was described as an amazing 118 feet. All of this made it eminently possible to provide the Victorians with the spectacle they craved for – from shipwrecks to earthquakes – in the greatest, grandest of style. Other 'mod-cons' of the day included heating provided by steam pipes – the concept of open fires having been dispensed with; lighting provided by gas – with 15 miles of piping and 400 gas jets; and a further few miles of speaking tubes to connect different areas of the theatre. Incidentally, electric lighting was partly introduced in 1884 and was subsequently gradually added to in varying degrees, prior to taking over entirely in the early years of the next century.

One further marvel of Victorian invention – a quirky novelty still in evidence today – was the manager's office situated just backstage at dress circle level with seven doors leading off allowing him to access virtually all parts of the building in any direction, quickly and easily:

(1) to the front of house, to enable him to meet the audience

(2) to a small private staircase which led down to the visiting company manager's office immediately below (used extensively to conduct private negotiations over the final settlement contra account on the last night of a show's run. Visiting producers liked to be paid off before they left the theatre!)

(3) to the private manager's eight-seater box in the dress circle, to see the shows

(4) to a gallery overlooking the stage area, to ensure that staff and artists were performing as they should

(5) to a corridor leading to the backstage dressing rooms, to welcome artistes, etc.

(6) to his secretary's office, immediately next door

(7) to the private cash and document safe cupboard, in which the company's share certificates were also held

And the 'stars' who have graced its stage are as celebrated as this remarkable house. There have been classical 'greats', 'greats' of the music hall, 'greats' from the world of ballet, musical comedy 'greats', dramatic 'greats' and, later, 'greats' from the silver screen. Those providing the drama in the early days include such notables as H. Beerbohm Tree, Ellen Terry, Sarah Bernhardt, Henry Irving, Lillie Langtry, and a good peppering of the music hall from Marie Lloyd, Little Tich, Gertie Millar and Dan Leno. As the twentieth century unfolded, many repeated their visits over and over again, to be joined by others – Lupino Lane, Julia Neilson and Fred Terry, Cicely Courtneidge and Jack Buchanan are just a few. The list is endless – Evelyn Laye, Ralph Richardson, Jessie Matthews, Sybil Thorndike – from all areas of theatricality – Tommy Trinder, Donald Wolfit, Wilfred Pickles, Ivor Novello. From the ballet stage came Anna Pavlova and Margot Fonteyn. From those who made it big on screen include – Claude Rains, Robert Donat, Rex Harrison, Greer Garson and Sean Connery. Later bills continue with the diversity: Peter Ustinov, Julie Andrews, Frankie Vaughan, Harry Secombe, Brian Rix, Cliff Richard, Tommy Steele, Billy Connolly, Bruce Forsyth, Elton John, Hank Marvin, Frank Skinner, Eddie Izzard, Jasper Carrott, etc.

Equally as important are the famous companies which have visited Leeds on so many occasions: opera companies which would include D'Oyly Carte, Carl Rosa, Sadler's Wells, Glyndebourne, English National Opera. The ballets include the Russian Imperial Ballet, the Vic Wells Ballet, the Royal Ballet, Ballet Rambert and the London Festival Ballet. For dramatic effect, try Henry Baynton's Shakespearian Company, the Old Vic Company, or the National Theatre. The Grand has also played host to many of the big 'milestone' musicals on their first great tours – the Novello repertoire, *Annie Get Your Gun, My Fair Lady* and *Oliver* representing just a few.

One aspect that should not go unmentioned due to its exceptional popularity is that phenomenon called pantomime – indeed, upon countless occasions this entertainment has saved many a venue's annual balance sheet from dipping into the red. The Grand's pantomime story is no different and spectacularly occupied the panto season of its first century almost consecutively.

But the salad days of houses packed to the ceiling night after night were not to last. The main problems at the Grand started as late as the 1960s, really, due to a lack of product. (Many managements had had problems before this.)

Gaps began to appear between presentations – particularly during summer months. Audiences, too, generally throughout the country, had become a commodity that no longer could be counted upon by theatres. Their aspirations and expectations – probably stemming back to the end of the war – were changing in a changing world. New things were suddenly becoming attainable which people had never dreamt of before – such as foreign holidays or outings in their own motorcars – all distracting from

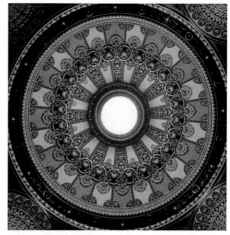

The ceiling centre.

conventional, out-of-date, pastimes. And all in addition to the lure of the new radio, luxury cinema and television!

As with all managements, the Grand braced itself against these difficult times.

A close-up of the dress circle front highlights its thickly encrusted ornamentation, appropriately lit by Gothic-style torches.

Indeed one of the measures, ironically, was to turn to the stars of television itself who, when not on the 'box', were hugely popular with theatre audiences who could actually come and see their favourites 'in the flesh'. This, together with the lucky coincidence of some of the big and popular musical tours, and some careful programming, bailed the theatre out for another few years. But, as elsewhere, the situation did not improve long-term and near the end of the 'sixties there was talk of demolition – even consideration of the Grand's replacement with a block of shops and offices! Fortunately, partly due to the building's listed status – a situation which may have helped save many an ailing venue – this irreversible action did not materialise.

What did happen was – and becoming increasingly a sign of the times of the decade – council intervention. In the first instance Leeds City Council took a lease on the theatre (guaranteeing the finances in conjunction with the Arts Council), with arrangements for its operation by a Theatre Trust. This was to prove a happy partnership leading eventually, by 1973, to the Council purchase of the building. Howard & Wyndham, the famous and very successful booking circuit through whom the Grand had booked its tours for years, was to remain in that role.

An important and unusual innovation then occurred in 1978 when, for the first time in more than thirty years, a new full-time opera company was founded – its principal objective to bring opera to the north of England. Opera North, as it is now known, was an offshoot of the English National Opera Company (formerly Sadler's Wells) based at the London Coliseum – this northern counterpart to make its home at the Grand in Leeds! Today it is still a thriving company, still *in situ*, and also touring to other houses in towns and cities such as Nottingham, Newcastle, Sheffield, Salford Quays and Hull. In addition it performs on the concert platform and enhances the educational and cultural life of the region generally via special projects, collaborations, schools, colleges and the community, etc. The Grand Theatre and Opera House, of course, had come into its own!

And the final instalment of the story continues the happy note. At the time of writing a massive improvement and refurbishment scheme is planned, designed to restore the venue to its former glory and to bring it technically into the twenty-first century. Backstage areas will include better dressing-room accommodation; improved flying facilities; an enlarged orchestra pit; and a hydraulic lorry-lift capable of raising lorries full of scenery, etc. from street to stage and rehearsal-room level. Administration accommodation and rehearsal rooms will be provided over the street (at the side) in and around Premier House, which will be incorporated into the plan and linked to the Grand by a bridge. The Assembly Rooms – for so long an important part of the cultural life of the city, then the home of the Plaza cinema before it closed in the 'seventies – will also be restored, bringing back into use a 'grand' room capable of housing performances, educational pursuits, entertaining, and even rehearsals. And lastly, but certainly not least, will be the grand refurbishment of the main auditorium; a resuscitation of original plasterwork and features, which will spectacularly reveal the true artistry of the Victorian craftsman and a golden age.

Up to now a well-mixed programme of plays, musicals, operas, ballets and concerts etc. has continued to delight Leeds audiences and the exciting promise of the future, with its Victorian yet all-mod-cons splendours, will no doubt ensure a place for this amazing and prestigious "magnificent temple of drama" well into its second century of success...

Amongst the highest seating in the house ... the upper-slips.

A view of the amphitheatre circle from the upper-slips.

Wakefield Theatre Royal and Opera House

The saying that good things come in small packages can certainly be verified in Wakefield, West Yorkshire, where stands the smallest Matcham House in existence, possibly the smallest Frank Matcham ever designed. It incorporates all of the expected Matcham traits, however, there being no small measure here, and sports a façade in warm red brick with stone dressings, typical of some of his other ventures and, moving inside, the usual generous amount of thickly encrusted rococo plasterwork.

Entertainment on the site has been traced back to long before the present building, in fact to 1775 when the actor-manager Tate Wilkinson leased a theatre as part of his York circuit (see part 1 – York Theatre Royal), but which would play only for a few weeks in the annual calendar to coincide with local race meetings when sufficient patronage could be relied upon. Some of the most famous 'stars' of the time appeared in that original building, notable examples including Mrs Sarah Siddons, Mrs Jordan, John Philip Kemble and Edmund Kean and the 'Theatre, Wakefield' as it was initially billed was renamed 'Theatre Royal' in the nineteenth century – reflecting the popular choice of

title of the period, whether truly 'Royal' or not generically implying respectability – this still being retained today. Another chapter in the old theatre's life began in 1871 when it became a beerhouse and music hall, and a further change came in 1883 when a refurbished building reopened as 'The Royal Theatre & Opera House', the proprietor now being one Benjamin Sherwood, a local councillor and hotelier.

The business would remain under control of the Sherwood family for more than fifty years but it was only after the first ten years or so of operation that the theatre's licence was revoked by magistrates owing to its poor structural condition. This state of affairs obviously required immediate and major action, the result being the creation of a new (the present) building which was designed by Frank Matcham. Nine months and £13,000 later it opened (15th October 1894) with Horace Lingard's No. 1 Comic Opera Company playing the burlesque opera *Brother Pelican.*

The new theatre presented touring companies in an assortment of entertainments: musical comedies, plays and grand opera. Notables include the D'Oyly Carte and Arthur Rousbey opera companies, drama from Frederick Melville's company and, later on, touring repertory from Harry Hanson's or Frank H. Fortescue's players interspersed with road shows and revues. Names famous enough still to be remembered and who have graced the stage at one time or another range from Robert Donat, Stan Laurel and Julie Andrews through to later personalities Hylda

Wakefield Theatre Royal and Opera House: in the smallest of Frank Matcham's auditoriums in existence, the stage drapery extravagantly dresses the house.

Baker and Harry Worth who became television favourites, and Jill Summers and Arthur Leslie to become known for their roles in *Coronation Street.*

Naturally the theatre followed the fortunes of the majority of its contemporaries, shaped by the demands (or lack of) of its patrons, and eventually went on the, not uncommon, route of film shows (as early as 1916 for a trial period) in an attempt to survive against the emerging and fierce contest from cinema. In 1947 the Sherwoods sold the Opera House to the Gateshead Empire Palace Ltd. (the Essoldo cinema chain) and although it remained a live theatre until 1954 it was then finally converted to full time cinema, reopening in 1955 as the 'Essoldo'. Of course TV was the next medium to have a serious effect upon the proceedings of live theatre and, indeed, cinema and the venue eventually resorted to seedy films for a time, prior to another conversion – on this occasion for bingo, reopening for that purpose in September 1966 – as the 'Lucky Seven'!

Perhaps the theatre was comparatively 'lucky' for although it was no longer occupied for its original purpose at least the diversions of cinema and bingo had kept the wonderful fabric basically intact. Further protection came in 1979 when the Department of the Environment awarded it a Grade II* listing as a building of special architectural or historic interest. The venue had actually passed into the hands of Ladbrokes some years before, but by 1980 they decided to terminate their bingo operation there which, in turn, stirred a whole burst of activity within the local community!

Times had changed since the theatre had closed its doors to live entertainment in 1954 and by the 'eighties was a resurgence of interest within the public at large and, perhaps, not a few regrets regarding some of the material losses for which the preceding quarter of a century was responsible. Naturally where theatres are concerned it would not have been practical for them all to have survived, but undoubtedly some were lost unnecessarily. In Wakefield the situation and the time were now right to avoid the mistakes of others – already there was a local discontent concerning the city's lack of a live theatre, and discussions about a remedy. The closure of the 'Lucky Seven' then prompted an amazing reaction!

The ball really started rolling with a public meeting in 1981 and there was obviously an overwhelming desire that the theatre should be revived. What followed during the next five years is a story within itself – basically a steering committee was formed and the Wakefield Theatre Trust established. With huge financial and practical help from numerous professional and amateur bodies and individuals, the immense task of acquisition, reversal, refurbishment, administration, etc. eventually resulted, on the 16th March 1986, in the official reopening of the Wakefield Theatre Royal and Opera House as a live theatre.

Several features or snippets of information may be of interest. Obviously attention falls firstly upon the auditorium which, with its original plasterwork, has been lovingly restored to its Victorian past, and forms a delightfully intimate space for its 504 seats. The existing gas 'sunburner' was found still to be *in situ* in the centre of the ceiling (similar to that described at Buxton Opera House – see part 4), once responsible for ventilation as well as lighting, and Messrs Totterton & Co of

Leeds – engineers to the gas lighting at the Grand Theatre there (see previous chapter) – were similarly employed at Wakefield, prior to the installation of electric lighting in 1898. A new orchestra pit has been installed, as has a counterweight flying system. Entrances to the stalls and dress circle are made via the existing, charming, bijou, foyer and exits from the gallery still lead around the corner as in the olden days! Backstage a new dressing room block has been added and another significant addition front of house follows the acquisition of adjacent shops which now connect internally with the theatre building and provide excellent refreshment areas. The restoration is a credit, with replacement items carefully matching originals as far as possible and, of course where practicable, retaining existing fabric (e.g. stained glass work and so on).

Congratulations must be extended to the many, many hugely enthusiastic and energetic people who campaigned, supported and worked for the restoration, for today the venue still flourishes, bringing live professional theatre back to the city, and providing a platform for the immense amount of amateur talent that exists in the area. Of course the work is never-ending, with development, improvements and renewals continually being made in order to preserve this theatrical gem for future generations.

A painting and plasterwork on the dress circle front.

Wolverhampton Grand Theatre

Not only does the Grand superbly illustrate the characteristics of a typical late-Victorian auditorium, with its rounded style, it also showcases another important work by one of the most prominent architects of his time – John Charles Phipps – which has been considered as one of his finest accomplishments. Additionally, this theatre's history completes all of the tick-boxes ever likely to be encountered in the life of an old survivor, highlighting ups and downs ranging from appearances by the most eminent luminaries, to closure, to local authority ownership and ultimate magnificent refurbishment, so that the building truly has a notable and relevant tale to tell.

When the curtain rose for the first time on 10th December 1894 to the strains of the D'Oyly Carte Opera Company playing in Gilbert & Sullivan's *Utopia, Limited,* the audience were thrilled with what they saw – both on stage and off – for the auditorium in cream, gold and claret was a sight to behold. One hundred and four years later – on 17th December 1998 – audiences were equally thrilled following the latest brilliant refurbishment which, costing £8 million, had faithfully restored historical features and simultaneously brought the theatre, technically, to a standard required by the impending 21st century.

Originally having well over 2,000 seats the various parts of the house were,

Wolverhampton Grand Theatre: another Phipps achievement – a sumptuous scene of cream and gold and warm red topped by a beautiful saucer-dome ceiling, richly embellished and complemented by an elegant chandelier.

as always in those days, carefully segregated so that the opposing classes did not have to mix! Today, of course, things are vastly different, for although the existing facade – with its impressive 123 foot length to Lichfield Street – remains practically the same in appearance, this original 'grand' entrance now serves *all* seats (and compare its present total number of approximately 1,200). The streetscape initially included four shops but these have since been turned over to the theatre's own use, and with glazing to the central arches and tweaking of the internal arrangements, the extra space has allowed the introduction of modern bars, lounges, staircases, lifts, foyer space, and improved disability facilities so that the front of house amenities are second to none!

Backstage the story is equally impressive: one of the most notable improvements being the replacement of the fly tower with one much taller that now ensures the theatre can receive the biggest of shows and the most impressive sets! So Wulfrunians now have the pick of the entertainment crop! Add to this an orchestra pit which can rise to stage level to form an apron, modern dressing rooms and administrative accommodation, air conditioning in the auditorium and a great attention to detail, such as careful restoration of the chandelier and Phipps' typical saucer-dome ceiling, and we have here a historically important house preserved to excellent standards for posterity.

"Nothing succeeds like success" – and the refurbishments bear out the old adage – but this was not always the case and in 1980, the Grand reaching its lowest ebb, with audiences at an all-time low, was forced to close. This illustrates the precarious and fickle nature of show business, which in Wolverhampton had always been generally popular and in plentiful supply, with records showing not only the Grand to have sailed through periods of immense appeal, but a number of neighbouring contemporaries to have accompanied it! Indeed there are accounts of dramatic performances from as far back as 1779, and music hall in the public houses (all being subject to the licensing requirements and resorting to the usual ploys to differentiate 'drama' from 'music'). Then reports show a Theatre Royal from 1845 to 1894 just prior to the Grand's existence; a purpose-built music hall from the 1860s – 'variety' subsequently being catered for from 1898 by the Empire Theatre until 1956; and from the 1860s until 1982 there was a always a popular theatre in Bilston Street with various names ranging from 'Star Theatre', 'Hippodrome', 'Prince of Wales' and 'Theatre Royal'. Alas, only the Grand remains today to tell the story!

Following the initial starry opening night in 1894 the Grand settled down to the life of a typical provincial touring house presenting, for many years, a variety of works from musicals to Shakespeare, but later on changing policy when it went over to repertory. Notably, in 1936, the rep was run by Leon Salberg from Birmingham's Alexandra Theatre (see later chapter) so the two houses were able to benefit each other – for example by having two groups, actors and even productions could potentially be interchangeable, thus raising standards of production. Some of those to become well known via the rep include Peggy Mount, Kenneth Moore, June Whitfield and Leonard Rossiter. Other famous names include, from the early days, Sir Henry Irving and Charlie Chaplin and, later on, Sean Connery, Michael Caine, Terrance Stamp and David Whitfield. From other walks of life speeches were made by Winston Churchill and David Lloyd George upon which (separate) occasions the theatre was utilised as a meeting hall. So the Grand has hosted a diversity of programme in an attempt to remain popular – touring, repertory, politics (!), pantomime and, by the 'fifties, variety.

In 1969, however, troubled by the universal problems of theatres in that era, with audiences swiftly diminishing, the Grand was sold to the local authority and run by a trust, thus ending 75 years of ownership by the Myatt family. Some refurbishments were carried out and the theatre remained open chiefly as a touring house – and often quite successfully – for more than ten years until, again, dwindling spectators brought difficulties, this time so great that the Grand had to close. It also spelt the closure of another era – that of professional theatre in

Wolverhampton – but luckily, waiting in the wings, was a determination from a nucleus of locals who were not prepared simply to sit back and accept the situation.

This led to the formation of the 'Save the Grand Action Group' which, along with the borough council, took stock and their 'action' plan would predominantly include funding issues involving grants and annual subsidy, making possible a programme of rebuilding and restoration and future successful operation of the venue. The Grand reopened in 1982 noted as one of the country's best venues – now attractive to touring companies and audiences alike – and went on to celebrate its one hundredth birthday in style on 10th December 1994 when the D'Oyly Carte Opera Company returned to play exactly to the date it had opened the theatre a century before!

The opportunity for promoting longevity was now at its strongest and decisions were taken to this effect, resulting in the latest fabulous refit – designed by RHWL, leading experts in such schemes. With all mod-cons at both sides of the curtain, interspersed with carefully preserved and restored Victorian characteristics the Grand, in its originating touring role, continues to present the number-one companies, stars and productions. Will there be cause for further celebration 10th December 2094? Only time will tell!

THE GRAND THEATRE

THIS COMMEMORATION STONE
WAS LAID BY
MRS C.T. MANDER
MAYORESS OF WOLVERHAMPTON
JUNE 28TH 1894
C.J. PHIPPS, F.S.A. ARCHITECT. — H. COUCH, BUILDER

THIS BUILDING HAS BEEN ERECTED BY
THE WOLVERHAMPTON NEW THEATRE COMPANY, LTD.

DIRECTORS
C.A. NEWNHAM J.P. CHAIRMAN
C.T. MANDER J.P. MAYOR OF WOLVERHAMPTON
B.G. CLARK. JOSEPH EVANS, L.W. HODSON

SOLICITORS
MESSRS FOWLER & LANGLEY

SECRETARY
THOMAS J. BARNETT

THE THEATRE OPENED ON DECEMBER 10TH 1894
UNDER THE MANAGEMENT OF E.H. BULL

Sheffield Lyceum Theatre

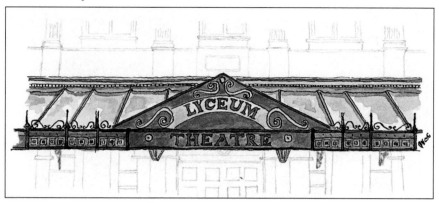

The chief contribution that the Sheffield Lyceum makes to this book is the fact that it has, in my opinion, one of the most superb auditoriums in the country. Indeed, so gloriously carried out is the grand rococo plasterwork – in the style of Italian Renaissance and Louis Quatorze, which also incorporates one of the most extravagant proscenium arches ever likely to be viewed – that this fact almost exclusively may be held responsible for the theatre's survival today (it gained listed status in 1972 at a time when its future was precariously hanging in the balance).

It will come as no surprise, therefore, to learn that its creator – W. G. R. Sprague – was one of the leading theatrical architects of his time, also leaving a legacy of important London theatres (for example the Albery, Aldwych, New Ambassadors, Gielgud, St Martin's, Strand (Novello), Wyndham's), and was a protégé of Frank Matcham's, to boot. In addition there were once a number of provincial Sprague houses all of which, alas, have since disappeared, making the survival of the Lyceum all the more momentous and significant. The history of the Lyceum also supports the trends which have become apparent from the studies of other venues in the book, confirming the ups and downs of theatrical tastes, social and economic standings and traditions, and resultant effects on the dramatic and operatic lives, companies and venues in Britain's show-business story.

When the Lyceum opened on Monday 11th October 1897, to the strains of the eminent Royal Carl Rosa Opera Company playing in *Carmen* with "some of the finest English and continental singers of the time" (*Sheffield and Rotherham Independent*), Mr Sprague was in attendance. The evening

Sheffield Lyceum Theatre: safety curtain and colour scheme by Clare Ferraby, consultant designer to the Arts Team, RHWL. Inspired by the commedia dell' arte, a masquerade before an Old English view of Sheffield. The balustrade is copied from the top of the exterior of the building. The artist's signature – a mouse (his trade mark) – is concealed within the artwork.

sparkled with an array of other VIPs including the Master Cutler and many "ladies and gentlemen of the professional and commercial classes of the city" – and in addition, "several well-known theatrical managers from other towns also attended to wish success to the efforts of their colleagues in Sheffield." These included "Mr R. G. Crawford of Edinburgh", "Mr F. W. Wyndham, well known in connection with theatrical houses in Newcastle, Edinburgh and Glasgow; Mr J. M. Chute, of the Prince's Theatre, Bristol; Captain Rogers, of the Prince of Wales's Theatre, Birmingham; Mr Arthur Hart, London; Mr H. E. Moss, the well-known director of 'Empires'; Mr Asquith and Mr Wanless, directors of the Hull Grand Theatre."

The (*Sheffield and Rotherham Independent's*) account of the evening goes on to say that "after the third act there were loud calls of "Hart" and in response Mr John Hart, the managing director" (who, previously, "with Mr Hopcutt, the local manager, were busy in every part of the house personally superintending the arrangements for the accommodation and comfort of the audience") "came in front of the curtain and was received with loud applause".

The Sheffield Daily Telegraph confirms what followed: "The theatrical public of the country had shown their welcome of the new enterprise by bushels of telegrams, from which it is merely possible here to cite a few. Sir Henry Irving, who will next week tread its boards, wired congratulations; so did Mr and Mrs Beerbohm Tree, Mr D'Oyly Carte, Mr Forbes-Robertson, Mr Arthur Roberts, Mr George Alexander, the directors of the Carl Rosa Company, Mr and Mrs Kendal, Mr Wilson Barrett, Mr and Mrs Edward Compton, Miss Fortescue, Messrs. Dawes and Little Tich, Mr Arthur Collins (of Drury Lane), Mr Mulholland (of the Metropole), Mr Brickwell (of the Garrick), and many others of light and leading as actors or managers. When Mr Hart made an end of reading these he called forth Mr W. G. R. Sprague, the architect, whose work was rewarded with a double call before the curtain." (Interestingly, his age at this time was 31 or 32!)

And so the Lyceum Theatre was launched upon its illustrious career! Its site was not new to the show-business theme either. It had started off in 1879 as a circus, which was destroyed by fire in May 1893, then Mr Stacey (to whom it was let) built a theatre – 'The City Theatre', designed by Walter Emden (another notable theatrical architect!). He sold this to the Lyceum Theatre Company in autumn 1896 which opened it in January 1897; closed it by Easter 1897 for substantial structural conversions and reopened it (probably encouraged by the massively successful nearby Empire Palace, opened only two years earlier) in all its, quite breathtaking, Sprague glory, as stated above.

Prominence, in the mind of the 1897 theatre-goer, seems to have been centred around such things as the electric lighting (albeit backed up by a "system of gas lighting" … "provided as a safeguard against any temporary failure of the electric light"); the lack of pillars to support the balconies (thus making for a better view of the stage than in many other theatrical venues of the time) and the iron, steel, concrete and brick (fire-proof) construction. Moreover, its present-day seating capacity of around eleven hundred was boasted as holding over three thousand persons. So much for regulation!

As this is the story not just of the Lyceum, but of theatres' generally unrolling progress, one particular aspect that occurred frequently in the early years, and to whose statistic the Lyceum was to contribute, can appropriately be mentioned here – the fire hazard! In many cases, of course, fire had completely destroyed theatres, often with the unfortunate loss of life. In the Lyceum's case, however, although the fire – which broke out at teatime on Monday 6th November 1899 – apparently destroyed much of the backstage area, only a handful of people were in the building, and the alarm was quickly raised. An account – which praises the work of the Sheffield Fire Brigade – was given in the *Sheffield and Rotherham Independent* on 7th November 1899 and makes interesting reading, both from its style and substantial coverage.

Even before the opening night there had been high hopes for the success of the Lyceum, and for this to attract quality performers for the people of Sheffield via a feast of Shakespeare, opera, ballet, society plays, comedies and pantomime. This was easily

A view upwards through the newly formed stairwell which now links the entire house, sweeping away the former segregation of the classes, highlights swish lighting and décor which sits happily alongside Victorian counterparts.

achieved and eminencies such as Sir Henry and Madame Sarah Bernhardt would soon appear – many of the famous names and companies returning over the following years time and time again. Sir Henry, incidentally, along with Miss Ellen Terry and the (London) Lyceum Company played the week after the Carl Rosa opening. When he was to make his final visit, in October 1905, this was to mark his last *full* week anywhere, since he died in Bradford a short time after.

A flip through the *Sheffield Year Book and Record*, and lists of productions held in the Sheffield Theatres' Archive, demonstrates how the Lyceum soon settled down as a touring theatre, receiving the best companies, productions and actors and actresses. (It is interesting to note the prices of admission in 1905: Private Boxes, £2.2s. and £1.11s.6d.; Grand Circle, 4s.; Orchestra Stalls, 3s. (if booked, 3s. 6d.); Upper Circle, 2s;. Balcony, 1s.6d.; Pit, 1s.; Gallery, 6d. Half-price at 9 o'clock to Grand Circle, 2s.; Orchestra Stalls, 1s.6d.; and upper circle, 1s. Early doors to all parts at 6.45p.m., 6d. extra, except gallery. Early doors to Gallery 3d. extra. Telephone 640.)

Let me select a few of the famous at random. Of the companies the Royal Carl Rosa, already mentioned, was to become a very frequent visitor. Opera was, additionally, brought by other notables, including the D'Oyly Carte and Sadler's Wells Opera Company. Sadler's Wells also provided their Theatre Ballet Company, as did The Royal Ballet and Ballet Rambert. Plays, too numerous to mention, were here in abundance – many of them now unheard of, but including those which have stood the test of time such as *Charley's Aunt*, *Lady Windermere's Fan*, *The Passing of the Third Floor Back* and, of course, the Shakespearean repertoire. And then all of the lighter musicals must have played here: in the early years those which, still, can be remembered and which are occasionally revived by amateur companies, but which at the time would have been hot stuff – the equivalent of *The Rocky Horror Show* or *Les Miserables* playing today. The lists show production after production of *The Earl and the Girl*, *The Belle of New York*, *Floradora*, *The Merry Widow*, *The Arcadians*, *The Count of Luxembourg*, *The Quaker Girl*, *The Maid of the Mountains*, etc.

And the players? Again a brief selection: Charlie Chaplin, Mr Forbes-Robertson, Mrs Patrick Campbell, Mr Seymour Hicks, Miss Phyllis Dare, Anna Pavlova the prima ballerina, Miss Julia Neilson and Mr Fred Terry, Lillie Langtry, Miss Ada Reeve and Mr Edmund Keane have all graced its boards … the list goes on!

After the Second World War, the old favourites still came, and new ones – just a few more selected at random, many returning in later years: 1948 Donald Wolfit, 1949 Michael Denison and Dulcie Gray, the husband and wife team, 1950 Margaret Lockwood, Evelyn Laye, Emlyn Williams, Dora Bryan, Sybil Thorndike, 1952 Wilfred Pickles, 1953 John Hanson, 1954 Irene Handl, 1958 Thora Hird, 1959 Michael Caine, Cicely Courteneidge, 1969 Flora Robson, John Mills and Anthony Quayle.

Pantomime has played an important part here too, as in nearly every other theatre in the land, with spectacular productions packing houses from Christmas until Easter, and providing ample competition for Matcham's Empire Palace pantomimes a few streets away. The posters, again, (selected at random) show famous names and will no doubt bring back happy memories to those who were fortunate enough to see them: 1948 *Mother Goose* - Frank Randle; 1951 *Jack And The Beanstalk* – Harry Secombe; 1952 Dick Whittington – Ken Platt, Tony Heaton, Morecambe and Wise; 1955 *Little Red Riding Hood* – Ken Dodd; 1961 *Beauty and the Beast* – Nat Jackley, Jack Douglas, Hope and Keen; 1962 *Aladdin* – Jimmy Clitheroe; 1963 *Goldilocks and the Three Bears* – David Whitfield, Peter Goodwright; 1964 *Humpty Dumpty* – Ronnie Hilton, Ted Rogers, Wyn Calvin; 1965 *The Sleeping Beauty* – Edmund Hockridge, Roy Hudd; 1966 *Cinderella* – Dickie Valentine, Cardew Robinson, Joe Black.

As I mentioned earlier, it was at the pantomime here that I became captured by the wonderfully coloured and magical world of the theatre. I can also remember little peculiarities about this particular theatre: the way that, when one entered the warm and glowing auditorium, an advertisement sheet – extolling the virtues of local businesses – was always in place upon the stage, so extravagantly painted that it was completely at home in its surroundings. When the show was due to start, the house curtain would then be lowered in front of it, in readiness for the performance. In complete contrast, the safety curtain would be lowered in the interval (presumably to comply with fire regulations) and this was an awful, somewhat dirty, structure, upon which was written in Old English script "For Thine Especial Safety" (an inscription, I believe, that once used to grace many Victorian theatres' safety curtains). Again, in complete contrast, the present safety curtain is painted just as extravagantly, with its local scene, as was the advert drop of the old days!

The fortunes of the Lyceum eventually came to resemble the general trend of Britain's theatrical tale. Glancing back to the lists of shows after the Second World War, three months of the year's fare had by now been taken up by repertory – in the shape of Harry Hanson's Court Players, who presented a different play every week. They are still remembered with great warmth by the locals, and a number of Court Players' (and other) companies operated in several parts of the country for quite a few years – a genre of 'out-of-town' commercial repertory which would play at local touring theatres for periods ranging from a week to several months. Of course, the alternative attraction of cinema was now in full swing. Then in 1954 the repertory season was increased to six months – by now TV had begun to gain momentum. And in 1959 the annual list of weekly shows becomes shorter since, for the first time, the theatre went 'dark' for about six weeks for a 'summer vacation'. This was to be repeated during the next few years – with the 'vacation' in some of the years in the early 60s extending from the end of May until early September. In 1969 the struggle became too great, and the theatre eventually closed its doors for theatrical productions.

Already bingo had taken the stage – with pantomime returning the boards momentarily to theatrical use at Christmas – and at the time this must have seemed a severe blow. Not so severe as some of the blows that were still to come! So many theatres in the country were going (or had gone) the same way! In retrospect, Bingo was one of the factors that allowed the Lyceum, by the skin of its teeth, to become one of the lucky ones, and survive to tell the tale. Many at this time were lost for ever – indeed, the land upon which

the theatre stood was wanted for redevelopment – but in 1972 the importance of the fantastic interior was finally acknowledged and the Lyceum achieved listed status, thus reprieving it from any immediate threat of demolition. Nevertheless, the building was to stand empty for many years to come, and was by no means out of the wood yet.

The next twenty-odd years or so are a complete story in themselves but it will suffice to give the basic points. Within two years of the Lyceum's demise for theatrical use a brand new theatre – the Crucible (see part 6) – was opened literally within a few yards of the Lyceum's main entrance. The Crucible was everything that the Lyceum was not, and *vice-versa*! By now, however, a strong and lively campaigning group had been formed which was fighting tirelessly to keep traditional theatre (in the form of the Lyceum's exceptional example) in the city.

Eventually the group formed a trust and the aim, of course, was always to reopen and refurbish the theatre and many ideas were mooted. However, despite its efforts, and the scuffles and skirmishes of the ensuing years, involving public enquiries and the like and much dissension, the venue was eventually sold to another bidder for more than the trust could afford, and opened as a scene for rock music in 1981. This venture was to be short lived, however, and the major reason for its failure – the inability to obtain a drinks licence – was to be repeated around 1985 when another serious project, to turn the Lyceum into a disco and restaurant, was abandoned. Now, with the fate of the Lyceum once again up in the air, came a change of fortune. Briefly, two of the original campaigners, having put up their homes as security, and with other backing including the city council, were successful in purchasing the building. A new trust was formed, the Lyceum and Crucible trusts joined forces, and funding was obtained – involving a package which was to include refurbishment to Tudor Square – from the Council, the EEC, and the private, voluntary and public sectors.

About £12 million was expended solely upon the Lyceum refurbishment, and the result – seen by the public for the first time in a series of grand gala evenings during week commencing 10th December 1990 – is breathtaking. Of course the auditorium has to be the *chef-d'oeuvre* for the theatre-goer, its 1897 grand rococo plasterwork having been brilliantly restored, obviously after much research, with principal colours of cream, white and gold, and hangings in a complementary dusky-pink. Copies of original lighting appliances and replenishment of long-ago painted-out pictorial decorations, together with a carpet predominant in burgundy which incorporates designs to be seen in some of the plasterwork, complete the overall appearance to perfection.

Typically, in line with modern-day theatrical renovations, steps were also taken to remove the conglomeration of passages. These had originally existed in order to ensure complete segregation of the Victorian classes by providing them with individual entrances to their respective parts of the house. Even I can remember the separate brick stairway that still remained for the galleryites, with its little paybox at the top, flickering gaslights and entrance around the corner away from the main 'grand' foyer! The refurbishment has provided, in its place, a grand entrance for the entire house.

The Lyceum, being characteristic of many of Sprague's other houses, originally had its principal entrance on a corner, but this has now been moved to the front of the building under a jolly coloured glass and iron canopy. The foyers that lead off are contained both in the existing part of the building and in a newly created space, and their decorations are in a style complementary to their respective areas. This means that Louis Quatorze is carried along throughout the original, and a completely contrasting ultramodern theme within the new, comprising bars at each tier-level, and an impressive stainless steel and glass stairway to connect the whole.

Equally as impressive are the backstage areas which were mostly demolished and replaced with every modern requirement. The stage itself was enlarged so as to become compatible with the needs of the majority of touring companies, and provided with a new counterweight flying system. A new orchestra pit was formed, with a hydraulic elevator which can be raised to any height, including stage level, and with the option to extend the size so as to contain even the largest ballet or opera orchestra. Dressing rooms with all mod-cons, wardrobe and storage spaces, and an excellent rehearsal room have all been constructed behind the proscenium arch making the Lyceum one of the most enviable theatrical spaces in the country.

As mentioned earlier, the Lyceum and Crucible Theatre buildings are situated within yards of each other, and this has obviously contributed greatly to their ability to merge under one management umbrella, known as 'Sheffield Theatres'. Moreover, the venues' contrasting designs provide the opportunity to present a wide variety of theatrical fare, which, in principle, allows their work to be complementary rather than competitive. The Lyceum's external refurbishment has restored the original sparkle splendidly and, together with the Crucible's clean lines, Tudor Square provides the perfect prologue to any theatrical occasion, and an optimistic epilogue in a story with such a chequered history.

Sunderland Empire Theatre

Here is a splendid example of a large variety house built in the Edwardian era which, with a somewhat unusual architectural style employing flamboyant ornamentation from stalls to steeply-raked third-tier gallery, and incorporating several gloriously vulgar features upon the way, captures perfectly the quintessence of the music hall and, indeed, the people whom it has entertained for so long. While Sunderland remains typical of the North East's cordiality, its industrial heritage reminds us of its famed days as a world shipbuilding centre, and the Empire continues to serve its modern-day customers just as faithfully as it did its hardened shipbuilders and coal miners of the past. Indeed, with eyes tightly closed, one can almost stand amid this 'palace of varieties' and still hear the jubilant cries and applause of audiences which over the years have been delighted in the Empire's commodious auditorium, and talked and laughed loudly in its halls and bars, promenades and crush rooms.

The theatre was the brainchild of Richard ("Dicky" to his friends) Thornton, originally from South Shields. He was a theatrical enterpriser so successful that from his modest start busking on the sea front at Marsden, he had risen to the great heights of controlling the other theatres in Sunderland, and also entering into partnership with Edward Moss, thus initiating the famous Moss'

Empires chain. (It is notable, therefore, that he was party to the building of other Empire Palaces in such places as Newcastle, Edinburgh, Birmingham, Sheffield, Liverpool, Glasgow, Hull, Nottingham, Leeds and Bradford. Moreover, that the chain was greatly responsible for the vastly ameliorating conditions appearing in theatres and music halls at the time, providing ever-more sumptuous establishments conducive to family entertainment at prices they could afford.) But the Sunderland Empire was his own baby of which he had total control, and which he ran with a policy of twice-nightly variety bills. He used a firm of local architects to design the building, W. & T. R. Milburn (see later chapter which shows off their Liverpool Empire).

Today, patrons will enter for all parts of the house under the bright green dome of its bold corner tower, topped with the figure of Terpsichore – but this was not always the case. Even in Sunderland there was class distinction at the time of the Empire's inauguration, and this demanded separate entrances – by now a British tradition anyway – complete with separate payboxes, separate bars (except for the gallery which had none), and separate lavatories, etc. so as to segregate each distinct area of the house and spare the classier members of the public from coming face to face with the hoi polloi! Today these entrances are still very much in evidence in the streets surrounding the theatre, many retained as vomitory exits and fire escapes. Those which served the cheaper areas each had, typically, small arched hatches in the wall for payboxes, along narrow passages through which the punters would individually file. Only those pursuing seats in the dress circle would initially experience the grand staircase and all of its finer trappings. The remaining clientele, apart from the front stalls customers who, additionally, had their own posh entrance and crush hall, would laboriously queue for seats. This was because only the better class areas were bookable in advance, leading to a mad dash for the best seats from the pittites or galleryites every time the house was opened! But at least the buskers kept the queues entertained as they tucked into their purchases of hot chestnuts or roast potatoes who, once in, could apparently also buy hot Bovril from the bars in addition to the usual beverages, to help dispel the cold night air.

The house was opened for the very first time, incidentally, on the 1st July 1907 when music hall star Vesta Tilley – having laid the foundation stone on the 29th September of the previous year – was to officially perform the opening ceremony. Her appearance was to originate a cavalcade of stars and performers for years to come. And as the century progressed through the inevitable changes and tastes that its decades would bring – from the stars of the music hall, the monuments of ragtime or jazz, the glamorous Hollywood and American favourites and the wartime themes of the 'forties, the lavish London and Broadway musicals and the Big Bands, the 'fifties and its rock and roll stars and those of the so-called 'swinging' 'sixties – the Empire would move with the times in an attempt to cater to the popular demand.

After the initial burst of success and comfortable early years, and following a general trend, audiences eventually began to diminish. Steps were taken to try to lure them back – indeed, by the early 'thirties, a projection box had been installed and films, which had in many music halls started out as one of the 'turns' on the variety bill, took over completely. *All Quiet On The Western Front* was the first film to be shown at the Empire and the 'talkies' were to continue for several years although, it is said, not always entirely successfully due to the long throw and steep rake of the auditorium, resulting in inferior presentation. Eventually, however, normality was gradually restored as variety and films began to share the Empire's stage, with stage shows finally winning the day. Many of the names that appeared at this time were a result of the audience's desire to see the stars of their wirelesses or films – a practice that would be repeated in later years in relation to the small screen (TV) when that likewise became the craze.

By 1939 things would again change completely with the outbreak of the Second World War – a black cloud that, fortunately for many theatres, would also have a silver lining. Initially it closed them down altogether (usually, for a matter of only weeks), and then came the general wartime limitations such as rationing, blackouts and travelling difficulties, etc. But at the same time it created a mass market for entertainment – which establishments like the Empire were only too happy to supply!

If the war years did not present enough problems then the following decade certainly did. Not only had the public's interest in cinema developed in leaps and bounds but now the arrival of television would have its disastrous effect. While many theatres had to close – some for good – the Empire struggled on, but with rising costs and loss of income this led to down-market productions and eventually it stooped to the level of presenting strip shows! Perhaps this was the lowest time in the Empire's history? But, as the old show-biz adage has it – *"It's not where you start, it's where you finish!"* – and when you're at the bottom, there's only one way to go! The Empire's owners had finally taken the decision to close – but as in all good stories (and in *all* of the Empire's

Sunderland Empire Theatre: an unusual but pleasing and impressive auditorium. Note the side seating which replaces the conventional box configuration, and the little boxes attractively contrived along each side of the dress circle. A massive refurbishment has somewhat altered the colour scheme since this photograph was taken.

pantomimes) the good fairy waves her magic wand in a puff of smoke, and in the nick of time, to save the day!

The good fairy in this case was the Sunderland Corporation which took the then extremely unusual step of buying the theatre. The move – the first of its kind in the country – led to national speculation, and was not without its local critics (for example, the rate payers). It was to reopen approximately six months later (Boxing Day 1959) as the first *number-one* theatre under *civic* control. The gesture undoubtedly saved the theatre from destruction or radical alteration and, although not without its ongoing financial worries, therefore preserved an important piece of heritage towards happier times. A gradual, but almost continuous, programme of refurbishment and improvement followed over the ensuing years – together with a similar recovery in presentations. In 1972 the Sunderland Empire Theatre Trust Ltd. was formed to take over the day-to-day management.

Then came yet another first! In 2000 there was a reversal of the situation when private management was reintroduced – in the shape of Apollo Leisure (UK) Ltd, part of the American SFX conglomerate (subsequently taken over by Clear Channel Entertainment UK). Despite the aforementioned comeback the theatre had still been hampered by problems of funding and adequate audience numbers, perhaps aggravated by pressures including those which related to local government boundaries and competition and opposition from its near-neighbour, the Theatre Royal, Newcastle (featured in part 1). In the end, the Council, although retaining ownership and a financial commitment, contracted out the management to the private company (following tendering processes, etc.) which, with its major status in the field, could likely provide the most optimistic future.

Although many excellent and major works had taken place to the theatre's fabric during its period under civic control, in April 2004 the Empire was closed for a £4.5 million redevelopment, with funding from various sources. It reopened in December 2004 with one of the best and most technically equipped stages in the country, together with vastly enhanced backstage and front of house facilities, including new air conditioning and revised safety measures. As a venue with a prime intention of becoming a leader on the North East entertainment front capable of receiving the best and biggest touring companies on offer, including the latest West End successes as well as world class opera and ballet, in addition to local community projects, family and one-night shows, the result has not been disappointing. Indeed, the opening productions set the scene with presentations of no less rank than Andrew Lloyd

Webber's *Starlight Express*, closely followed by Cameron Mackintosh's *Miss Saigon*, and the current *What's on* list continues with a healthy and varied programme of equally prestigious events (for example, the National tour of *Chitty Chitty Bang Bang*), while admirably fulfilling the theatre's objectives.

But the presentation of 'stars' and quality productions is nothing new at the Empire for we already know that Vesta Tilley began it all in 1907. In her own generation, all of the popular music hall greats played the Empire Palace (as it was originally known) – some upon several occasions – from singers to comedy acts, jugglers, magicians, ventriloquists, even animal acts, etc. A selection in no particular order could include Marie Lloyd, Wee Georgie Wood, Hetty King, George Formby Snr., Florrie Forde, Fred Karno Company, Harry Lauder, Gertie Gitana. The 'twenties and 'thirties brought their film and radio stars, such as George Formby Jnr., Fred Emney, Sandy Powell, Tommy Handley, Betty Driver, Ted Ray, and a pleasant story also tells how Gracie Fields, while playing at the Empire, stopped the traffic when she appeared in a local shop to sign copies of her latest record!

The Big Bands would include Jack Hylton and Joe Loss and, of course, a great wartime favourite was Vera Lynn. Later, and more recent celebs include Marlene Dietrich, Harry Secombe, Reg Varney, Ruby Murray, Harry Worth, Tony Hancock, Frankie Vaughan, Des O'Connor, Pat Phoenix, Brian Rix, Charlie Williams, Jimmy Tarbuck, Helen Shapiro, Morecambe and Wise, Benny Hill, Tommy Cooper, Cliff Richard, Les Dawson, Bill Maynard, Su Pollard, Michael Crawford, Cilla Black, Billy Connolly, Cannon and Ball, The Krankies and Ant and Dec. Of course drama, repertory, opera, ballet and classical concerts have also played – Margaret Lockwood, Helen Mirren, Timothy West, Derek Jacobi, the Royal Ballet, D'Oyly Carte Opera Company, Birmingham Royal Ballet and Scottish Opera, to mention only a random few.

A number of other 'people' stories and facts show that the famous Laurel and Hardy duo played the Empire twice – in 1952 and 1954; Tommy Steele made his professional debut here in 1956; the Beatles played in 1963 when a local newspaper critic apparently described the Fab Four as "going nowhere" and "eminently forgettable"; sadly Sid James, the well known and much loved comic, died here on stage in April 1975 during a performance of *The Mating Season*.

And so as the Empire approaches its centenary birthday its colourful history lives on. Built as an old, but sumptuous, variety house it is another fine example of just how far the old music hall tradition had developed by the time of its opening, illustrating the transformation from the old song and supper rooms to that of the high class variety theatres. And a theatre of such stature that it is perfectly suited to its present requirements as a number-one touring venue. Now, state-of-the-art and equipped for the expectations, desires and demands of the twenty first century, it will hopefully continue to lure only the very best in entertainment for the enjoyment of many, many more generations to follow.

Bradford Alhambra Theatre

Externally, the Alhambra is one of the most impressive theatres I have ever seen, with its dramatic three domes – its principal one supported upon Corinthian columns which enclose a visible grand staircase – towering above a classical façade in cream and blue-grey faience with gilt trimmings, and more modern, but equally striking, glass extension. Originally totally in white, it must have shone against the darkness of the woollen mills that provided its audiences, in those days (opening March 1914) typically reaching their posh seats via a main grand corner entrance – then, situated under the principal dome – or cheaper ones via separate doors along the street.

Today all parts of the house are accessed from the main foyer, provided impressively by the new glass wing through which, upon the approaches, patrons can be seen circulating between the staircases and various levels that generally relate to the different areas of the auditorium. Each floor contains its own ancillary and entertaining arrangements (such as bars/buffet, etc.) thus the warm glow of conviviality of any occasion is experienced in advance of entering the theatre.

The structural changes mentioned formed part of a massive and life-saving improvement and refurbishment scheme that ousted the Alhambra from the doldrums and put it firmly on the theatrical map. It cost approximately £8.2

million (including upwards of £2 million from the EEC), took 21 months to complete, and the official reopening was on Thursday 30th October 1986.

One of the most significant problems had been that the theatre had simply been overtaken by technology – no longer attractive to the larger and more important touring companies it was missing out on some of the major, popular and lucrative shows – in turn, reducing audience appeal. All this, together with the usual problems that theatres were facing following the arrival of television, the package holiday, the motor car, the clubs, etc., finally brought things to a head. The alternatives seemed to be either to go out of business, or to spend money to create a theatre of the time – one that would hopefully bring back the customers – on both sides of the curtain! Fortunately a decision in favour of the latter won the day!

The improvement works were startling, and I can speak from personal experience as a member of the theatre audience. My first visits to the Alhambra were in the pre-improvement days and I remember a rather uninviting small

Bradford Alhambra Theatre: the opulent paintings and an abundance of fine plasterwork are enhanced by the present warm colour scheme.

foyer, very steep steps to the dress circle, and a decidedly icy auditorium – the upholstery being entirely in deep blue. Post-improvement brings a completely different story – and one that pleasingly retains all of the important 'old' bits alongside streamlined and swish 'new'.

In the Edwardian era small foyers were the norm – they didn't need to be any bigger as large portions of audiences entered their respective parts of the house via other doors. The Alhambra's refurbishment – typical of many of the others that I have seen, even featured within these pages – not only makes for much pleasanter access to all seats (capacity 1464), but additionally provides areas for eating, drinking, exhibitions, concerts, shop, etc. and daytime activity – in a hugely attractive setting.

And the house? Well, it is absolutely gorgeous – preserving the original fantastic plasterwork and Edwardian ambience. And with a new colour scheme in warm red with just a hint of blue to the backgrounds, superbly restored allegorical paintings above the boxes and proscenium depicting art, music and literature, the whole effect is no less than spectacular!

The 1986 refurbishment took the opportunity to provide a stage large enough to satisfy the modern demands of large scale opera, ballet and blockbuster musicals.

This picture demonstrates how technology, by now, had allowed theatre balconies to become much deeper and free from obstructing columns. The era of the horseshoe and its attendant pillars was gone.

The opportunity was also taken to acquire adjoining property which has allowed the existing stage to be greatly enlarged, and for a new studio space to be included. The backstage accommodation was revamped with all mod-cons, and with a new and much enlarged orchestra pit and the installation of the very latest in stage technology, the building was – is! – a showpiece!

In its heyday the Alhambra, which opened as a variety theatre, had been hugely successful despite plenty of competition from other entertainments in the city (supplied by the Theatre Royal, the Prince's, the Palace and the Empire) and, not surprisingly, all of the 'greats' appeared. In 1914 it compared quite magnificently with all of the other major and most spectacular houses that had by now sprung up in various parts of the country – as it still does today with those that remain. The architect was Chadwick and Watson of Leeds, and the auditorium with almost 1800 seats (then) was noted particularly for such features as its absence of pillars, the pit-stalls actually having carpets and tip-up seats (not benches), and its extravagant plaster decoration (by Felix de Jong & Co Ltd. of London – prolific and well known in top theatrical circles for exceptional quality décor).

The general shape of the house also reflected the engineering achievements of the period – with its deeper, cantilevered, balconies by now having succeeded the ubiquitous horseshoe designs of the previous century. Electricity was installed from the outset – with a back-up gas system in certain areas, should the electricity fail! Equally talked about was the fact that all seats could be

A section of the circle-front.

booked in advance – eliminating 'early doors' – and 'twice-nightly' shows were the order of the day from the start, with prices: boxes 15s (0.75p) and 10s (0.50p); orchestra stalls 1/6d (0.7½p); dress circle 1/- (0.5p); pit-stalls 9d (approx. 0.4p), so that, all-in-all, the Alhambra was clearly considered to be quite a trend-setter of the time! The official opening was conducted at 2pm on March 18th 1914, and the first performances were presented on Monday 23rd March 1914 – a special matinee in the afternoon before a VIP audience, and in the evening's show a notable name on the bill was Nellie Wallace, the famous comedienne who, incidentally, had also been on the opening bill of the London Palladium in 1910.

Now the Bradford Alhambra story cannot go further without mention of Mr Francis Laidler – the man responsible for its birth and, indeed, its operation for more than forty years. Unusually, he was 35 years old (in 1902) before he had any professional connection with the theatre and music hall business for which he would have such an obvious flair, and eventually his interests included the Leeds Theatre Royal, Keighley Hippodrome and, of course, the Alhambra. His route to the Alhambra came via the Prince's Theatre where his first managerial talents were realised, and where he presented his first pantomimes, the medium for which he was soon to become so famous. He obviously had much vision,

and seeing the changing face of music hall and popularity of family-orientated variety, the ameliorating conditions and sumptuous houses that were resulting, decided to progress his interests to equal only the best. In his building of the Alhambra, that, he certainly achieved!

From the beginning quality acts were brought to the Alhambra and, initially, Mr Laidler's booking partner was Walter De Freece (who, actually, was the husband of Vesta Tilley the great music hall/variety star) but from 1916, and for more than 40 years, Moss' Empires became the booking agents. Another important event for the theatre came in 1930/31 at which point Francis Laidler brought his pantomimes to the Alhambra's stage. His excellence in that field was already well known (as were his 'Sunbeams' – little local girls' dancing troupes who appeared every year) and, still today, quality pantomime is synonymous with the Bradford Alhambra.

The theatre has also played host to the many other forms of entertainment through the years – opera, drama, ballet, musicals – notable companies including the Carl Rosa Opera Company, D'Oyly Carte Opera Company, Sadler's Wells Opera Company, The Royal Ballet, Ballet Rambert, London Festival Ballet, Scottish Theatre Ballet, Birmingham Royal Ballet, Northern Ballet Theatre, Royal Shakespeare Company, National Theatre, Bristol Old Vic Company among many others. The musicals are, really, too numerous to mention for they have all been presented – and would feature the most notable stars of the day! The 'new', hi-tech, Alhambra receives the best and top smash hits have included works such as *Jesus Christ Superstar, The Sound of Music, Blood Brothers, Les Miserables* and *Phantom of the Opera.*

The 'stars' have shone just as brightly and names will, additionally, reflect the changing styles in entertainment through the years – e.g. the variety stars of the 'teens and 'twenties; the big bands of the 'thirties; the Second World War years; the Rock 'n' Roll of the 'fifties; the 'swinging' 'sixties and – throughout all of this – the pantomime! Here's merely a sprinkling: Vesta Tilley, Florrie Forde, George Robey, Nervo and Knox, Jose Collins, Sir John Martin-Harvey, Matheson Lang, Jack Warner, Elsie and Doris Waters, Wilfred Pickles, Jessie Matthews, Gracie Fields, Ivor Novello, Carl Brisson, Jack Hylton, Joe Loss, Billy Cotton, Sophie Tucker, Paul Robeson, Edmund Hockridge, John Hanson, Albert Modley, Arthur Askey, Frank Randle, Norman Evans, Laurel and Hardy, Tommy Cooper, Ken Dodd, Jimmy Clitheroe, Tommy Trinder, The Beverley Sisters, Pat Phoenix, Shirley Bassey, Michael Caine, Dame Margot Fonteyn, Rudolph Nureyev, Dudley Moore, Cannon and Ball, Les Dawson, Russ Abbot, The Krankies, Su Pollard, Tommy Steele.

Royal visits have featured upon special occasions, the Alhambra's portals having been graced by the Duke of Edinburgh (1969) and Princess Anne (1977).

In 1955 Francis Laidler died and his widow, Gwladys Laidler, took control of his theatrical interests – unfortunately also inheriting all of the problems that the mid-'fifties would bring – problems so extreme that by 1958 the Alhambra was up for sale! There were no takers and the theatre limped along until 1964 at which point, with liquidation of the company looming, Bradford Corporation saved the day by purchasing it and leasing it to a new company (a trust) set up for the purpose of management. But in 1974 the council itself took over the management, although it would be the 'eighties before the Alhambra was finally recognised as an obsolete 'time capsule' (the 1914 Edwardian version virtually remaining intact) when the tough decisions regarding the future were finally made.

The happy finale is that the 'showcase' Alhambra, as one of Britain's major touring theatres – its number-one status being famed over a wide area – continues to provide first class entertainment within an exceptional setting. If Mr Laidler could see his Bradford Alhambra today there is no doubt that he would be a very, very proud man.

Liverpool Empire Theatre

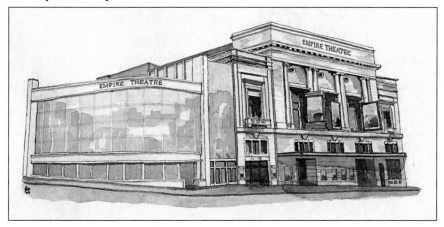

'The Mighty Empire' was the phrase that sprang to mind when I first entered this awe-inspiring house of curves brilliantly executed in, predominantly, warm crimson, pinks and gold with seating for 2,381 patrons on two sweeping levels. Curves in every direction imaginable – on the horizontal, the vertical, backwards, forwards, sideways, upwards, downwards – an all-encircling invention incorporating florid ornamentation from flamboyant fan vaults to marble balustrades. With a plethora of filigree, the eyes are feasted as they rise from the stalls of this great house – the largest two-tier theatre in the country – towards its sumptuous dome, launched with panache by its creators, W. and T. R. Milburn in 1925!

The style is not unlike the more extravagant cinema building which began to emerge in the 1920s, and is highly typical of other theatres that came from the Milburn 'factory'. Indeed, although traditional stage boxes are now included at each side on the proscenium walls, early photographs show how, at the ends of the circle, the seating at one time dipped towards the stage in a not dissimilar manner to that at Sunderland Empire, another Milburn creation featured earlier in this section. The treatment of the upper side-walls is also in some ways comparable with some of their other works, notably the Southampton Mayflower and Edinburgh Festival theatres and, of course, the gargantuan scale is ubiquitous.

Of equal stature are the stars and companies that have graced the 'Emmy's' (as it is colloquially known) stage, but in order to consider these properly we need to go back further than the present building, as theatrical tradition

Liverpool Empire Theatre: with echoes of the super-cinema, this enormous house is typical of its creators, W. & T. R. Milburn. This side view illustrates the enormity of the auditorium, enhanced by a brilliant colour scheme.

began on the site on the night of October 15th, 1866 with the opening of the New Prince of Wales Theatre and Opera House. A year later the venue was renamed the Royal Alexandra Theatre and Opera House, a name which lasted until 1896 when, following financial difficulties it changed ownership to that of Edward Moss and Richard Thornton – the company that would become the great Moss Empires conglomerate. They immediately introduced an extensive rebuilding and makeover job by Frank Matcham and, typically for Messrs Moss & Thornton, promoted fare that would "elevate the tone of variety entertainments" [with] "the absence of all that can be construed into vulgarity" in their new 'Empire Theatre of Varieties'.

Returning to 1866, the foundation stone had been laid by opera star Theresa Titiens and the theatre's first production was Gounod's Faust, presented by the Italian Opera Company. The building was only three-quarters of the size of the present and, reportedly, became almost self-sufficient with its own steam engine and forge – not an entirely unusual find, for some of the larger theatres of the time were positive backstage factories, having their own workshops and plant for the in-house manufacture of stock scenery, fittings, gas and, later, electricity, etc.

Notably, this was the first theatre in the country to install stage lighting using the fish-tailed gas burners supplied by Messrs Defries of London – electricity not being introduced until about the late eighteen-nineties – and it is said that at one time there were long rubber tubes to transport oxygen and hydrogen from tanks in the cellar to provide limelighting. Reports from similar venues also tell how limelight was sometimes produced in the wings by pouring powder into braziers – generating much smoke in the process – to create coloured lighting effects. All of this is a hazardous and precarious business – is it any wonder that theatres of this era were like time bombs waiting to go off? – and often did! Later improvements at the Alex also saw glass sealed gas footlights which apparently had their own chimney incorporated into a side wall to rid the fumes!

The stars of the period are repeats of many of those quoted as appearing in other great houses in this book, for example Sarah Bernhardt, Henry Irving and Ellen Terry, and it was at this theatre that Charles Kean made his final appearance. Of course the famous music hall stars of the day came here as well, including Vesta Tilley, Dan Leno and Little Tich, in addition to companies of renown such as the Carl Rosa Opera.

Scrolling through the following decades is rather like a 'roll of honour': Ivor

Novello, Gertrude Lawrence, Dame Sybil Thorndike, Fred Astaire, Gracie Fields, Jack Hulbert and Cicely Courtneidge, Jack Buchanan, Fred Emney, Arthur Askey, Tommy Trinder, Richard Tauber, Nat Jackley, are just some of the names that emerge. American favourites have included Bob Hope, Bing Crosby, Judy Garland, Danny Kaye and Frank Sinatra, and one story has it that Roy Rogers actually rode Trigger up to his bedroom in the Adelphi Hotel – much to the dismay of its staff! And all the big musicals, such as those from Drury Lane, came here too.

Having survived two wars, the 'Emmy' played an important part in the upkeep of Liverpudlian morale during those hard times, and while the city was getting it back together in the 'fifties, presented the big band shows for their delight, with names like Julie Andrews, Morecambe and Wise, Frankie Vaughan, Jimmy Clitheroe and Laurel and Hardy thrown in for good measure.

Then came the 'swinging' 'sixties when, of course, Liverpool was at the hub of the entertainment scene and their very own 'Beatles' raised the roof. The razzmatazz went on … and on … with the Rolling Stones, Diana Ross, Billy Connolly and Shirley Bassey – and there was 'culture' too – provided by, amongst others, the Welsh Opera Company and the London Festival Ballet. Other favourites have included Don Williams, Bruce Forsyth, Little and Large, Liverpool's own Cilla Black, and Tom O'Connor. The theatre has

Decoration details.

also staged Royal Command and Gala performances in the presence of Her Majesty the Queen, H.R.H. The Duke of Edinburgh and Prince Charles. Today the eminence continues ... Ken Dodd, Gemma Craven, Paul Nicholas, Victoria Wood, Welsh National Opera and English National Ballet in addition to the national tours of the big musicals such as *Doctor Dolittle, Beauty and the Beast, Whistle Down The Wind, Blood Brothers, Chicago, Sunset Boulevard, Miss Saigon, Starlight Express,* etc.

And so, as part of the great Moss' Empires chain, the theatre was on course from the outset and extensive demolition and rebuilding works which so spectacularly provided the present house in 1925 also gave Britain one of its finest and most prestigious venues. The opening show, a revue entitled *Better Days* starring Stanley Lupino, Maisie Gay and Ruth French, was packed to the ceiling and was the beginning of many years of success. This success, however, would eventually run out, for in 1977 Moss' Empires decided to part company with their theatre, it having sustained financial losses for a number of years.

As had become a feature in some other cities by this time, the day was saved by council intervention when Merseyside County Council stepped in to take over, with the running of the venue to be undertaken by a trust board, and the deal was finally sealed in 1979. Difficult decisions had first to be made, however, for another theatre in the city – the Royal Court – was going through a similarly bad patch. Which should the city support? The latter was a superb art deco creation with an equally impressive who's-who list of performers and visiting companies. In the end the Empire was favoured owing to its "greater income potential and adaptability". Today the Empire is owned by the Empire Theatre (Merseyside) Trust Ltd., managed by Clear Channel Entertainment UK, and the tale has a happy ending as the Royal Court also survived, up to now in use mostly as a music venue but with great future potential for a broader programme of arts and entertainment.

With the 1979 take-over came a grand refurbishment at the Empire, including state-of-the-art sound and lighting systems – said to equal those at the New York 'Met', new dressing rooms, new 60-foot orchestra pit to accommodate up to 84 players, redecoration, re-carpeting and reupholstering. This was financed with cash from the government, Arts Council, local authority and others, and the result was stunning. Here was a theatre that could now present any production that the country could throw at it – on a scale unparalleled. But the Empire has not rested upon its success and has since completed several phases of further improvement, development and refurbishment – both externally and internally.

One of the most exiting moments was the reopening in 1998 following a period of closure and cost of £10.5 million, during which a new stage and dressing rooms had been built, together with a splendid auditorium refurbishment, which provided the present quality house. And the latest phase has taken advantage of the demolition of old buildings to the left of the theatre, and has added an impressive three-storey-high glass atrium entrance and annex. This incorporates the latest in box office technology, has extended the circle bar and hospitality features, provided excellent conference and events facilities, and improved disablement access via the installation of a lift.

In the spirit of Liverpool's long maritime tradition it can now be said that The 'Mighty Empire' is sailing well into the twenty-first century, constantly adding exciting moments, memories and events to its already fascinating history!

Birmingham Hippodrome Theatre

Here is a house of national importance – a fact not only substantiated by a magnificent auditorium, its recently refurbished broad sweep resplendent in creams and silvers and brilliantly contrasting warm reds, but also as home to one of the country's major ballet companies – the Birmingham Royal Ballet, formerly the Sadler's Wells Royal Ballet – and incorporating prestigious associated and backstage facilities. Having undergone several major redevelopments in the last few years, the schemes have cunningly preserved the best of the priceless old alongside the handsome new, thus creating a collage of colourful yet coherent and exceedingly pleasing styles. Additionally, a reputation for entertainment stemming back for more than a hundred years places the venue well into the hearts of the people of the Midlands, from the days the chimneys of the industrial revolution had characterised the area as the 'Black Country', and created one of the most prolific and bustling manufacturing centres.

Ironically the present name – Hippodrome – is suggestive of circus, which is precisely what the building's first venture was. Opening on the 9th October 1899, it incorporated a ring thought to have been capable of being immersed for aquatic spectacles, and a proscenium stage – a format not entirely uncommon at this time – providing the opportunity for both circus and music hall presentations. It was advertised as the "Tower of Varieties and Circus" and its façade, indeed, included a Moorish tower – a dominant feature that would remain until the early 1960s, and which obviously would become notable as a local landmark.

In 1900 came major internal reconstructions, and, together with a name change – 'The Tivoli Theatre of Varieties' – the venue dispensed with circus and set the scene that would preside over the next half-century in favour of music hall and variety. It was in 1903 that it acquired its name 'Hippodrome': by now under the control of Tom Barrasford, already a rising star in the music-hall-chain-world who was to bestow many of his other establishments with the same title. He is especially noted as an exponent of the twice-nightly performance format, and a promoter of low admission prices. Many of the music hall greats appeared, such as Vesta Victoria, the Fred Karno Company, George Robey and Gertie Gitana but nevertheless it wasn't all plain-sailing, with competition from other venues, the introduction of films, including cine-variety programmes, and several periods of closure.

In 1924 the Hippodrome came into ownership of the increasingly important Moss' Empires chain. They were able to lavish money on it, and so in 1925 following major works the doors reopened into a completely rebuilt auditorium – the one that still stands today – in Roman neo-classical design, with its huge and impressive single circle, spacious stalls and pleasing arrangement of boxes. The opening show was a revue entitled *Happy Hours* starring Clarkson Rose, and the theatre was now at last on course for a good spell of success – as the city's major variety house! Indeed it catered so admirably to the demands of the various changing styles and tastes that everybody of note appeared and selected at random are a sprinkling of names that will still be instantly recognised: Laurel and Hardy, Duke Ellington, Billy Cotton, Jack Hylton, Joe Loss, George Formby, Gracie Fields, Danny Kaye, Frank Sinatra, Vera Lynn, Lena Horne, Evelyn Laye, Ted Ray, Arthur Askey and Max Bygraves.

Of course, the 'Variety' bubble burst towards the late 'fifties, as everywhere

Birmingham Hippodrome Theatre: the splendid vibrant auditorium originates from 1925. Above the side boxes are cut-glass chandeliers which once lit the old foyer, now cleverly preserved. A temporary structure installed into the ceiling provides a hoist for Aladdin's carpet to magically fly between the stage and the upper circle in a pantomime.

else, but the Hippodrome changed tack and began to receive the big musicals that were on tour – examples such as *Brigadoon* and *Carousel* – its large stage presenting them to effect. Probably the most important musical to be staged was in 1964 when *My Fair Lady* played for six months, and broke box office records. And one-off shows or pantomime also brought in the biggest star names of the day – examples can feature John Hanson, Norman Wisdom, Harry Worth, Mike and Bernie Winters, Dick Emery, Les Dawson, Danny La Rue, Simon and Garfunkel, Gerry and the Pacemakers, Sammy Davis Jnr., Cleo Laine, Tommy Steele, Elton John, The Beatles, Cilla Black, Cliff Richard, The Rolling Stones and Ken Dodd.

But as we have learned in other chapters these were hard times for theatres, and the Hippodrome was no exception and although seemingly doing well with its musicals another problem, specific to the Hippodrome, was becoming apparent. It could no longer satisfy either the staging or accommodation demands of the modern musical, or a major theatrical touring company. The theatre, however, did struggle on – continuing to present big names and big shows and, indeed, miraculously escaping demolition – until things came to a head in 1979.

This turned out to be the watershed year for the Hippodrome in which its future would finally be decided! In the event, Birmingham City Council purchased the building and leased it to the Birmingham Hippodrome Theatre Trust Ltd., a non-profit-making charitable body charged with the tasks of future operation and development. The fateful decision proved to be one of good fortune, paving the way for opportunity – the product of which has manifested itself in an abundance of ways since – so that today stands not only a building of esteem, but a centre of theatrical importance. The achievements did not occur overnight, and major building works – involving the purchase

Plaster silver motifs adorning each of the fronts of the lower central boxes. At one side of the stage inscribed 1899 – the date of the original theatre, at the other 2001 – the date of its renaissance following extensive refurbishment.

of adjacent properties/land, including occasional periods of closure – took place intermittently in just over two decades, the latest lasting for 22 months during 2000/01 at a cost of nearly £30 million.

The final result, however, is astonishing, and the following features and improvements are especially to be noted: a splendid auditorium seating 1,847, magnificently restored and retaining its original 1925 features; a much larger stage with all of the modern technical advancements; state-of-the-art dance studios; accommodation for the Birmingham Royal Ballet; a centre for the treatment and prevention of dance injuries; excellent backstage and administration facilities; a studio theatre with seating for 206; a fabulous foyer with emphasis on steel, wood and glass; a luxury restaurant; luxury bars, glass lifts which also create disablement access to all levels; a completely new exterior, and a feeling of spaciousness and light throughout.

Naturally, the wonders on offer are attractive not only to audiences, but also to visiting companies, the level of technology and amenity enabling the presentation of all types of production to best effect. The Hippodrome, therefore, is a popular host to the whole range of available works, including the major musicals, opera, ballet and pantomime. To give a taster, here is just a small selection of those who have played: the companies including the Birmingham Royal Ballet, Welsh National Opera, Opera North, Scottish Opera, Glyndebourne Touring Opera; the latest blockbuster musicals including *The Phantom of the Opera, Les Miserables, Sunset Boulevard* and *Miss Saigon*; and individual performers comprising the top star names from the worlds of drama, music, dance and comedy.

In 1999 the Hippodrome was proud to celebrate its centenary year with the 69th Royal Command Variety Show, at which Her Majesty the Queen and His Royal Highness The Duke of Edinburgh were present. Another 'gala' night was *The Silver Gala* presented by the Birmingham Royal Ballet for the November 2001 reopening ceremonies, in which many of the audience – both ladies and gentlemen – were clad in appropriate silver apparel.

Finally, the theatre has an excellent reputation for educational and outreach work, together with the amenities to facilitate, with numerous projects geared towards the involvement of young people. In line with modern-day practice this prestigious building is generally accessible to the public during the daytime providing conference facilities, catering, live concerts, theatre tours, exhibitions or just simply a meeting place thus, additionally, fulfilling an all-important community role in the life of Birmingham and the Midlands.

Birmingham Alexandra Theatre

Mention the 'Alex', as it is colloquially known, to the theatre-goers of Birmingham and district and, not least, to any of its performers, and they will doubtless respond with tales and memories of great warmth – for the theatre, during the last century or so, has truly established itself as something special within the hearts of the people.

The present interior, with its wide (42ft) proscenium, remains quite intimate due to its comparatively narrow depth, and with a predominance of art deco harks back to the days of the super-cinema – not surprisingly since the present house was built only in 1935, almost entirely replacing a former, typically Edwardian, one. With ever increasing competition in the 'thirties from the talkies and their emergent luxurious venues, the need to move with the times had been recognised, and today's house, predominantly in blue, cream and gold, with splashes of pink, is a delightful example of its period. It is a pity that the same cannot be said externally, for city centre redevelopment has taken its toll with restructured priorities placing the venue in an awkward position, although a pleasant modern foyer block fronts the theatre and cunningly devised bridge (1968) attempts to retrieve the situation, which originally sported a main entrance in a once bustling John Bright Street.

The theatre's history tells us much about the life of any typical provincial theatre to be found in any of Britain's major cities and in his book *Alexandra Theatre – the story of a popular playhouse* published in 1947, M.F.K. Fraser conjures the most luscious pictures of early twentieth century theatrical life. He describes the popularity of melodrama at that time – the 'Blood Tub' world – essentially the province of the 'Number Two's' (into which category the Alexandra fell), as opposed to the West End and the 'Number One's' who had their *Chu Chin Chows* and their *Maids of the Mountains*. Well the Alexandra, born in the heyday of melodrama, might have served its apprenticeship with the 'Blood Tubs' but it went on to achieve the status of "a handsome modern home of reputable drama and outstanding pantomime" and, today, that of a major touring house! "From Blood Tub to Number One"?

Actually the building, which opened on Whit Monday 27th May 1901, and costing £10,000, was originally called the Lyceum Theatre. It was the brainchild of William Coutts who, hitherto, had 'dabbled' in theatricals in connection with his involvement with the Temperance Institution, in providing local people with an alternative pastime immersed in sobriety. These previous dramatic ventures were extremely successful and led to him building the new theatre.

M.F.K. Fraser tells us that: "The Lyceum, in the fashion of the time, was a flamboyant, heavily ornamented structure, outside and inside. It went in freely for scarlet and gold, and for dust-collecting draperies. It was said to have room for two-thousand people, but of course that was computed in terms of an elastic-sided gallery, with a capacity on a popular night of just as many people as the expert packers could crush into the backless, undivided rows by most ruthless persuasion and practical demonstration."

But despite Mr Coutts' previous successes, his fare did not suit the Lyceum audiences: "not at all what they wanted in the fourpennies and sixpennies, let alone the two bobs" (Fraser), and although a mixture of touring was put on, by November 1902 the place was up for sale. Admittedly there was also much competition within a few miles at that time from other venues, with names like the Empire Palace, Gaiety, Grand, Imperial, Tivoli, Prince of Wales, Queens, Royal, etc., etc.

The theatre's next chapter in life, reopening on 22nd December 1902, was more optimistic, brought about by its purchaser (for £4,450) Lester Collingwood who, with much previous theatrical experience was apparently an extremely popular 'showman' in every sense of the word. He immediately had the theatre refurbished, renamed the 'Alexandra' (after Queen Alexandra), and restocked with popular fare at popular prices. To quote again from M.F.K. Fraser:

> *"The classes still fought shy of the Alexandra, which was frowned on in Edgbaston for what it was. Collingwood, with the increasing support of the masses, didn't worry. His theatre, still essentially a Blood Tub, was truly a popular house, the resort of the publicans and sinners, the tradesmen, the sports, the jolly lads who fancied a rowdy, raucous, totally unrepressed night out.*
>
> *"The Alexandra stayed open all year round. You could get in for fourpence – tuppence if you were young enough and yet had tuppence. You could book a seat for eighteenpence. Otherwise you queued.*
>
> *"There were two queues for each unreserved part, the early door queue and the ordinary door queue. The former was admitted half an hour before the latter, and paid a few coppers for the certainty, or at worst the chance, of being in the first hard shiny row of the pit, or well down towards the front of the gaunt bare gallery, where, on a busy night, up to thirteen hundred of you could be squeezed, pushed, shoved and concertina'd along the hard bare boards which passed for seating up there.*
>
> *"You might with luck find yourself on the very front tread of the gallery, with your nose glued to the rail, your young buttocks maltreated by the heavy boots of the gentleman just behind you, who had nowhere else to rest his feet. You sucked oranges. You chewed sweets. You cast peel and sticky wrappings down on to the heads of the nobs in the circle – 'dress' circle, of course, though only the manager and the bandsmen wore evening dress at the Alexandra (the bandsmen only down to the waist)."*

This era lasted until the 14th September 1910 when, sadly, Lester Collingwood at 56 was killed in a car accident, on his way to see a play in Sheffield. It should be noted that one of the legacies he left to the Alexandra, besides putting it on its feet, was the tradition of annual pantomime, which he had begun in 1903, and which was to prove a financial saviour on more than one occasion, growing in immense popularity and status, and at one time running for up to four months of the year.

Up for sale again, another name illustrious in the annals of the Alex enters the story – Salberg – whose managerial skills, father then son, would last until 1977. Leon Salberg purchased the theatre along with two brothers-in-law in 1911, and although he came without any previous experience of the theatre

Birmingham Alexandra Theatre: the flavour of art deco is much in evidence here, consistent with the period of the theatre's construction.

business he was obviously very shrewd and successfully steered the venue through the changes that the following decades would bring. For example, by the 'twenties, with interest in melodrama dwindling, he brought in touring musical revues – some featuring names that will still be remembered – e.g. Florrie Forde, Flanagan and Allen, Gertie Gitana, Randolph Sutton, Gracie Fields: not all of them by then having achieved their ultimate fame.

In 1927 came a further innovation, when Leon Salberg began his own repertory company presenting a tortuous programme of a play-a-week and twice-nightly shows. Although the system was not without its weaknesses (for example so little production time) and initial teething troubles (when it was replaced by a short, disastrous, spell of *Cabarevue* – " a repertory of song, dance and laughter"), it eventually flourished, bringing a period of golden days to the Alexandra in terms of good box-office, good productions, and good reputation. And with pantomime doing rip-roaring business from year to year, the time became right to build for the future, to replace the old house, albeit much loved by all, with a new and modern venue. And so *Dick Whittington* brought down the final curtain on the old Alex on April 6th 1935 and *Cinderella* raised the opening curtain on the new the following December.

This (the present) house was vastly different, costing more than £40,000, designed by Roland Satchwell (Birmingham), and with all of the streamlined mod-cons of the day. To accommodate it the previous building was demolished, apart from the dressing-room block whose original wall can still be seen in Station Street. Multi-coloured seats were in evidence throughout – even replacing the benches of the former pit and gallery and the new house, comprising stalls, dress-circle and gallery, was arranged in an impressive sweep without the need for obstructive pillars. It had all of its seats accessible from the main entrance hall, where previously the gallery and pit benches had had their own doors in Station Street around the corner. The seating capacity (1530) was much reduced and the place far more comfortable.

In 1937 Leon Salberg died and his son, Derek, who had joined the theatre in 1931, became director. By now repertory was doing extremely well and as Leon Salberg had started a further company in 1936 based at the Grand Theatre in Wolverhampton (see earlier chapter), a 'mix-and-match' policy was possible, allowing a sharing of resources between the two venues. But then the war years intervened bringing problems of their own: the black-out; air raids; theatres ordered to close early; performance time changes – even *morning* matinees; lack of audiences – lack of *personnel*. But, with the surrounding streets devastated, the Alex survived – and never closed – and in 1940 'twice-nightly' performances became '*once*-nightly' and, in 1943, 'weekly' became 'fortnightly' – helping production standards to improve.

In 1941 another innovation was the visit of a ballet company – a 'first' in John Bright Street – the Ballet Rambert. With good business this would lead to further visits and, indeed, to the introduction of future weeks of more highbrow fare, for example from Sadler's Wells opera and ballet companies in this, once, 'Blood Tub'. And to seasons of other tours of note, including plays, comedy and musicals all of which would bring the top stars in their field to the stage of the Alexandra Theatre. But for the time being repertory continued to be the mainstay (not forgetting the annual pantomime) achieving huge prestige over a long period. In the 1960s things began to decline, however, (a sign of the times, outlined in other pages) and the bubble finally burst in 1973 when it was taken off – and touring took over entirely not long after.

In 1968, the financial situation became impossible, and the City Council purchased the theatre for £85,000, saving it from imminent closure, and leasing

The rear of the dress circle where the art deco theme continues.

Ceiling detail at the rear of the dress circle.

it to a non-profit making trust, with grants from the City and the Arts Council. Since that time there have been several refurbishments notably in 1979 and 1990, ensuring that the venue is ably equipped to cater for the demands of its changed role as a modern touring house. (At the time of writing the proprietors are Clear Channel Entertainment UK.) The Alex's story has truly been a 'rags to riches' one – and her rise from the 'Blood Tubs' and the 'second-rates', to her supremacy as a producing theatre and success as a principal touring house is to be applauded.

The names of the stars and major companies who have graced her boards will further acknowledge her renown, and I select a hotchpotch from programmes as far back as the 1940s to the present: Sadler's Wells Opera, Sadler's Wells Ballet, Ballet Rambert, Old Vic Company, Young Vic Company, D'Oyly Carte Opera Company, Royal Ballet, Royal Shakespeare Company. Margo Fonteyn, Irene Vanbrugh, Evelyn Laye, Irene Handl, John Gielgud, Flora Robson, Sybil Thorndike, Peter Ustinov, Donald Wolfit, Alec Guinness, Joan Greenwood, John Mills, Paul Schofield, Peggy Ashcroft, Margaret Rutherford, Jack Hulbert, Michael Denison, Dulcie Gray, Hayley Mills, Elspet Gray, Robert Lindsay, Derek Jacobi, Richard Todd, Albert Finney, Richard Burton, Sean Connery, Jon Pertwee, Leslie Philips, Frank Windsor, Leonard Rossiter, Dora Bryan,

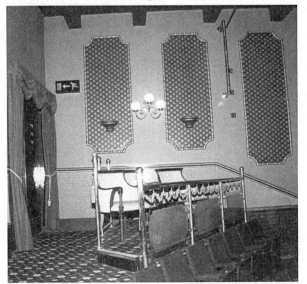

Thelma Barlow, Penelope Keith, Brian Rix, Anthony Newley, Norman Wisdom, Tessie O'Shay, Pearl Carr and Teddy Johnson, Jack Douglas, Millicent Martin, Eric Morecambe and Ernie Wise, Ronnie Corbett, Ted Rogers, Ian Lavender, the Drifters, Lisa Goddard, Joanna Lumley, John Hanson, Prunella Scales, Paul Nicholas, Robert Powell, Topol and Christopher Timothy.

These unusual but charming 'boxes' are placed halfway up the dress circle at either side.

Stoke-on-Trent Regent Theatre

My attention was first attracted to this theatre after seeing a simple black and white photograph of its interior. Not only did it look quite impressive but it would also provide, I thought, an interesting example of the décor of the super-cinema style of the late 'twenties and 'thirties. Upon eventually entering its fine auditorium I was certainly not disappointed, for here is a house that not only illustrates

the genre to perfection – its original innovations intact – an overwhelming refurbishment presents it to today's onlooker with a stupendous pizzazz! And after some investigation I would additionally learn that there were other important factors not so immediately apparent – notably, that it initially opened as a cinema (hence the cinema-look) but with a big stage beyond the screen; that it has played host to a significant number of top stars; and that a massive engineering programme was needed to produce the venue as it stands today.

The prerequisites of the luxury cinema period are well represented in the body of the house with typical filigree panels, which would once have concealed ranks of Wurlitzer pipes, and other quintessences picked out in white and various shades of cream. These, then, are boldly accentuated by the use of strong and vibrant colours in the scarlets of the recesses and house tabs and the golds of the upholstery, which work well together in creating a hugely cheery appearance. But the *magnum opus* has to be the fine ceiling – a huge dome that covers the whole area above the stalls – in white and purple which, with concealed lighting, corroborates the architectural theme.

The cinema/theatre was the product of Provincial Cinematograph Theatres (PCT) who are noted as being the first national circuit, and as one of the ones for making a mark on many a British High Street with their chain of 'Regents', trend-setting in ever increasing opulence! The company's chief architect, W.E. Trent, was responsible for a large number of them (many, actually, named 'Gaumont' following a takeover of PCT in 1929 by Gaumont-British), including the design here at Hanley.

The refurbishment that transformed the theatre to its present form was undertaken in 1996 and as might be expected, retains and emphasises original features wherever possible whilst, on the other hand, introducing

Stoke-on-Trent Regent Theatre: even before entering the auditorium, the scene is set in the elegant foyer and bar. In 1929 the original foyer flooring elegantly sported a chequer-board of black and white marble. Here, tiles that have stood the test of time are cleverly recycled to form the surrounds to the bars – a further touch that links the present with the past.

Almost the entire repertoire of the cinema age is immaculately preserved in this marvellous auditorium, its vibrant colours dominated by an impressive central dome.

facilities commensurate with the expectations of the modern world. Major reconstructions included the reversal of earlier works (1972) which had converted the original, single-screen, cinema configuration into three separate screens (an unusual departure), and the provision of an entirely new state-of-the-art backstage area capable of accommodating the most demanding of theatrical production (all-in-all no doubt a mammoth undertaking). Indeed the fly tower, a large one bearing the words 'The Regent', is visible from many approaches to the town! The theatre is situated within a triangle of streets with various accesses to each, with its main façade – charmingly that of its white faience origination – remaining in Piccadilly.

The first audiences to enter these portals did so on Monday 11th February 1929 following an official opening by the Lord Mayor of Stoke-on-Trent. These were still the days of comparative movie infancy when silent films continued to be presented alongside live entertainment, and so it was not unusual to find the theatre stage in addition to the 'silver screen', and that

Seating in a broad sweep ensures a fine view from every part of the house.

many a performance would comprise the films, an orchestra, music-hall-type acts, and a Wurlitzer which would rise through the floor for good measure! But the *theatrical* houses of Britain were by now in some state of flux as the new 'talkies' were taking off, which would result in many closures and cinema-conversions. The immediate future of the Hanley Regent was secure, however, as the luxurious 'picture palace' was chosen to screen the first sound picture in the area, Al Jolson in *The Singing Fool*, in July of that year, which apparently created quite a stir as patrons descended upon the town in their masses!

With both a screen and a stage the Regent had more than one string to its bow within its opulent surroundings, and would therefore go on to great success. Not only was it *the* venue to see the best films, its stage became a platform for the popular live entertainment of the day, diversifying as required. The big bands and dance bands would sell-out in the 'thirties and 'forties – with top names, Joe Loss and his Orchestra being just one such example; the 'fifties could boast international stardom with a visit from Count Basie and his Orchestra; and the 'sixties began a long and happy tradition when the amateurs moved in with their annual shows, presenting countless sell-out musicals to great effect.

A favourite with the audiences, of course, was the Wurlitzer and its fame spread when live radio broadcasts began to be made from 1931. Many, many performances were given by Mr E. Felton Rapley, and other famous organists played too, including Reginald Dixon from the Blackpool Tower.

The 'sixties also brought more great names, some via pantomime – a hugely popular venture from 1963 – and live shows which continued into the 'eighties. Here, randomly selected, are a just few names that will illustrate she sheer prestige of the house: Max Wall, John Hanson, Ken Dodd, Freddie and the Dreamers, Gerry and the Pacemakers, Shirley Bassey, Matt Munro, Roy Orbison, Cliff Richard, Engelbert Humperdink, Gene Pitney, The Seekers, Tony Bennett, The Rolling Stones, Morecambe and Wise and Tom Jones.

But let us get up to date with the main housekeeping events of the building itself. Firstly, in 1950 it was no longer the 'Regent' – now having changed to the 'Gaumont' – a name that would last until 1976 when it then became the 'Odeon Film Centre'. Secondly, in 1974 the theatre was 'tripled' – in other words it was converted to three separate houses all showing films simultaneously – a feature that happened to scores of cinemas, most of them, as in Hanley, achieved by dropping a wall in the back stalls to create two studios underneath (or, in some cases, above) the balcony in addition to the main house. (Of course, live shows also continued at Hanley.) Thirdly in 1986 the, now, 'Odeon' – no doubt doing "very well" – was given a £500,000 refurbishment, but seemingly doing too well for, together with a greater availability of films, the owners (now 'Rank') opted to close the Odeon in 1989 in favour of a brand-new six-screen venue across town. Thus, the prestigious 'Odeon' closed in October of that year with a charity performance of *The Sound of Music*.

There is, however, a further exciting instalment! Some local people never forgot the attributes of the – shall we call it 'Regent' again – the original name to which it will revert. A few years later, possibly prompted by the, then, precarious position of the Theatre Royal, Hanley's other professional house, the lack of artistic stimulus in the town was recognised, and suitable accommodation in which to promote it. Perhaps the 'Regent', languishing and boarded-up, could solve the problem? Ideas were mooted; negotiations were held with Rank, campaigns were started, a registered trust was formed, fund raising began, listing by the English Heritage was achieved (Grade II), and the City Council's interest was engaged – etc., etc. This paragraph can certainly not do justice to the foresight and work of the people who fought to revive the Regent, and make it what it is today – a top class, number one, touring house – and they should be held in esteem!

In short, the Regent was finally considered along with two other venues, as a chance to create a cultural quarter to satisfy those needs of the town, and in the end was selected along with the Victoria Hall to do just that, and to be managed as a joint operation. The chief funders were the National Lottery, along with the European Development Fund, English Heritage and City Council – supported, of course, by many others. The Regent, with its resplendent art deco decoration brushed up, opened its doors again on the 22 September 1999, to be followed by an official opening in the October by no less than Her Majesty the Queen.

Today a flip through the current *What's on* brochure clearly demonstrates that the top shows, companies and 'stars' have returned to the Regent. In the heart of the new Cultural Quarter – a superb blend of trendy pedestrianised streets and bars and shops and restaurants and museum and art gallery and outdoor chessboard and Victoria Hall – the Regent, as of old, again provides the Potteries' people and their neighbours, with a quality and varied entertainment unsurpassed!

3 MUSIC HALL AND VARIETY

Music Hall flourished with the working classes – (often envied by their 'superiors') – and provided an escape from the pressures of their overworked and overcrowded conditions. Smoke-filled, beer-swilling pub entertainment gave way to purpose-built halls and, in turn, to the sumptuous houses of the Moss' Empires era. Eventually all classes came to patronise music hall, from every walk of life, even to royalty…

- *Leeds, City Varieties Music Hall (1865)*
- *Bristol Hippodrome Theatre (1912)*

Leeds City Varieties Music Hall

Within the very heart of Leeds lies a little gem. A jewel from the past. A treasure, indeed, surrounded by many other treasures – for Leeds does have its share of elegant Victorian buildings in the vicinity, the upkeep of which must be applauded – including several fine shopping arcades (one even designed by Frank Matcham – the County Arcade), and the brilliant Grand Theatre and Opera House just around the corner (see part 2). Many of these may well embrace the legacy of the typical northern 'where there's muck there's brass' trait stemming from Leeds' days as a successful industrial woollen city. But few can boast that their roots extend so distant as the 'little gem' in question – the City Varieties Music Hall – which almost certainly dates from around 1750.

A treasure perfectly preserved – and one which, at least during the three decades from 1953 thanks to B.B.C. television, has certainly not hidden its light under a bushel! The Varieties went out into the homes of millions of people on countless occasions in the popular TV series *The Good Old Days*. Here, the artistes, complete with the exuberant chairman, would perform in traditional music hall manner, suitably aided and abetted by an enthusiastic audience made up of a crowd especially invited for each occasion and, of course, specially dressed in appropriate period costume. I was once privileged to be in that crowd and what a time we had! I went along with a member of a local operatic society – I suppose they chose people from such organisations due to their prowess for singing and acting the part – and we were all given perfect seats in the front stalls. I must confess that many of us hired only the top half of the costume, for that was all that could be seen by the television

Leeds City Varieties Music Hall: a gaudy interior provides a deliciously effulgent atmosphere for the music hall.

Balcony front detail: if only she could talk.

cameras, and I remember that Arthur Askey was one of the main turns on that particular bill.

As I explained in my introductory chapter, many music halls started life as taverns, some with adjacent singing rooms, and the City Varieties was no exception. The White Swan Inn, thought to have been built around 1750, was an old coaching inn which had acquired its singing room and about a hundred years later, in 1865, at a time when such entertainment was becoming increasingly fashionable, this was revamped and opened as 'Thornton's New Music Hall and Fashionable Lounge'.

Of course Leeds was synonymous with many other great cities at the

"The girl I love is up in the Gallery".

time, fuelled by a growth of industry that provided a rapidly increasing population ever anxious to exchange the rigours of the day for a world of comparative glamour. This, the proprietor was able to furnish. His name was Charles Thornton – not the same Thornton who was to open the Sunderland Empire in 1907 (see part 2) whose name, in any case, was 'Dicky' and not 'Charlie'! – although Charles was to retire from the music hall business in 1876, in part due to rivalry from other thriving concert venues which had sprung up in the area. This closed the Varieties for a short time, which then became available for sale by auction. (Thornton, incidentally, re-directed his efforts into 'Thornton's Arcade' just down the street, the first of the Leeds arcades to be built, which is still very much in evidence today and well worth a visit. Look for its charming 'Robin Hood's clock' which depicts characters from Sir Walter Scott's Ivanhoe, and who continue to strike away the passing hours. Charles Thornton died in 1881.)

The next proprietor was a Mr Stansfield, succeeded by several hosts over the following few decades most of whom, generally, also had other entertainment connections, and who reigned with varying degrees of success, coping with the pressures of their own times. One such pressure came on Monday 27th August 1898 in the form of the newly opened Leeds Empire Palace, a little way down Briggate. Here was a house built by Frank Matcham for the famous Moss' Empires circuit – incorporating all of the usual Matcham magnificences – and which presented equally impressive fare. This did take its toll on the Varieties although later that year it was purchased by Fred W. Wood (who, in addition, was subsequently to have interests in the Queens' Theatre in Holbeck not too far away), and under whose ownership it was to regain some of its former success. Mr Wood died in 1913.

The next decades – the nineteen-twenties, 'thirties and 'forties – were to see several changes in ownership and control of the 'City Palace of Varieties' as it had become known, including the White Swan Estates Company of Leeds, the British Union Varieties and Harry Joseph. As times changed, they also saw changes in prosperity, especially during the period when the only way to keep the place alive was to present strip-tease shows – a new cultural dimension! But at least these seem to have kept the wolf from the door until it became possible to 'list' buildings of 'special and architectural interest' and thus to offer a measure of protection to the Varieties, from demolition or radical structural alteration. Following the death of Harry Joseph in 1962, his sons took charge. The reign of the Joseph family is documented as being abundantly successful.

It goes without saying that many great names have played the Varieties over the years — just take a look at the fading bills. One of the most famous, who appeared at the age of eight in 1897 before having achieved his later fame, was Charlie Chaplin. The list, however, is endless and includes such luminaries as Marie Lloyd, Charles Coburn, George Formby Senior, George H. Elliot, Harry Lauder, Houdini, Lillie Langtry, Vesta Victoria, Bud Flanaghan, Florrie Forde, Fred Karno, Vesta Tilley, Nellie Wallace and Dan Leno. A glance at the bills of other music halls and old theatres which were in existence at the time – not only the many alternative venues in Leeds, but those in the towns and cities further afield – reveal many of the same names, as they toured the music hall chains and circuits. (For example, compare some of those at Sunderland Empire, Bradford Alhambra or Bristol Hippodrome in other pages.) Today you'll find that the bills are equally entertaining, with a lively and varied programme of music, comedy, one-night stands, music hall shows and pantomimes – and top stars – try Ken Dodd and Cannon and Ball, as an instance!

In 1987 the hall was sold to the Leeds Grand Theatre and Opera House Ltd.. and the years that followed saw a continual programme of improvements, including new circle seats purchased by the City Varieties Friends in 1991, re-roofing and stalls seating and carpeting in 1992 and re-wiring in 1993. A further innovation closed the entrance to the hall on the Headrow and replaced it with the original Victorian entrance in Swan Street on the opposite side of the building. And more recently…

A visit to the 'Verts' – as it was lovingly known by the locals for years – in person or via their publicity blurb and website, etc. – oozes a tremendous enthusiasm. Currently they are campaigning to raise a £4 million sum to restore the building to its former glory, and to install those all-important mod-cons and technical facilities demanded by the present century – especially being mindful of the Disability Discrimination Act. And to promote this and to share their unique venue with everybody else they have loads of schemes in place such as an active 'Friends' group – with meetings, socials and guest speakers; 'Volunteers' who help run the place by augmenting the front of house staffing, and various fund-raising ventures (e.g. donations, sponsor/ buy-a-seat etc.). Well who said that Music Hall was dead? In Leeds, it certainly isn't!

Bristol Hippodrome Theatre

Not only does this theatre showcase the last major project to emerge from the Frank Matcham 'works' – opening as a sumptuous variety house in 1912, it also clearly illustrates how Music Hall and Variety entertainment had been transformed by the time it was nearing the end of its boom period. The entertainment, having originated in the public houses of a generation before, with its attendant vulgarities and male working-class dominance, had by now come a long way. Through the pleasure gardens and song and supper rooms, the gas-lit, smoke filled, beer-swilling saloon theatres and tavern concerts, the food, drink, tables and chairs, had emerged a much higher-class locale, more akin to a quality theatre, ever increasing in luxury and attracting a more family-orientated clientele. This amelioration, aided by the 1878 Act, was fostered by proprietors keen to promote and tap into an improving market, and certain entrepreneurs, not least the famous Moss and Stoll duo, were prominent in its realisation. Indeed all classes came to patronise the variety houses, from every walk of life, even to royalty, and when the first Royal Command Performance took place at London's Palace Theatre in 1912, Sir Oswald Stoll is said to have commented that the "Cinderella of the arts had at last gone to the ball"!

It was Sir Oswald who was responsible for bringing the Hippodrome to Bristol. With a background in entertainment stemming from his childhood, upon the death of his father he and his mother continued the operation, and they opened several music halls in various parts of the country and were successful.

Meanwhile, another up-and-coming proprietor was similarly successful – Edward Moss who eventually teamed up with Richard Thornton (see Sunderland Empire chapter, part 2), and another chain of halls was emerging. In 1899 Stoll joined Moss and Thornton, rather than becoming opposition, and this led to the birth of Moss' Empires Ltd. A while later Thornton left the company to pursue his own interests – Moss' Empires went on to become the most prolific and highly successful music hall conglomerate in history. Stoll also had separate theatrical irons in the fire and eventually, in 1910, left the combine to concentrate on them – but not before making his mark on the British music hall scene along with Moss, aided and abetted in most instances by Mr Matcham who designed the majority of their buildings. Both Stoll and Moss were advocates of good clean family entertainment, eliminating any trace of vulgarity from their houses; indeed it has been said that Stoll conducted himself more like a Sunday School teacher than a music hall proprietor – and their tasteful establishments encompassed and encouraged this sentiment.

Much fine building resulted all over the country from the above mentioned partnerships – all run on good, clean, family-orientated lines. And in 1904 under the Stoll banner, came the pinnacle of all music halls – the London Coliseum, a Matcham house which opened to sensation. More halls would follow and among them, in 1912, Stoll turned towards Bristol, where he brought another wonder of extravagance – incorporating many of the innovations found in existing Stoll-Moss-Matcham successes, proclaiming just as much spectacle, though by now with a more restrained embellishment reflective of the later age.

One, much talked about, innovation was a gigantic water tank – a masterpiece of ingenuity and engineering – and photographs still exist which show how it formed the front area of the stage, once the floor had slid backwards under the rear section. Equipped with elevators and a six-foot high, fifty-foot wide, glass screen which would rise in front to shelter those positioned nearest from the waves and spray, equine-aquatic displays took place in absolute spectacular fashion. The first occasion was on the opening night on Monday 16th December 1912 when *Sands o' Dee,* an aquatic melodrama, was performed as part of the variety bill. Involving real horses, which plunged into the raging waves, transporting the hero to rescue his heroine, the effects would no doubt have to have been seen to be believed! Prices were: Orchestra Stalls 2/- and 1/6; Parterre 1/-; Grand Tier 1/- and 9d; Balcony 6d and Boxes (to seat 5) 7/6.

Matcham was the master of such devices and had installed them in previous

Bristol Hippodrome Theatre: a house that sums up the sheer quality of music hall that became synonymous with Stoll and Matcham in their heyday – so spectacular that even today the repertoire remains equally relevant, now providing a magnificent home for large-scale opera, ballet and blockbuster musicals.

commissions, for example in his London Hippodrome in 1900 and Manchester Hippodrome in 1904. These were 'true Hippodromes', both of which opened to ovation, and incorporated circus arenas in addition to the proscenium arch, thus making possible a range of entertainments. With hydraulic lifts, water jets, kaleidoscopic fountains, waterfalls, sliding stages, and at Manchester an 'automatic mechanical circus-mat

At each side of the rear stalls is an interesting group of private boxes divided by gold figureheads, not unlike the prows of ships, reflecting the city's maritime connections.

remover', they were the talk of their times. Another contrivance at Bristol was the extravagant dome above the auditorium whose centrepiece was designed to slide open, thus aiding ventilation in hot weather: Matcham's famous

London Victoria Palace which opened in November 1911 – only weeks before the Bristol venue – had a similar arrangement. Further Bristol novelties included a 'handsome lounge', a tea-room, and the possibility of booking all tickets via an advance booking office – suitably divided into separate areas to avoid "the mixing of the different classes". The façade, meagre in comparison to the magnificences beyond, perhaps illustrates how Matcham always made the most of limited street frontages and awkward sites. A grand entrance paved in black and white marble was via a tower topped with gigantic sculptures bearing an electrically lit revolving globe proclaiming 'Hippodrome' – not unlike his London Coliseum of a few years earlier.

Although the Hippodrome obviously eventually became redundant as a variety house, its exceptional features remain equally relevant today in its present role as a number-one touring date – thus the craftsmanship of a bygone era lives on to benefit and delight current customers. (The same can be said of many former music halls.) Perhaps not surprisingly, in almost a century, there have been some changes – for example the tank disappeared many years ago, as did the illuminated sign and, sadly, some of the finer detailing in the auditorium has been lost. But the basic fabric, well intact, with its excellently raked stalls and sweeping cantilevered balconies, seating for almost 2,000 and a huge stage (proscenium 48ft) still provides the ultimate accommodation – now for the big blockbuster musicals, opera, ballet and concerts etc. which these days frequent. And a faded elegance harks back to the glamorous and golden days.

Even at the beginning of the Hippodrome's golden days its policy of music hall and variety was already threatened, however, as elsewhere, by other forms of entertainment – not least, the silent film. Indeed projection equipment was integral to the initial plans – perhaps an indication that from the start the theatre was prepared to move with the times in order to survive. Bills that included a whole array of novelties – ranging from star turns, drama, circus, animal acts, water spectacle, film, etc. – found themselves gradually replaced as the tastes of the various decades hankered after ragtime, revue, cabaret, radio personalities, dance bands and musical comedy. All of the biggest stars and shows played and, together with the sheer standing of the theatre, it managed to keep 'live' longer than most. Only for a six-year spell during the 'thirties did it have to resort to full-time cinema – otherwise it can pride itself upon having provided an almost continuous programme of live entertainment, even through two wars.

At times the Hippodrome's success story was naturally tinged by events of both fortune and dilemma. It emerged from the Second World War without serious damage and was also lucky enough to survive neighbouring theatres which closed in difficult circumstances – for example the Prince's, blitzed in the war, and the Empire during the diminishing audiences crisis of the television era – on each occasion happily taking over the competitor's role. On the other hand, a serious fire gutted the stage in the late 'forties, which so easily could have spelled closure and, as a struggling provincial house during the second half of the last century, it faced closure on frequent occasions. With escalating production and maintenance costs, a dearth of good touring productions, low audiences, obsolete backstage facilities and cramped conditions and the consequent refusal of some companies to appear, the future was often bleak to say the least. Many efforts were made by many people in attempts to resolve the situation. Happily, in 1979 Stoll Moss Theatres, the then owners, finally made the decision to continue to run the Hippodrome – by now, having sold off their other provincial interests (a sign of the times); the Bristol venue would be their flagship of the regions.

The Hippodrome underwent a renaissance and today proudly stands firm having received a gradual programme of improvement and refurbishment. The present proprietors are Clear Channel Entertainment UK. All of the top London shows play – either pre or post-West End – the magnificent house presenting them to perfection. Opera and ballet also abound, taking advantage of the spacious facilities. As in other chapters, the selection of a role of honour of distinguished players is a difficulty and can only begin to give a flavour. The ghosts of the old days would include Vesta Tilley, Wee Georgie Wood, George Robey, Fred Karno – to be gradually overtaken by Cicely Courtneidge, Sandy Powell, Gracie Fields, George Formby, Max Miller, Tommy Handley, Stanley Holloway and Ted Ray. Then there were the stars of the dance band era such as Joe Loss and Billy Cotton and his Band Show – while Sir Thomas Beecham catered for the more serious. Another mixture – Dame Sybil Thorndike,

Richard Attenborough, Michael Redgrave, John Mills, Ralph Richardson, Tyrone Power, Sam Wanamaker, Peter O'Toole … Jimmy Edwards, Mike and Bernie Winters, Dame Edna Everage.

The house has always excelled in the spectacular – featuring the entire range of lavish musicals – *Chu Chin Chow*, *The Maid of the Mountains*, *The Desert Song* and *White Horse Inn* are but a few from a myriad of old greats. Some were gigantic productions direct from Stoll's other great house, the London Coliseum, others were even presented as ice shows! The new Broadway musicals making their way in the 'fifties were equally at home, for example, *South Pacific*, *Carousel*, *The King and I* and *Guys and Dolls*, the latter of which was its British premiere. And more recent productions have included such hits as *Phantom of the Opera* and *Mary Poppins* – shows so lavish that they have played for complete seasons. Eminent companies have included Sadler's Wells Opera and Ballet, Covent Garden Opera, Welsh National Opera, the Bolshoi Ballet, London Festival Ballet, English National Opera, the National Theatre, etc., etc. Today, as a major touring venue the Bristol Hippodrome continues to revel in the spectacular and lives on to recreate the charm and magnificence of a past and lost era – the 'golden days' – for the delight and enlightenment of future generations.

A mirror, placed in an alcove at the edge of the dress circle, reflects the proscenium and upper circle opposite.

4 SEASIDES AND SPAS

As with much commercial enterprise, the business of theatre building has been greatly influenced by the economic and social climates of the day which, at various times, have resulted in a supply and demand in specific areas (that is, a supply of customers and their demand to be entertained!). At opposite ends of the scale these can be traced to the working classes in the great industrial conurbations – the masses seeking respite from the toils and labours of their 'satanic mills', and the leisured classes in their constant search for recreation and amusement.

It is the latter which we shall now consider: the salubrious environs which sprang from the wealthy – as early as the seventeenth century the inland spa town which was to develop, not just as a place where the diseased could venture to be eased by the curative waters, but where they could also partake in the 'round' of social activities which became the norm, eventually to be overtaken in the advent of the seaside as the place of fashionable entertainment.

In actual fact their splendid playgrounds did not remain exclusive for an indefinite period, for when these became accessible – via the transport revolution and improving social and working conditions – the lower classes came to rub shoulders with their 'betters', and not entirely to their betters' satisfaction!

Where the seaside is concerned, I cannot help but to choose

Blackpool in Lancashire as the most expressive example – for Blackpool, in my opinion, became a phenomenon! Utilising every possible accoutrement of leisure, from the beach to its famous Tower, it provided theatres galore for the masses of people who came year in, year out, from the industrial towns. And although it developed a reputation for a somewhat brassy and colourful clientele, many of these venues were of an exceptional and sumptuous standard, providing a quality of entertainment unsurpassed.

And so a wonderful legacy of fine and elaborate buildings resulted – many surviving as a tribute to a bygone age of hedonistic magnificence…

- *Buxton Opera House (1903)*
- *Scarborough Spa Theatre (1880)*
- *Blackpool North Pier Pavilion Theatre (1939)*
- *Blackpool Winter Gardens Pavilion (1878/1896)*
- *Blackpool Opera House (1889/1939)*
- *Blackpool Grand Theatre (1894)*

Buxton Opera House

When it comes to the finer trappings of the typical spa town – the leafy walks and parklands, the elegant structures of shops and hotels, pump room and pleasure gardens, museums and art galleries, etc. Buxton, in its extremely privileged Peak District position, can indeed be said to be very well served. Add to this a beautifully preserved Edwardian theatre – in fact no less than a 'Matcham', highly reminiscent of its initial glory, and today presenting a regular programme of entertainment appropriate to its surroundings – and the town can be well recommended as *the* place to visit.

The Opera House, in keeping with its neighbours, is built in solid stone and its architecture is characteristically that of entertainment, with a jolly beckoning canopy over the main entrance, and a dome surmounting each corner of the front elevation. An added attraction, to the left, is the adjacent Pavilion Gardens conservatory-style entrance of iron and glass which leads towards the Pavilion itself (1871), modelled on the Crystal Palace and the Palm House at Kew, and situated in the beautiful Pavilion gardens which mark the work of two important gardener-architects, Edward Milner and Sir Joseph Paxton. (See also following chapter for detail of Sir Joseph Paxton's contribution to the Spa complex at Scarborough, opened in 1858.) Although entrances to all parts of the theatre are now gained via the front grand foyer, the Opera House was built in the traditional style of its 1903 opening, with the usual segregation of pit and gallery audiences from those who frequented the more expensive seats.

In 1979 the Opera House reopened its doors following an extensive programme of restoration and redecoration. Unlike many modern revampings of old theatres, which often include the wholesale alteration of the front-of-house arrangements, with provision of large bar areas, etc, this was not to be at Buxton. The result is that the patron is greeted with a grand entrance from the Edwardian era, small, but still crammed with the sumptuous marbles, alabaster, polished brass and mahogany, gilded mouldings and painted ceilings that have come to be expected of Matcham. What a brilliant prelude to the delights to follow!

The story of the Opera House is not dissimilar to many of its contemporaries – except that it survives today to tell the tale, whereas scores of others were not so lucky – and its fortunes closely follow the well-trodden path of early success, then decline in later difficult years, salvaged by the introduction of the 'talkies' (in 1932), until eventual closure (1976). Although there was a consequent loss of regular theatrical production during the extensive forty-odd years' cinema use, this change in direction subconsciously preserved the building for its happy sequel of glorious regeneration (1979), keeping all of its essential features intact albeit, cosmetically, in a rather sorry state towards the end. More recently, notably between 1999 and 2001, further programmes of restoration work have built upon these previous rejuvinations, so that today is presented a house of complete magnificence!

In order for any eighteenth century spa town to flourish, it had to provide more than the abundance of health-giving waters with which its Roman ancestors may once have been content. Clearly a major component in development was the provision of adequate social and pleasurable opportunity for the rich, and

Buxton Opera House: view from the 'gods' reveals an elegant auditorium, rich in decoration. A recent refurbishment has modified the colour scheme since the picture was taken.

thus it was not unusual to find the inclusion of grand palaces for music and drama emerging in such localities.

Many spa towns can still today show evidence of a theatre stemming from its heyday (for example see part 1, Bath Theatre Royal), and Cheltenham can even boast, as at Buxton, the survival of a, still successfully operating, Matcham house (the Everyman Theatre, (formerly the New Theatre and Opera House, opened 1891)). Buxton's inauguration into luxurious spa status was due to the 5th Duke of Devonshire who, in the 1780s, set the ball rolling by erecting The Crescent, closely followed by other fine buildings. But before another hundred years were out, developments were made over to the Buxton Gardens and Improvement Company which became responsible for the recreational advancement of the town, including the building of the Opera House. (Today the House is operated by the High Peak Theatre Trust Ltd.)

And so, although there is evidence of earlier theatrical life in the neighbourhood, it was the Opera House that really established Buxton as an important 'touring date'. This was aided, of course, by moves in general progress – the railways had arrived here in 1863 being just one example – and the town developed with a great deal of success as an eminently suitable locale and home for a festival.

In Buxton, the crowning glory from the start – and to the present day, following its grand refurbishments – has to be the magnificent auditorium with seating, currently, for 938. The photograph shows it as it was after the 1979 refurbishment, predominantly in cream, white, gold and brown – a colour scheme reflecting contemporary press descriptions at the original opening and materials (such as tiles and carpet) which had survived and were still intact. (It is a pity that the house valance is incongruously plain, in no way representing the original, especially when photographs can still be seen in old programmes that could have been copied, and this is somewhat disappointing.) The latest (2001) refurbishment, however, has brought the auditorium even more closely towards its original design of blue, cream and gold by utilising information from paint-scrapings etc., and much of the seating has been renewed in a hue also in keeping with the initial plan.

Colour schemes apart, the many 'Matchamisms' uniquely remain with bravura (onion-domes, concave arches, painted ceiling panels, etc.) and although the whole is less intricate than some of his earlier work (for example Blackpool Grand 1894, see later chapter) this is a gem of Edwardian theatricality, still watched over by carefully placed cherubs and voluptuous caryatids. An unusual retention is the 'gasalier' in the centre of the ceiling which is the original that has been restored and converted to North Sea gas and is again in working condition. It was used not only for its lighting ability, but for its assistance in ventilation, the heat from its burners causing the foul air to rise, to be ejected via the exhaust above. As it represents and demonstrates a ventilation and lighting technique frequently used in the theatres of its time, its survival – a rarity – is commendable.

The 1979 resuscitation was designed by Arup Associates, in liaison with Theatre Projects Consultants Ltd., and Bovis Construction Ltd. executed much of the work. The chief elements, obviously intended to bring the Opera House up to date, technically, whilst preserving its Edwardian charm, paid particular attention to such mundane, yet admittedly indispensable, areas as electrical rewiring and improved central heating. More interestingly, the orchestra pit

The auditorium ceiling with fully-working 'sunburner' gaslight fitting.

was enlarged to accommodate up to 85 players (and it can be covered over to produce a forestage, as in the photographs), and the raked stage (a feature of so many theatres from this era) was cleverly retained, thus preserving the existing good sightlines. It is a pity that the traps – originally a feature of the stage – had been removed some years earlier. The flying system, with its original timber grid, was found to be in good condition and therefore the theatre remains, essentially, a 'hemp house', utilising the initial method of raising and lowering scenery, without the use of modern counterweighted assistance.

One point of curiosity lies with the lighting – which, from the start, was electric – but initially backed up by a co-existing system of gas. This was piped to the gasalier, the dressing rooms and the 'floats' (footlights). The floats were provided with the 'triple' system of ignition where a pilot lit the flash which, in turn, lit the extent of the footlights. This obviated the necessity of the explosive leap from one end of the lights to the other, often found in this day and age with less efficient systems. The control was in the form of a distributor set up in the prompt corner which survived until 1938 when the Opera House was lit entirely by electricity, with a Grand Master board from Stand Electric providing the controls. The current lighting system has been computerised since 1981 but the Grand Master was, remarkably, intact until this replacement when it was then relegated to become a period 'prop', hired out for use in television and films. Further curiosities lie with the open spring which meanders under the stage and, front of house, the dumb-waiter that was once used to convey drinks from the downstairs bar to the upper levels – but which makes its deliveries inside the ladies' toilet!

The Opera House has opened its doors to a myriad of entertainment during its long existence. All of the great names and companies have appeared – some many times – as old programmes, available for public viewing in Buxton library, will tell. Pantomime – the first in 1903/4 *Babes In The Wood*, with prices of: Boxes £2.2/- and £1.1/-, Dress Circle 3/- (first three rows 4/-), Pit Stalls (reserved) 2/-, Upper Circle 1/6, Gallery 6d. Other offerings were billed as "a Musical Comedy", "a Play", "a Farcical Comedy", "Non Stop Farce", "Variety Entertainment", "Great Detective Play", "Vaudeville Concert Party", "All Star Combination", and, of course, the usual diet of opera, Shakespeare and ballet.

Just a selection of entries from the early years give a very vivid flavour of what they must have been like. "For three nights and one matinee commencing Thursday September 25th 1913 – The Farewell Visit of Mr George Edwardes' Company, in the Play with Music – *The Merry Widow*, Direct from Daly's

Theatre, London, with Augmented Orchestra and Powerful Chorus". Also in 1913 the "London Criterian Farce Company", "West End Company", "World Famous Imperial Russian Ballet", "Comic Opera", etc.

On Monday May 12, 1913 for six nights the D'Oyly Carte Principal Repertory Opera Company presented *The Mikado, The Yeomen of the Guard* and *The Gondoliers* all in the same week. For six nights Monday June 29, 1914 "The Cavaliere f. Castellano English and Italian Grand Opera Company, From Drury Lane Theatre, London" similarly gave a cornucopia of goodies: Monday *Faust*; Wednesday *Il Travatore*; Thursday *Rigoletto*; Friday *Cavalleria Rusticana*. On Saturday afternoon at 3pm, July 26, 1913, was a "display of Morris and Country Sword Dancing".

The prices for musicals in 1913 seemed to average as follows: Boxes £1.1/- and 10/6, Stalls 4/-, Dress Circle 3/- (first three rows 4/-), Pit stalls (reserved) 2/6, Upper Circle 1/6, Pit 1/-, Gallery 6d, while a play would be somewhat cheaper at Stalls 3/-, Dress Circle 2/6, Pit Stalls 1/6, Pit 1/-, Upper Circle 6d, Gallery 4d.

Equally enterprising for their feats of repertoire were some of the play companies: in July 1915 "Esme Percy and Kirsteen Graeme's Repertory Season" presented ten plays during their run – with most featuring the same names in the cast!

Week, March 2, 1914 announces: "*Smoking Permitted This Week*; Twice Nightly 6.50 and 9": [a variety bill] includes: "Carl Hertz – Important Expensive Engagement of the World's Famous Illusionist in a Conflux of apparent Miracles and Sensational Illusions that has never been attempted by any other Artist". More genteelly, sometimes there was a "Tea Matinee on Saturday at 3 - *each lady in the stalls and dress circle will be presented with a cup of tea*" and often, ladies were reminded that "*No Hats or Bonnets allowed in the Stalls or First Three Rows of the Dress Circle*".

The programmes are also typical of those produced in theatres during first half of the twentieth century – with the theatrical content almost taking second place in a limited centre-page spread, to the advertisements crammed around its perimeter. The Spa connection was obviously still significant with "The Buxton Water and Treatments. Buxton Aerated Water may be had at the Opera House Bars and Gardens Café", and "Buxton Laxative Salt @ 1/6 and 2/6 per bottle". Some advertisers featured in Opera House programmes for years, such as "Fish and Joule, High Class Family Butchers" selling "Pickled Tongues, Calves' Heads and Corned Beef". Happy days!

In 1937 the 'talkies', by then *in situ* at the Opera House, were punctuated by a few weeks of festival in late summer – and the first Buxton Festival was born. A spa town being the perfect location to host such an event, with its attendant conveniences and salubrious surroundings, must have contributed greatly to its success. So much so, that the festival idea was repeated in the ensuing years, until just after the outbreak of the Second World War. When the Opera House was to return to full theatrical use, following its marvellous regeneration and restoration in 1979, the event continued – The Buxton International Arts Festival – and this has become one of the largest opera and classical music festivals in the country. Since 1994 the International Gilbert and Sullivan Festival has, additionally, taken centre stage. Add to these the array and diversity of production available throughout the year generally, catering both for education and the needs of the local people as well as the visitor, attracting the highest standards in performer and company, and I am sure that Mr Matcham's attendant cherubs and caryatids are safe to continue their thoughtful gaze for many generations to come.

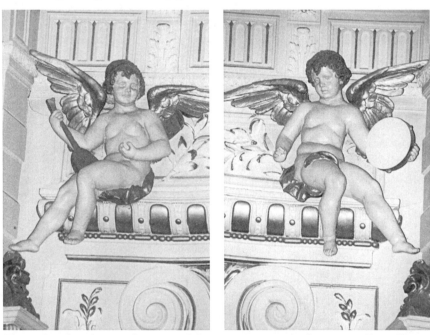

These cherubs adorn each corner of the proscenium arch; the one one the right is said to hold a real tambourine.

Scarborough Spa Theatre

The seaside is a very remarkable place, with which no inland town or even idyllic country spot can be compared. Think of the sand and the sea; the prom, 'white horses', cliff tops and lighthouses, fishing boats and pleasure trips with stiff sea-breezes; Punch and Judy and penny arcades and what-the-butler-saw and buckets and spades; piers, fairgrounds, bathing huts, sand-castles, flags, windmills and sea gulls, candy-floss and landladies. And in all of this there developed an equally remarkable style of entertainment not to be found, quite in any shape or form, anywhere else but at the seaside.

There have been pierrots, minstrels, concert-parties, variety shows, dancers, comedians, a huge emphasis upon music – bands, orchestras and singers – and often presented with small groups of people, each taking a turn in the chorus or helping out backstage in addition to giving their own solo performances. And, of course, alongside, evolved a genus of edifice in which the remarkable should be housed encompassing a variety of spaces from, for example, elaborately emblazoned bandstands and concert rooms, to equally ornamented pier theatres and pavilions. It is the latter which shall be considered in this chapter and although the years (and, no doubt, the weather) may have diminished the number of venues and particular entertainment form presently under scrutiny, a few excellent examples still remain for our cogitation.

The Spa Theatre in Scarborough is one of them, carefully preserved, and still presenting successful summer seasons of 'seaside shows', such as minstrel shows, old time music hall and songs from the shows, in typical 'seaside' tradition. It forms part of the superb Spa complex which today also houses excellent conference facilities incorporating the Grand Hall, the Ocean Room, ballrooms, bars, restaurants and cafes, in addition to delightful outdoor terraces where holiday-makers can simply sit back in their striped deck-chairs and listen to the strains of a band or an orchestra whilst simultaneously enjoying the sea view.

The origins of the Spa date back as far as 1626 when a Mrs Farrow (Farrer) had noticed that a spring flowing out of the rocks had discoloured them and, along with its unpleasant taste, considered there must surely also be medicinal qualities. It was towards the end of the 1600s that the Corporation first took steps to market the 'miracle' waters on a commercial basis, installing cisterns, and by 1700 a Spaw (as it was then known) House for the Governor had emerged. Thus in Scarborough were the beginnings, as in many other parts of the country during this period, of the development of a Spa town – a fashion which was to become enormously popular in England during the eighteenth

Scarborough Spa Theatre: the house curtain rises on typical seaside fun. This isn't the end of the pier, but it almost could be!

century, giving way to more seaside orientated pursuits in the nineteenth (although in Scarborough's case, the pump room did survive until 1939).

The Scarborough Spa, however, did not proceed over the next hundred years or so entirely without mishap, suffering landslide and high tides and several storms, sometimes necessitating rebuilding. But the attraction of the resort was ever increasing and in 1826 the Cliff Bridge Company was formed which erected the bridge which joins the town with the exquisite hotels on the south cliff, and which also took over control of the Spa. (The bridge, incidentally, opened on the 19th July 1827.)

(Some notable points that contributed to the growth of Scarborough – and to seaside towns generally – cannot be dismissed, for they have ultimately affected the success and shaping of the theatre. In particular they include the introduction of the railways – which in Scarborough's case was in 1845 – bringing in countless visitors, often from the overcrowded industrial areas. Linked to this the gradually ameliorating working conditions began to give

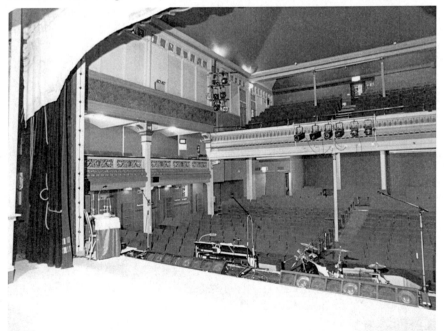

For well over a hundred years pierrots, minstrels, concert-parties, variety shows, dancers, comedians, bands, orchestras and singers have all played to this jolly house.

access no longer just to the idle rich, but also to the middle classes and eventually to the working classes, via a rise in disposable income and shorter working hours. (Bank holidays – first introduced by the 1871 Act – were always considered to be important at the Spa.) Thus, a trip to the seaside, becoming increasingly achievable by nearly all sections of the community, developed into a very healthy and popular tradition.)

A Gothic Saloon opened on the 16th August 1839 to the designs of Henry Wyatt – and it was in the 1830s that the first orchestra was heard – and as the Spa prospered, several additions and improvements were made by Sir Joseph Paxton (designer of the Crystal Palace, see previous chapter) including, in 1858, a grand concert hall. This was to be gutted by fire, however, on the 8th September 1876, making way for construction of the present Spa building – designed by Thomas Verity & Hunt, London – incorporating the remnants of the former structure. The official opening was on the 2nd August 1880.

During the last hundred years, not surprisingly, many additions, re-buildings, refurbishments, etc. have been carried out to make the Spa what it is today. The Spa came back into Council control in 1957 and with continued and careful planning, the building has gradually been restored to the grandeur of its Victorian heyday. Its typically seaside theatre, originating in 1879, was completely renovated in 1972. Seating (620) is on stalls and circle levels and, of particular note, is the charming mural which extends the full width over the proscenium arch.

A host of famous names have appeared at the Spa including Sir Henry Irving in 1882, Sir Charles Halle in 1893, Irene Vanbrugh in 1897, Mrs Pat Campbell in 1903, Sir J. Forbes-Robertson in 1903, Lillie Langtry in 1904, Vesta Victoria in 1913, and Ivor Novello in 1925. (See also sections on music hall, touring and legitimate theatre which include some of the same names, and consider what sort of lives they all must have had in the context of performing, audience behaviour and touring, etc.!) Of course the name Max Jaffa is synonymous with the building. The Spa also staged Scarborough's longest running summer show *Dazzle,* and this was first presented in 1958.

Today it is good to see that the old style traditional seaside entertainment is not only alive and kicking, but is being presented in exactly the same surroundings as it was more than a hundred years ago. It has survived weathers and wars, political, economical and social changes, competition from more up-to-date entertainments and holidays abroad and yet, in spite of all of this…the band plays on!

Blackpool North Pier Pavilion Theatre

Although those acquainted with the popular Lancashire seaside resort of Blackpool may find it difficult to believe today, its origins lay in quite the different environment of comparative tranquillity. As the nineteenth century was dawning the town was steadily beginning to grow, but by the time it was half way through a very different picture was emerging. The major influence, of course, was the railway – first arriving nearby in the 1840s. Up to now, seaside resorts generally had been largely frequented by the better classes, who had in many cases almost replicated their fashionable spa towns of the previous era in their new coastal discoveries. The accessibility now provided by the countless links between the great industrial areas and the seaside, however, together with the improvements in the social access to leisure activity, brought an entirely different order. In turn, a new species in the working class society had been spawned – the excursionist and holidaymaker – and as time progressed many were to arrange themselves into groups and organisations such as the Sunday School outing or factory outing so that, aided and abetted by cheap tickets offered by rail companies, seaside towns found themselves deluged by the masses! In 1863 Blackpool Central Station was opened which, almost quite literally, decanted all of its passengers at the head of the North Pier!

Naturally the entrepreneurs were keen to take advantage and so, in time, developed all of the infrastructure of the seaside leisure industry: the beaches, the promenades, the boarding houses and hotels, the donkeys, the rides, the theatres, etc. – Blackpool proving always to be at the forefront. One of the first attractions to adorn the seafronts was the pier and, again, not to do things by halves, Blackpool built three! It is the North Pier, opened in May 1863 by the Mayor of Preston, which I draw on to illustrate this area of entertainment, the North Pier Pavilion at its seaward end having presented shows typical of the seaside fare to countless millions in its time. (A second, smaller, theatre – the Arcade Theatre – also operated at the prom-end for many years.)

The early piers were initially conceived as landing stages for the steamers, additionally providing a "walk upon the waves" for pedestrians – a pursuit that became exceedingly popular. Only later was their entertainment potential realised, and on the North Pier this tradition was to begin with the building of the Indian Pavilion in the 1870s with, some have claimed, space for 2,000 spectators, and modelled upon a Hindu temple. A perusal of the local newspapers of the period, whose advertisement columns publicise "grand concert", "promenade concert", "grand orchestra", will reveal that much of the fare was for high class music, featuring only the best in orchestral playing and from the world of opera. Perhaps the most notable performer, in August 1881, was the famous Covent Garden opera singer Adelina Patti. With such 'grand' fare on offer, were the powers-that-be trying to maintain a certain level of decorum? By the early decades of the twentieth century, Pierrot groups and concert parties had become a ubiquitous attraction at the British seaside, and these were to feature at the North Pier as well. In September 1921, however, calamity struck – when the Indian Pavilion caught fire and was completely destroyed.

Its replacement came within a few years and not long after saw the beginning of a Blackpool legend – *On With The Show* – presented by Lawrence Wright, a songwriter musician/publisher whose name was to become synonymous with the pier. The show, whose format consisted of music more in tune with the time, comedy and variety (at least one programme described it as "a new style entertainment"), was hugely popular, so much so that it literally did go 'on' – for more than thirty years! Calamity struck again in June 1938, when another fire ridded the pier of its seaward theatre!

This time the replacement – the present theatre – was ready for the following summer season. To date it must have provided millions with magical holiday memories – throughout the Second World War, and changing its format with the times, it has presented quality shows with the top names of the day. In the 'fifties, following the retirement of Lawrence Wright, another successful 'institution' began with Bernard Delfont's *Show Time,* which was to run for twenty-five summer seasons. The North Pier Pavilion has certainly been consistent! In more recent times the summer format, though still of a high quality, and featuring equally notable stars, has been more varied, and produced individually.

Let me mention just a few of the names associated with the pier's entertainments, some of

An attractive foyer provides a very welcome reception to the show.

A cheery atmosphere is conjured up immediately, high above the waves at the end of the pier!

which might jog a happy memory! In the early days Monsieur Speelman (conductor and musical director), Mr Sims Reeves, Madame Lori Recoschewitz and Mr W. Riley (vocalists), Charles Halle, Madame Adelina Patti. The *On With The Show* editions – (some of these returning upon many an occasion) – (1932 - "8th edition") e.g. Bob and Alf Pearson, Sidney Firman, Roy Barbour; (1937- "13th edition") e.g. Tessie O'Shay (1939 – "15th edition") e.g. Frank Randle; (1945 - "21st consecutive year") e.g. Dave Morris, Ingrid Hageman, Robert Wilson; (1950 - 26th) e.g. Albert Modley, Betty Jummel, Maureen Rose, Tano Ferendinos; (1952 - 28th) e.g. Ernest Arnley, Gloria Day, Sylvia Gaye, Tudor Evans, John Tiller Girls, Reco & May, Henry Lytton, Larry Macklin, (1953 - 29th) e.g. Beverley Sisters; (1954 - "30th Anniversary Show") e.g. Lenny the Lion with Terry Hall, Anne Shelton, Tiller Girls; (1956 – "32nd edition") e.g. Ted Lune, Frankie Vaughan. The Show Time summer seasons – David Nixon, Billy Dainty, Joan Regan, Edmund Hockridge, Charlie Drake, Bert Weedon, Harry Worth, Mike and Bernie Winters, Joe (Mr Piano) Henderson, Jimmy Clitheroe, Freddie and the Dreamers, Freddie Starr, Janet Brown, Paul Melba, Ken Goodwin, Peters & Lee, The Black Abbots, Russ Abbot, The Krankies, Cannon & Ball, Lenny Henry, Roger de-Courcey & Nookie Bear, The Grumbleweeds, David Copperfield, Stan Stennett, Dickie Henderson, Andy Stewart, Hope & Keen, Tom O'Connor, Bella Emberg, Stan Boardman, Rose Marie, Bobby Crush, Roy Walker, Dana, Joe Longthorne, Jim Davidson, Brian Conley, Su Pollard, Lily Savage, Hale & Pace, Duggie Chapman.

The Pavilion has been refurbished in the last few years, along with the pier itself, and its other attractions. It shares its jolly seaside outlook with other goodies such as the Sun Lounge, where patrons can relax and listen to live organ music, restaurants, the Merrie England Show Bar, shops, amusements, etc. and a tram runs from the promenade end to the theatre, especially welcome to patrons in bad weather. Here is a very specialised form of British entertainment, at its best, beautifully preserved, yet still playing full-tilt to delighted audiences.

Seating is provided for around 1,500 patrons on one sweeping level, which rises in a comfortable rake from the stage towards the rear of the house.

Blackpool Winter Gardens Pavilion Theatre

Although this venue no longer performs the traditional function of a theatre in the strict sense of the word, I have selected it because of its important contribution to British stage entertainment in the past, and its continuing use for a host of activity that still incorporates some theatrical presentation. Moreover, its history and relationship to the famous names of yesteryear and to the Winter Gardens complex as a whole, and the fact that its splendid Victorian auditorium remains, beautifully preserved, as a living example of all of the above, are equally important factors.

Turning the clock back to the Blackpool of 1875 when the Winter Gardens and Pavilion Company was founded, we find direct evidence of a rapidly growing resort, synonymous with its coastal contemporaries in other parts of the country, it already having acquired two of its three piers – the North Pier in 1863 (see previous chapter), and the Central Pier (then known as the South Pier) in 1868. The Company was obviously well aware of this situation and its prospectus gives us some clues … that "revenue might be estimated from the fact that 938,000 persons visited Blackpool by rail alone in 1873 and over 1,000,000 in 1874 … which number will probably increase from year to year". And its objectives: "This company is formed to provide in Blackpool superior Gardens and Pleasure Grounds, with a magnificent Pavilion and other accessories of the kind now so popular" … and … "The Pavilion is intended for first class musical entertainments (as leading artistes would be engaged) and other purposes of public recreation". The architect, from Oldham, was Thomas Mitchell.

And, indeed, the opening proceedings took place on the 11th and 12th July 1878, and can only be described as 'mega' – performed by the Lord Mayor of London, complete with horses and carriage; in excess of 60 mayors from other towns; civic guests, officials and dignitaries; bands etc., in ceremonies that included processions, a firework display and, of course, an inaugural concert. But before focusing specifically upon the Pavilion's story, it is necessary to acquaint the reader with the complex as a whole.

It has been described as "a lavish arrangement of crystal domes, theatres, ballrooms, gardens, dancing fountains and florid promenades – a masterpiece of the Victorian era". Today the four-and-a-half acre entertainment and conference venue includes the Pavilion Piazza and Horseshoe, the Floral Hall, the Empress Ballroom, the Arena, the Opera House (see following chapter), the Olympia Exhibition Centre, the Spanish Hall suite, bars and restaurants, the eclecticisms interconnected by spacious and sweeping promenades. Notably, the home of many a political party conference, the complex – restored and refurbished to the tune of £4 million in 1989 – has provided unparalleled

Blackpool Winter Gardens Pavilion: the floor, now levelled, offers multipurpose use and continues to be encompassed by rich Victorian decoration. Cleverly designed scenery closely copies the original plasterwork in creating a platform for cabaret performance, but the stage curtains will never rise again for they now conceal nothing more than a brick wall!

facilities for conference and exhibition activity over a great number of years, in addition to its obvious number-one position in the show-business field.

The Pavilion, very different now to that of 1878, has actually undergone several transformations in its hundred-and-some years, adapting its role to the changing world in an attempt to remain viable. It opened as a grand concert hall, and the *Blackpool and Fleetwood Gazette* for Friday July 12th 1878 tells us that it was "larger than the Manchester Free Trade Hall" and "it is calculated, will comfortably seat three thousand persons". "Outside the concert-room, and encircling it, is a promenade with a glass circular roof... This promenade is 30 feet wide, and is separated from the concert-room by a sort of wooden portcullis or sliding sash... The object of this is to enable the whole to be thrown into one great concert-room, should occasion require it to be done. In this way from 6,000 to 7,000 persons can be provided for. Ordinarily this portcullis will be down, with the exception of openings into the room here and there, so that those who like to listen to the music while promenading will not interfere with the comfort of those who wish to pay a closer and more careful attention to the performance."

One occasion when 'the whole' was thrown into one great concert room was on August 28th 1882 when the world famous French actress Sarah Bernhardt appeared. In a play in French, and with poor acoustics, so the story goes, the result was an increasingly restless audience, but the final straw came when a broad Lancashire accent was heard to declare "Speak up, lass!", after which the actress left the stage!

During its early years the Winter Gardens did not, apparently, reward its shareholders to any extent. Perhaps its taste was too highfalutin – indeed, perhaps so was that of Blackpool's at the time – but both would eventually learn how to cater to the popular demand.

In 1887 the Winter Gardens fortunes changed with the appointment of a new manager from London, Mr William (Bill) Holland whose stay, a comparatively short one owing to his sudden death in 1895, was no less than remarkable. He has been described as the "People's William", and the "British Barnum", such was his ingenuity and popularity and flair as a showman – not only bringing spectacle on the grandest scale to his entertainment palaces, but being greatly influential in the provision of some of those palaces from the outset! Several of the 'Gardens' major features stem from his imagination, not least the magnificent Empress Ballroom and the first Opera House building, and in 1889 during his reign, the Grand Pavilion being "ill adapted to theatrical representations", was reconstructed as a theatre.

These tablets, located in niches at the entrance to the horseshoe and depicting traditional scenes of music and dance, may have gone largely unnoticed by the countless thousands of visitors who have filed past them.

The ambulatory or 'horseshoe' which provides the promenade that encircles the Pavilion. The wall in the centre of the picture, formed from shutters, can be removed to unite the Pavilion and the ambulatory, thus creating one huge space as it did over a hundred years ago – now usually utilised, more successfully, for exhibitions, etc.

In actual fact the present auditorium of the Pavilion is the result of further reconstructions in 1896/97 by architects Wylson & Long – perhaps prompted by the standards boasted by the now hugely popular Her Majesty's Opera House, and the magnificent Grand Theatre (1894) just down the road? And its story has almost turned full circle for today, having gone through the usual ups and downs, it remains richly restored to its original Victorian brilliance. This is particularly commendable, since its ingredients encompass much of the theatricality of the age, with classical columns, caryatids, nymphs, gildings, and elaborately encrusted mouldings at every turn – which are now all securely preserved.

All of this is a consequence of, ironically, the Pavilion's most vulnerable time – the complex's 1989 refurbishment – when a serious decision had to be made as to its future. With two magnificent and flourishing theatres within five minutes' walk, and the Pavilion's uncertain location within the ambulatory and the complex, several alternative schemes were considered, such as a restaurant conversion, and ten-pin bowling, etc. Finally it was decided to utilise it as a multipurpose space, capable of housing exhibitions, conferences, and theatrical/cabaret-style performances (with some 600 seats – circle and balcony now out of use).

And so the raked floor – lowered during the earlier theatre conversions – was once again levelled to reach the height of the surrounding promenade. The perimeter wall of the hall at (former) stalls level is removable in sections, thus permitting the space to open out into the promenade area (not dissimilar to the 1878 'portcullis' idea), and the arrangement allows what has been considered to be the most important existing work of architects Wylson and Long to survive.

The original stage area, however, does not survive, having been converted to a restaurant (with a separate entrance), and cleverly hidden immediately behind the new extravagant draperies which now adorn the sumptuous 31ft 6ins wide proscenium arch, is a brick wall! An 'apron' stage has been constructed in front, and although the only access to it is from within the hall itself, the present arrangement of flats, whose design is cunningly copied from the architecture of the auditorium, provides a limited backstage area and allows for entrances and exits.

In its heyday the Pavilion Theatre, and its companion along the hallway – the Opera House – presented shows twice nightly (in addition to all of the other theatres, and there were many, in the immediate vicinity). It has packed-in audiences to see and hear the top star names from every conceivable field of the business over a great number of years – opera and ballet, big-bands, drama, music hall and variety, radio, comedy, film and TV – to the top star names from the arena of the party political conference! Selected at random, the celebrities include: Tessie O'Shay, The Dave King Show, Terry Thomas, Freddie Frinton, David Whitfield, Arthur Haynes, Jimmy Edwards, Ken Platt, Tommy Cooper, Bob Monkhouse, The Kathy Kirby Show, with Ted Rogers, Johnny Hackett and Donald Peers, Morecambe and Wise, etc. One notable coup occurred in 1949 when *Annie Get Your Gun*, one of the first of the new American musicals, was obtained to play for the season.

It must be said, however, that the Pavilion did turn its back on live shows for a spell, and in 1929 succumbed to the talking picture! Although Blackpool's theatres, including the all-year-round venues, have always been cushioned by the summer-seasonal trade when balancing their annual books, by the late 'twenties their managements were becoming increasingly worried by the growing interest and advancements in the 'talkies'. A year earlier the Winter Gardens and Tower companies had merged and so now controlled several of the town's major theatres, and the Pavilion was the first that the new company had wired for sound. On a happier note the new, powerful, conglomerate instigated many extensive programmes of refurbishment, rebuilding and innovation on the complex over a lengthy period of time, thus creating a most lavish and prodigious centre of multiple entertainment. And eventually, the Pavilion would be reclaimed for theatrical use.

We have already considered in our theatrical story how, when war broke out in September 1939, theatres in all parts of the country were affected. Blackpool was no exception! Firstly, theatres were ordered to close, but while in the Capital it was some time before they would reopen, in Blackpool, and in other comparatively 'safe' areas, this would be nearer to a week. Secondly, evacuations from London meant that eminent theatrical artistes, managements and companies visited the provinces, bringing with them an array of delights! And thirdly, Blackpool and the surrounding area had an enormous influx of wartime personnel, from Service people to civil servants. All of these facts made the era for Blackpool – with a fantastic and prolific product on offer, an exceptional existing entertainment infrastructure, and a ready-made audience – an absolute boom time! The theatres, cinemas, ballrooms and restaurants were packed to capacity and the entertainment industry never looked back. Well, not until the 'fifties…

The story runs much the same as in other chapters, and for similar reasons, it is one of decline. New distractions and their accessibility – not least that of television – took over the priorities of the leisure time of potential customers. Even Blackpool's trump card – that of the summer-season boost – was challenged as the foreign package holiday grew in popularity. But the Pavilion pressed on, presenting variety in the 'fifties, then (ironically) featuring the stars of television during the 'sixties and 'seventies in stage adaptations of their own comedy television series, such as *Love Thy Neighbour* and *Are You Being Served?*

I had the good fortune to visit the Pavilion several times during the 'seventies (on one occasion to see the cast of *Are You Being Served?*), so I am able to give a first-hand account. There was an excellent ambience to the place, especially as its 1,700 seats were usually packed, although I do remember one visit being seated towards the upper slips, which didn't have terrific sightlines. The colour scheme at that time was creams, whites and gold, with upholstery and drapes in turquoise – especially appropriate for a warm summer season!

Today, almost thirty years on, there are undeniably fewer theatres in a Blackpool, which, naturally, has had to change with the times and adapt to altering fashions and tastes. But on the credit side, the ones that do remain are there, not as seedy relics to a faded and glorious past, but thanks to the modern-day wave of thinking which at last has acknowledged an intrinsic worth, have been lovingly refurbished and recognised as an asset for the future. And they continue to take up the gauntlet in an attempt to satisfy the ever-changing demands of present generations.

A good view of the beautifully restored plaster detail on the proscenium, upper stage box and balcony slips.

Blackpool Opera House

I always thought that the name 'Opera House' – conjuring up thoughts of gilt and plush and baroque grandeur – unusual for this mighty house of sweeping, more *moderne*, lines of art deco, until I learned that the present building is actually the third on site, its name being bequeathed by its predecessors, dating back to 10th June 1889. To give it its *official* title of the day, the 'Her Majesty's Opera House', according to local newspaper reports, undeniably lived up to its majestic name in all respects, which is hardly surprising when it is noted that her architect was no less than Frank Matcham! The Winter Gardens Company had it built as an addition to their pleasure grounds and pavilion operation.

The *Blackpool and Fleetwood Gazette*, on Friday 7th June 1889, was enthusing even before the official opening, drawing attention in particular to "the provisions made for safety, in case of fire or panic", and the "magnificence of decoration". A further account on Friday 14th June 1889, during the opening week, describes how "the large audiences … have declared in an unmistakable fashion their high appreciation of its admirable arrangement, its convenient appointments, and, above all, its superb beauty" ... "the delicate blue, the pale pink, and the white and gold of the decorations harmonise most exquisitely" and… "the ceiling is certainly a work of much magnificence".

Of further interest: "It should be stated that on Monday a party of journalists were excellently entertained by the directors of the Winter Gardens Company. They were conducted over the theatre by Mr Matcham, the architect, and later in the afternoon they partook of a sumptuous dinner at the Albion Hotel … "At the close of the [inaugural] performance there were loud calls for "Holland" and on the manager of the Winter Gardens making his appearance there was a burst of enthusiastic applause" … "Mr Matcham was also called, he briefly expressed the hope that the most complete success might ever attend that theatre and also the thriving town of Blackpool". The opening show, performed by the D'Oyly Carte Opera Company, was Gilbert and Sullivan's *Yeoman of the Guard.*

Now the Opera House had risen out of the enterprise of 'Bill' Holland (see also previous chapter) the great showman, who had foreseen the requirement for a large quality theatre. Perhaps influencing factors may have been the existing Winter Gardens Pavilion which, at the time, had been described as "ill adapted to theatrical representations", and also similar interests shown in the town's entertainment scene by another notable showman – Tom Sergenson – who had recently declared his intention to erect a 'Grand Theatre' on a nearby site. It was several years before the 'Grand Theatre' (see following chapter) was to come to fruition, however, but in any event as history would have it, the two venues would become great rivals over a very long period of time – indeed until a merger was to bring them under the same management in 1928.

But the period of time during which the *initial* Opera House building survived was comparatively short lived for in 1911, quite unusually, this Matcham house was rebuilt. The extensive alterations, designed by Mangnall & Littlewood of Manchester, were described in a local report which, again, enthused (*Gazette-News*, Tuesday 6th June 1911): "Her Majesty's Opera House, reopened to the public last night, after having been in the hands of the builders for many months, may truly be described as one of the most beautiful playhouses in the kingdom. Spaciousness and luxury are the characteristic points, and although the theatre has been about doubled in size, the construction is such that there is a clear and unobstructed view of the stage from every part of the house."

The Opera House's shows had been transferred to the Winter Gardens Pavilion during the rebuilding process and on completion, the opening attraction on the new stage was "that famous sensational detective play *Arsene Lupin* presented by the company of Miss Emma Hutchison and Mr Percy Hutchison". This building was to last longer than its predecessor – indeed

Blackpool Opera House: The elliptical proscenium and ceiling reflect the period of their design. In a majestic sweep the stalls, dress and upper circles accommodate nearly 3,000 persons with an uninterrupted view of the stage.

until 1938 – by which time the owners, the Blackpool Tower and Winter Gardens Companies (which had merged some years earlier – and there have been several changes in ownership since), had made the decision to demolish and go bigger and better!

The result was the present prodigious building of enormous proportion, contrastingly executed in a completely modern style (not unlike the new super-cinemas), which eliminated any hint of the Victorian or Edwardian, and incorporated all of the mod-cons of the day on both sides of the footlights! On its opening, it was said to be the largest purpose-built theatre in Europe! Reports out on July 14th and 15th 1939 hailed it as a "Wonder Building" and the "Last word in Modernity and Stage Equipment", and told us of the goodies to behold.

At a cost of £125,000 was a house of 110ft width, with a 100ft wide x 52ft deep stage and 45ft proscenium opening, seating almost 3,000. 6,000 yards of carpeting worth £4,000 adorned the floors and the general colour scheme was that of autumn – peach, beige, russet, copper, plum, gold and bronze. The walls of the stalls were in warm, wine-coloured, mahogany above which a series of continuous plain plaster arches formed the upper side walls and ceiling – each relieved in paler, complementary, hues and incorporating concealed house-lighting, stage lighting, and ventilation and acoustic techniques.

Other novelties of the time included projection equipment – the theatre could be immediately converted into a super-cinema; state of the art amplification; the 'wharf-way' – a promenade which enclosed the (huge) orchestra pit around which the cast might 'parade'; and a Wurlitzer organ. Backstage, four floors of dressing rooms could accommodate a cast of 250, with speakers relaying sound from the stage (quite an innovation at the time), and leg baths for the chorus; the largest lighting switchboard in any of the company's venues; spotlight "cages" high above in the wings – allowing the operators to remain out of sight; provision for 93 scenery cloths – 55 on counterweighted lines; and a stage area incorporating much elaborate apparatus. This was described as "the biggest reconstruction plan in the history of the Winter Gardens" … "built on the site of the old Opera House but occupying twice its area" and "a landmark in theatrical history".

And so the 'New Opera House', as it was advertised for a time, was on its way and, not unexpectedly, would experience many ups and downs, twists and turns, during the years to follow – some of the highlights of which can now be considered. The first highlight, then, must be the official opening on Friday

July 14th 1939 and as the 1,000 guests gathered, Reginald Dixon and Horace Finch played organ duets on the new £5,000 Wurlitzer. With the line up of official guests on stage, comprising civic dignitaries, representatives from the Winter Gardens and Tower Companies, the architects (C. H. MacKeith) and the world of show business, actress Miss Jessie Matthews presided.

A golden ribbon had been suspended across the proscenium and, in cutting the ribbon with a pair of golden scissors, from which hung a decorated horseshoe, Miss Matthews announced: "I have very great pleasure in declaring this lovely Opera House open". Upon returning to her seat she amusingly complied with an old superstition by handing the chairman a token penny as she placed the scissors into her handbag. Also at the opening was Mr George Formby and it was he who would star in the first show – a revue *Turned Out Nice Again*.

While the 'New' Opera House continued to present the big musicals that

A view from the top of the house illustrates the extravagant proportions which cannot fail to impress. The house curtain, now in traditional warm red, originally matched the copper hues of the upholstery.

its predecessors had staged: the likes of *The Arcadians* and *The Chocolate Soldier*, opera and ballet, and featured all of the eminent companies such as the D'Oyly Carte, Sadler's Wells, etc., its size and virtuosity soon gained it a reputation as *the* place to see spectacle! Right from the word 'go', and for the next two decades, the vast summer extravaganzas which would occupy the House were absolutely the last word, with exceptional sets utilising all the theatre's technical prowess (the stage-lifts and traps, the lighting. etc.), special effects, brilliant costumes, and such tremendous line-ups both in eminence and number, that they are still talked of today! Scenes featuring a train crash, a blazing oil-well and cascading waters were not unusual!

By the time the 'sixties were here, however, styles were changing and staging became simpler, though still lavish and featuring the top star names. Since then a variety of formats have been tried, influenced by the tastes of the day, from the traditional summer-shows to stage versions of popular television series, to short seasons of major London musicals. Sunday concerts have also played a large part in the Opera House's history, bringing to Blackpool a wealth of national and international stars.

Another highlight which should not be missed occurred on Wednesday April 15th 1955 when the first Royal Command Variety Show ever to be presented outside London was staged, with American singing star Eddie Fisher topping the bill. The Opera House did not possess a royal box, and so one had to be specially built – which was situated on the right hand side of the auditorium where it remained for a number of years before being removed. At the time of writing it has not been replaced. On that special night, it was occupied by Her Majesty the Queen and His Royal Highness the Duke of Edinburgh.

The theatre, of course, has undergone the usual highs and lows of popularity, on occasions resorting to its flexibility as a cinema, and most of them being the result of the external situations described in other chapters, which I need not repeat. An additional feature in its favour is its fine position in the Winter Gardens complex which promotes, particularly out of season, excellent facilities and an adaptability as a major conference venue.

To conclude, let me mention a just a handful of the players – a task of difficulty owing to the vast number of distinguished celebs – selected purely at random: Judy Garland, Paul Robeson, Shirley Bassey, Petula Clark, Frank Sinatra, Bob Hope, Tony Bennett, Sammy Davis Jnr., Arthur Askey, Gracie Fields, Wilfred Pickles, Alma Cogan, Vera Lynn, Max Bygraves, Bruce Forsyth, Harry Secombe, Tommy Steele, Tom Jones, Mike Yarwood, Freddie Starr, Cannon and Ball, Russ Abbot and Ken Dodd.

Blackpool Grand Theatre

One early publicity caption certainly got it right when, in its opening weeks, the Blackpool Grand Theatre was declared to be "the prettiest theatre in the world" – a statement which could probably still ring true even today! This particular example of a Frank Matcham theatre is considered by many to be one of his finest survivors – 'Matcham's Masterpiece' – and to this end many people have lavished much tender loving care in a variety of ways over the last few decades, fundamentally achieving that survival and, in the longer term, ensuring a gradual but 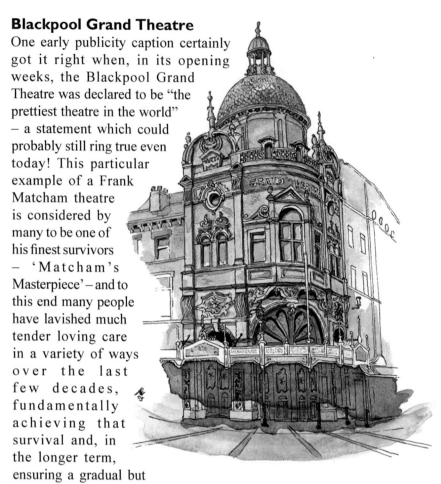 continuing programme of splendid restoration. So that today the interior remains a dazzling faithful Matcham spectacle at its best – largely attributable to the vigorous 'Friends of the Grand' organisation and their associates who, in 1972, began by halting the theatre's metamorphosis into a department-store as proposed by local planners! Their efforts must be applauded!

The Victorian Blackpool entertainment scene has already been set in previous chapters – it arose at a great speed, in less than a single lifetime – and by the latter portion of the nineteenth century the tastes of the well-to-do were already being well catered for at the North Pier, the Winter Gardens Pavilion and the Opera House. Opera, ballet, orchestral concerts and classical drama abounded

– but the tastes of the masses had yet to be adequately tapped!

Enter in 1876 another entrepreneur, who would successfully cash in on this burgeoning market for music hall and melodrama – one Thomas Sergenson. Events would lead to his eventual acquisition of the leases of two local theatres which, with no apparent theatrical know-how but an obvious business acumen, he was to run with the 'popular' fare to great success. A little later, he also increased his 'empire' by taking on the lease of the Prince's Theatre in Bradford (presumably prior to Mr Laidler's occupation of that building – see part 2 – Bradford Alhambra) but, with sights always higher, his real claim to fame was yet to be unleashed!

The first signs came in 1887 when he bought some old premises along Church Street and the following year declared his intention to build a new and modern 'Grand Theatre', but the project was not immediately realised. The Winter Gardens just down the road, at this point, proclaimed their latest venture – to build an opera house (see previous chapter). Perhaps this was prompted by Mr Sergenson's proposals, but were these proposals later mothballed in view of the impending new opera house? In any event, for the time being Thomas Sergenson built five shops on the plot – which had been planned anyway and would presumably provide an income and in July 1889, he also opened a makeshift circus. A couple of years later, however, he obviously assessed that there was still the need for another quality theatre – and by 1891 preparations were underway for the building of the Blackpool Tower whose complex would also include a circus – and so Sergenson's original plan was brought out of mothballs and Frank Matcham was instructed to produce "the best, prettiest and cosiest theatre possible".

When it arrived, the result was astonishing – opening around nine months later, on July 23rd 1894, and costing an immense £20,000 – and the *Blackpool Gazette and News* the following day gave a description of the building and an account of the opening night. With evening dress "general in the stalls, circle and boxes", and "there being but standing room only in the pit, while the extensive seating accommodation of the upper circle and gallery were well taken up" … "the scene presented at the rising of the curtain was a very brilliant one indeed". Obviously the VIPs were out in force, including "Members of the Town Council" and, interestingly, Mr W. Holland (from the Winter Gardens), and Mr Frank Matcham. The production was Shakespeare's *Hamlet*, the lead role performed by Mr Wilson Barrett, the famous actor-manager who, additionally, made the curtain speech. Mr Barrett was obviously equally at home with such officiations (see part 2 – the Leeds Grand Theatre and Opera House) which, besides praising the new theatre and those responsible, somewhat echoed his earlier themes concerning the morals of the masses!

The quality of the opening production set the pace for this touring house for the entire length of Thomas Sergenson's management and ownership – which was to last until 1909 at which point he apparently elected to retire. The new owner managers – the Blackpool Tower Company, with their ever increasing importance on the Blackpool entertainment front – achieved equal prestige in the heydays that would follow and, by 1928, in a merger that would bring the massive Winter Gardens complex into the fold, bookings for all of the theatres involved became complementary rather than competitive. Even the years of the World Wars proved to be heady periods, the unusual Blackpool wartime situation already having been mentioned in a previous chapter, with its magnetic propensity towards attractions and audiences alike. The list of eminent companies, stars and shows, is exhaustive but a few of the key players must be mentioned.

All of the big musicals came from the start – many of them supplied by the famous George Edwardes companies. The *Maids of the Mountains* and *Chu Chin Chows* were certainly out in force here! For those with a more serious liking there was also opera, and the regular visitor at the Grand was the Carl Rosa Company. The dramatic side has always been well represented – the Grand having spent much of its time as a drama house – and early records show performances by such luminaries as Herbert Beerbohm Tree and Frank Benson. And as the decades unfolded the theatre moved with them, continuing to present the popular fare of the day – ragtime, the new big American musicals, variety, summer shows – always featuring the top entertainers. Indeed, so highly regarded was the Grand that, for many years, it became a pre-London touring date, so that countless numbers of shows played in Blackpool even before the West End!

Here is a taster of entertainers – a hotchpotch from all walks simply to name-drop, simply to illustrate the Grand's high standing: Sarah Bernhardt, Ellen Terry, Lillie Langtry, Forbes-Robertson, Seymour Hicks, Irene Vanbrugh, Matheson Lang, Sybil Thorndike, Edith Evans, Jack Hulbert, Cicely Courtneidge, Gertrude Lawrence, Noel Coward, Evelyn Laye, Carl Brisson, Donald Wolfit, Flora Robson, John Gielgud, Rex Harrison, Michael Redgrave, Vivien Leigh, Alec Guinness, Richard Todd, Michael Denison and Dulcie Gray, John Hanson, Margot Fonteyn, Gracie Fields, Arthur Askey, Wilfred Pickles,

Blackpool Grand Theatre: "Matcham's Masterpiece"!

202 Theatres of Achievement

Jimmy Clitheroe, Thora Hird, Hylda Baker, Sid James, Timothy West, Prunella Scales, Les Dawson, The Grumbleweeds, Cannon and Ball, The Krankies, Billy Pearce and Ken Dodd. There are so, so many more!

Even with all of this going for it, however, the Grand has not been without its share of storm clouds – many of them resulting from the same issues that would affect numerous similar venues. One example, the cinema, posed obvious problems towards the end of the 'twenties but the theatre overcame this by 'kitting-out' for the 'talkies' and so was versatile enough to either show full seasons of films, or intersperse them with live shows as the need arose. The other major obstacle – that of television, coupled with other distractions of the time – caused audiences in the late 'fifties to dwindle and by the early 'sixties the Grand, up to now an open-all-year-round house, began to close out-of-season. But the really bad news came later in the 'sixties when the theatre was included in a redevelopment plan for the town centre, and in July 1972 when it closed full-time, and when permission was sought to demolish it!

A very fortunate fact in the Grand's favour at this point was that it was a DOE Grade II Listed Building – which precluded any such immediate notions and, as it turned out, provided the time which allowed for the formation of a very successful 'Friends of the Grand' group, which was to emerge fighting on its behalf from all corners! The chief points of the story tell how the matter was therefore put to a public enquiry, and that the outcome was in the Grand's favour, as it was considered that it "… could be successfully run by a trust or the Corporation as a combined civic and commercial theatre …" and "… put to the best possible use for the benefit of local residents and holiday-makers alike".

By the mid-'seventies, however, the theatre was still closed and quickly decaying, but eventually came an arrangement whereby EMI (the now owners following an earlier takeover bid of the Tower Company) would refurbish and run it as a bingo house, allowing the opportunity for the Friends to lease, stage a number of performances and, ultimately, purchase the theatre. Basically, this is what happened, and the building is now owned and run by the Grand Theatre Trust Ltd. (of Friends origination) – a limited company with charitable status.

The story is a too long to include here but, if told, would reveal an enormous amount of hard work (from the administrative aspects down to the physical 'scrubbing out'), and support – including much generous financial assistance – from other bodies and organisations. This work has, over recent years, not

With an abundance of fine art and plasterwork, here the Grand could be mistaken for one of the world's great temples or palaces; however the sumptuous heavy house draperies quickly restore the air of theatricality.

Exceptionally decorated circle-fronts curve in a most pleasing manner, ensuring an intimacy is maintained in a house that has a fairly large seating capacity.

only gradually built up audience and professional confidence but has also resulted in a continuing programme of excellent restoration, so that the building presented today – and in particular its auditorium – is truly an amazing work of art!

Here, also, is another example of a theatre where bingo has, ironically, helped to save the day. In many cases the fabric of theatres has been preserved through such activity, but in Blackpool it has to be said that EMI, additionally, performed an absolutely wonderful makeover prior to its 1977 reopening which, of course, provided an excellent foundation for what would follow.

The colour scheme was quite dramatically changed and, as a life-long visitor to Blackpool and the Grand I have personal recollections. From childhood visits in the late 'fifties I can still hear the two piano-players hammering away in the pit prior to the first curtain of a play, then the interval clinking of teacups in the dress circle, but most of all I remember the quite unusual (to me) colour of the upholstery – which was entirely in turquoise. Upon muscling in on the bingo crowds some years later, I was delighted to find that my Grand of earlier was still in excellent condition – but had my memory failed me, for although the original turquoise house tabs and extravagant pelmet seemed to be in place, the seating and carpets were now in a warm red? In actual fact my memory was quite correct – and the present wine upholstery is admittedly much warmer than before, though I must confess to still having a soft spot for the original! The latest bout of refurbishment, which has notably restored original paintings, has also replaced the complete set of house curtains, which I am pleased to see remain in the former style and colour! To turn it all on its head, *blue* is actually the colour reported to have been predominant in 1894!

The Grand has also hosted visits from the royal household – notably on Friday 29th May 1981 when the Prince of Wales attended a Royal Variety Performance and formally reopened the theatre; in June 1989 when Prince Edward was present at a charity performance; in July 1994 – the centenary year – when the Queen and the Duke of Edinburgh were present at a rehearsal for the Gala Centenary show.

In 1993 the Grand hatched another feature with the opening of a further space – the Annex Studio Theatre – which, in addition to the main house, and situated in converted rooms upstairs, provides for alternative activity. The raked seating for 108 can be retracted so that the contrastingly modern space with its Canadian maple floor and prolific use of mirror is ideal for a multitude of events from smaller theatre, poetry, music, dance, etc., to conference, meeting, rehearsal and workshop use, etc.

It has to be said that the building is exceptional! The Victorian elements in the auditorium have received a sensitive programme of extensive restoration and, together with modern sympathetic lighting techniques, are extraordinary! The supporting acts – the bars, foyer and staircases – also utilised for some daytime activity and catering, additionally, complement the star attraction perfectly. And together with the external features, the original stone corner entrance topped with its green dome and now sporting a reproduction of the original glass and iron canopy at street level, and the creation of the 'kiosk' shops and 'Matcham Court', the overall package can be described as nothing less than a showpiece! Indeed, it is 'Matcham's Masterpiece'!

Matcham's Masterpiece – 'the prettiest theatre in the world'.

5 REPERTORY DAYS

Early in the twentieth century an attempt to provide an alternative to the commercial product of the provincial touring house by presenting work motivated, rather, by artistic merit, led to small theatres springing up all over the country. Whether or not the policy was always achieved, local communities were supplied with a range of drama that became lovingly known as 'weekly rep!', and its theatrical participants with a first-class training ground...

- *Liverpool Playhouse (1866)*
- *Birmingham Old Rep Theatre (1913)*
- *Oldham Coliseum Theatre (1885)*
- *Coventry Belgrade Theatre (1958)*

Liverpool Playhouse

When, in the second part of the 1990s, I prepared my list of theatres that would feature in this volume, the Liverpool Playhouse was home to the longest surviving repertory company in Britain, and would therefore be a good choice. It also, I thought, in structure, was quite archetypal as a residence to such a phenomenon, and so would ideally illustrate, as a whole, the life-work and development of the non-commercial side of professional theatre and the repertory movement. Sadly, in 1998 the Liverpool Repertory Company went into liquidation, thus terminating almost eighty-seven years of continuous business (save for short war-time or summer periods of dark) and a marvellous record of service to the community and theatrical fraternity alike.

Today, however, the operation continues with the newly formed Liverpool and Merseyside Theatres Trust, which, jointly administering the Playhouse and Everyman theatres, fortunately keeps the doors of the Playhouse open and so thankfully, the good work proceeds. Notwithstanding this situation my original aims are still achieved – for nothing can rewrite the illustrious history associated with this grand building and its inhabitants – a tale that owes a debt of gratitude to an abundance of pioneers, players, and stalwarts. I hope that I will be forgiven for mentioning none of them, save for some of the famous – whom I name only to illustrate the depth of success of the venture, for there are other volumes which will sing their praises, and this book is essentially about buildings.

The playhouse actually began life as a music hall – the New Star Music Hall – erected in 1866, designed by a local architect, Edward Davies. As with many other entertainment ventures, the site was already associated with recreational amusement, its predecessor being a concert room known as the Star Concert Hall. And the music hall spectacle was to continue, reportedly in sumptuous style – the new venue seemingly lavishly appointed (of note, the new scenery and drop curtain painted by William Telbin – see also Leeds Grand, part 2, for mention of other works), sporting only the best in decoration and upholstery, with fine paining, ornament, glasswork and mirrors, etc.

It is said to have accommodated up to 2,000 people and, with stalls equipped with tables and chairs in addition to gallery and traditional theatre seating, refreshment bars on various levels, waiters, and chairman complete with gavel, a mental picture is conjured which is not too distant from television's portrayal, *The Good Old Days*. (At the opening night (26th December 1866)

Liverpool Playhouse: an intimate auditorium – the home of outstanding contribution to British theatre.

prices of admission were reserved stalls 1/6d, balconies 1/-, body of the hall 6d and admission to the stalls at 1/- was to gentlemen only by the Houghton Street entrance.)

The 'fare' was reputedly of equal excellence comprising a miscellany of opera, ballet, orchestral and choral music, comedy, variety, and vaudeville, etc., and with the growth and importance of Liverpool's seaport, commercial, and industrial populace, it was to enjoy success as one of the premier 'halls' for a good number of years. There were inevitable changes in ownership from time to time, and in name – in 1896 it would become the New Star Theatre of Varieties – and although there were also major internal refurbishments, the exterior that we see today is largely that from 1866.

Another name change came in May 1898 and brought also with it a change in policy – the Star Theatre, reflecting a switch from music hall to drama – thus ending a long and successful association with the former, and launching what was to become an extensive and celebrated career as a drama house. The first play was a Wilson Barrett success from London – *Hoodman Blind* – and melodrama featured prominently, until a further change of hands in 1911.

But early in the twentieth century were coming new ideas concerning drama,

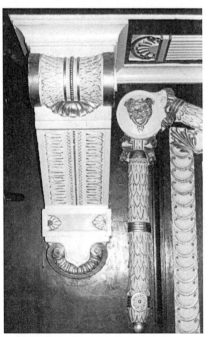

with the desire of some to break away from melodrama, the presiding touring scene, the 'London' preoccupation with long runs – in particular a theatre that relied upon or was motivated by profit – to allow the development of a theatre on artistic merit that would promote, rather than suppress, new or non-commercial ideas. Thus the repertory movement was born which, in its heyday, would proliferate more than a hundred local companies throughout the country and Liverpool, based upon these principles, was one of the forerunners. Said to have been prompted by the success of Annie Horniman's repertory company formed at the Gaiety Theatre in Manchester in 1908, the Liverpool Repertory Company moved into the Star Theatre, which subsequently would undergo a further name change – to the Liverpool Repertory Theatre.

The interior of the theatre at this time was remodelled, the architect of note being Stanley D. Adshead of Liverpool University, and it is his 760-seater auditorium in the Greek revival style that remains intact. Of course there have been several refurbishments and alternative colour schemes over the years, but the present house is chiefly that which was packed out on the evening of 11th November, 1911 for the new company's first production at the theatre – *The Admirable Crichton* by J. M. Barrie. In attendance, of course, was the Lord Mayor of Liverpool, Lord Derby, and other local dignitaries. Interestingly, the ticket prices of this period were stalls 4/-, dress circle 3/-, boxes £2/2/- and gallery 1/-.

Now the stories of many, many repertory companies share a host of common facts, often originating from amateur roots (as some of the following chapters will testify). With their numbers growing to more than a hundred in their heyday they became the chief source of theatre outside London, thus markedly enhancing the cultural scene of the provinces. While the concept of being able to produce for art's sake as opposed to profit, as already mentioned did allow new productions and ideas to emerge, many companies were also run on tight budgets, and had to produce more well known works as well. Often their measure of success fluctuated against external influences – such as wars, cinema and television to mention just three, and I have scarcely heard of any company that did not, at some time or other, have its financial worries. And although the quality would sometimes vary – from "shaky scenery" at one end of the scale to companies of renown at the other – it is clear that, in many cases, communities were to grow very fond of, and patronise avidly, their own, local, repertory theatres.

Their 'weekly rep' (so called because most produced a new play every week) almost became a British institution – like Sunday lunch of meat and two veg. – and not only provided excellent training opportunities for those involved, via the sheer diversity of works made available, it frequently supplied audiences with a good range of drama at affordable prices. Many a famous name would also emerge from the process, though the 'system' was geared towards teamwork and the company rather than the 'star' and eventually, the spirited (nay gruelling), practice of playing one play in the evening while rehearsing another during the day gradually gave way to runs of two, three, or more weeks.

State financial aid, firstly becoming available in the 1940s, had played its part and as time progressed, notably within the decades following the end of the Second World War, encouraged the new ideas that began to brew with a civic and community orientated thinking – e.g. theatres open all day encompassing much more than the evening's performance – and many schemes led to the building of new theatres, often involving new and innovative theatre forms. Examples of some of those which excel are shown in part 5 - Coventry Belgrade (1958), part 6 - Sheffield Crucible (1971), part 7 - Manchester Royal Exchange (1976) and part 6 - West Yorkshire Playhouse (1990).

The Liverpool Repertory Company, however, remained *in situ* at the Liverpool Repertory Theatre (in 1917 a further name change to the Liverpool Playhouse) throughout its existence, and went on to become a company of renown. Alongside its contemporaries, it took on appropriate measures as necessary in order to survive the ups and downs of life. One such example was during World War II when the Old Vic Company took up residence who, for approximately four years – having been evacuated from London, and filling a gap created by the wartime activities – provided Liverpool with an extremely successful period of plays, involving many notable personnel.

Another difficult time, of course, was the mass arrival of TV in the 'fifties, but having weathered that storm the Playhouse joined the rest of the country during the 'sixties in a period of forward thinking and renewal, and embarked upon several schemes of major improvement and redevelopment. Of significance was a new lighting system, state-of-the-art for the time and operated from the rear of the dress circle; refurbished auditorium; new dressing rooms and larger stage; and conversion of a rehearsal room to become a second performing space – the Playhouse Studio (or the "Theatre Upstairs"!)

But perhaps most strikingly came the building of a new extension to the left of the existing theatre which, incorporating a glass cylinder supported upon a central pillar, and equal to the theatre's own height and approximately half its width, has ever since provided the main entrances to *all* levels, together with bars, restaurants, cloaks, etc. Of course, when adding new structures to old comes the daunting task of matching the two, hence the reason for a *completely* differing design, which does not have to profess to do this.

The Playhouse continued through the 'seventies and 'eighties but, by now, was experiencing financial difficulties, and there were several threats of closure – usually curtailed by the fortunate coincidence of a box office run of particular success, or government aid. Sadly, however, the Liverpool Repertory Company ultimately lost is battle against the odds, and its final curtain descended on the 3rd January 1998.

On a brighter note let us consider some of the momentous achievements occasioned by the Repertory Company at the Playhouse. Not only have the people of Liverpool benefited greatly from the provision of quality live theatre in the area – those taking part have likewise received an opportunity to air their talents, have them nurtured, including writers, directors, actors, technicians, etc. Often this has led to national and international acclaim. Additionally, established greats have, of course, trodden the Playhouse's boards along with the 'home-grown' talent. The wartime London Old Vic Company brought Bernard Miles, Sybil Thorndike, Alec Guiness, Lally Bowers, Michael Redgrave. Other notables have included Robert Donat, Rex Harrison, Peggy Mount, Patricia Routledge, Richard Briers, John Thaw, Jean Alexander, Thelma Barlow, Deryck Guyler, Patricia Hayes, Richard Todd, Penelope Keith, Hayley Mills, Warren Mitchell and Denis Waterman to name only a few. Famous writers include Willy Russell (e.g. *Blood Brothers*) and Alan Bleasdale (e.g. *Having A Ball*).

Checking out the blurb on the current ventures at the Everyman and the Playhouse reveals an absolute wealth of enthusiastic and wide-ranging activity – from 'home' and touring productions to a whole assortment of community-orientated and educational projects, partnerships, celebrations, festivals, etc. In 2005 they were named Best Performing Venue at the Mersey Partnership Annual Tourism Awards. Thus, the revitalised Playhouse, along with its Everyman counterpart, continues in the footsteps of its predecessors in producing exceptional works, hopefully ensuring that the theatre doors will remain wide open for the benefit of many, many more generations to come.

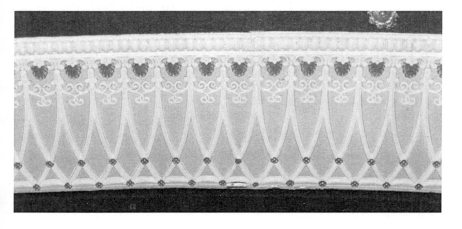

Birmingham Old Rep Theatre

Here is a true landmark of repertory theatres, being the original purpose-built rep venue to open in the country, and thus from the 15th February 1913, along with what was to become a most illustrious company – The Birmingham Repertory Theatre Company – started a near-on sixty year period of prestigious work, cultivating an equally esteemed roll of honour in the shape of actors, directors, plays and playwrights. Although the Company and the theatre separated in 1971, the story ends happily for both – the Old Rep Theatre (as it would become known) continuing today to entertain the public via a new resident company (The Birmingham Stage Company), while the Birmingham Repertory Theatre Ltd. (no longer having a resident playing company – in line with present-day trends) has an impressive new building in which to perform.

The Repertory Theatre was built by Barry Jackson, the son of the founder of the Maypole Dairies, to house his *Pilgrim Players*, an amateur company he had formed some years earlier, by now proceeding under its revised name. The first production on its stage was *Twelfth Night*. Not only was he endowed with money – which enabled him to fund his dream until its eventual transfer to a Board of Trustees in 1935 – he was equally endowed with a great talent, which also enabled him to successfully run and direct his theatre and company, and he was knighted in 1925 for services to theatre. The venture, it has been said, was no doubt motivated by the accomplishments of Annie Horniman's Manchester Company (1907) and the Liverpool Repertory Theatre (1911, see previous chapter) and its principles and aspirations followed on in the same vein, which I shall not repeat here as they are set out in several other areas of this book. And, needless to say, although the theatre met with great artistic success over a long period, it wasn't all plain sailing as the undertaking was obviously subject to the vicissitudes faced by similar operations, e.g. the arrival of the 'talkies', TV, etc. with which it had to contend.

The theatre was built on a restricted site with a very pleasant brick and stone facade to Station Street. The plainness, as compared with, say, Victorian predecessors is evident, and is particularly carried on throughout the interior, probably reflecting the proposed purpose and principles. It was designed by architect S. N. Cooke and originally seated 464 (currently 383) on two levels – the stalls accommodating the majority in one straight steep no-frills slope, all with good sightlines, and a small balcony at the back catering for the rest. The proscenium wall is equally understated, with an opening of 22 ft., and the comparatively small auditorium, almost of courtroom appearance, lends an intimate atmosphere to the productions.

In addition to that of Sir Barry Jackson, there are many distinguished names

Birmingham Old Rep Theatre: another house of achievement – the first purpose-built repertory theatre in the country. With a steep rake, plain furnishing and uninterrupted views, attention was firmly directed towards the stage from the outset.

that have been associated with the theatre, and I begin with John Drinkwater as he was its first general manager. He also, as a playwright, poet and actor had several of his plays tried out here – one of the most notable being *Abraham Lincoln* (1919) which transferred to London and eventually America. The Rep was to have many productions to fly the nest either to London, elsewhere, or on tour during its lifetime, and was also significant in the nurturing field, and as a springboard for talent in all areas, e.g. writing, acting, etc. It will take just a few names at random, from those instantly recognisable and who have trodden its boards at one time or another, to illustrate the eminence of this slice of British theatrical history: Laurence Olivier, Paul Schofield, Albert Finney, Ralph Richardson, Noel Coward, Derek Jacobi, Peggy Ashcroft, Edith Evans and Richard Chamberlain, in no particular order. Of equal distinction are many of the productions that graced the stage of The (Old) Rep, some of which explored far beyond the boundaries of commercial theatre, thus contributing greatly to the nation's cultural wealth. Additionally, perhaps significant moments would include modern dress Shakespeare (contentiously received by some!), and the English premier of Bernard Shaw's *Back to Methusalah*.

In 1971, following the donation of a city-centre site from Birmingham City Council, a new Birmingham Repertory Theatre opened a short distance away – in keeping with the pattern being set by the new wave of regional theatre

building, i.e. spacious and modern and containing all of the up-to-date requirements – leaving the Station Street property to become The *Old* Rep. Sadly, although utilised by local amateur operatic and dramatic companies, the "Old" Rep spent much of its time 'dark' until, in 1992, the Birmingham Stage Company took residence. It is considered that the track record of the BSC, which has produced classic, contemporary, new and, in particular, plays for children, has continued the excellent reputation with which the Old Rep Theatre has become associated.

Oldham Coliseum Theatre

The postal address of Fairbottom Street, Oldham, Lancashire does little to conjure up thoughts of drama, opera and fine theatre – more likely to portray the mental picture of a back street in a northern industrial town – yet here is established a little theatre with a big reputation. A theatre which, over more than one hundred years, has provided entertainment to countless thousands, and has, more importantly, been greatly instrumental in fostering the talents of new actors and playwrights, many of whom are the famous names from cinema and television. A positive workhorse amongst British theatres!

For the purposes of this book the Coliseum's tale has two chief themes: (a) the story of a building and, (b) the story of a unique repertory company. Where the building is concerned, like many others in this book it has had its trials, tribulations and successes, and has bowed to public and social taste in order to run the course of survival. Unlike many within these pages it is fairly plain and unpretentious – although extremely comfortable and completely at home in its purpose. No baroque or rococo here! No voluptuous caryatids supporting domed ceilings, or displays of flamboyant embellishment or attendant cherubs to keep a watch over the histrionics of past and present.

What you see is what you get! But the continued success of its work bears out that customers obviously do 'get' what they want! Here is a marriage of theatre and company, which has, over the years, contributed hugely to the British theatrical scene.

Let us pick up the threads in an Oldham just after the turn of the century – the Edwardian years – the theatre-building boom years! At this point the town was still adding to its stock of theatrical houses and the Colosseum (as it was then spelt) rubbed shoulders with no less than five neighbours, all with equally enticing names such as 'Theatre Royal', 'Gaiety' (at one time 'Adelphi'), 'Empire', 'Palace' and 'Grand'. Such was the call for entertainment from the inhabitants of Oldham's industrial town, with its pit stacks and myriad mill chimneys of the cotton trade, as they clamoured down the cobbled streets to fill them.

The Colosseum had started its life a number of years before – around 1885 – in Henshaw Street, to present circus shows. Its instigator had been a circus owner called Myers who, basically, could not afford to pay for the completed building, and so the builder Thomas Whittaker stayed on to try his hand with his 'inheritance'. He opened with a "Chinese Fair" and eventually presented music hall and stage plays. By 1887, however, the council was looking to build a market hall on the site, and so Mr Whittaker moved his building lock, stock and barrel to its present position in Fairbottom Street.

Now a notable point is that the building was constructed entirely of wood – and was to substantially remain so until the mid-1960s! This was to present certain licensing difficulties at times during its life – and we shall later see how these were overcome. Indeed, the fire aspect was considered from the start, and exit doors and fireproofing were significant factors brought to attention. It is also interesting to note how, at this time, the lighting was arranged, and the following extract – reprinted from *The First Hundred Years* by James Carter – from an eye-witness (Walter Wall, the son of Mr Whittaker's theatre manager, Stephen Wall) at the 1887 rebuilding tells us:

> *"All the wood used in the building was fire-proofed, and a good advertisement was obtained by publicising the fact that scrap ends of timber were of no use as chips for fire-lighting. Even the Fire Brigade could not light a fire with them. I remember them trying. On all day bills and programmes appeared the words, "The Safe Theatre", and also a statement by the chief of the Manchester Fire Brigade that a wooden staircase was safer in a fire than a stone one. Gas was used as an illuminant and the limelights for following the artistes were truly*

'limelights'. The gas used for them was produced on the premises, and the 'limes' shaped and drilled in a workshop under the stage. They were worked from 'lime shelves', two on each side behind the proscenium, and from the wings, the simple burners or mixers being enclosed in big clumsy boxes.

"The footlights were of gas (not incandescent mantles) with a pilot light at each end. Sometimes the lights would not run along and had to be encouraged by stagehands blowing the flame along from one burner to the next. There was a contrivance by which coloured glass could be raised between the footlights and the stage. The glass screens were amber, red and green.

"On the back wall of the stage was a huge frame on which canvas was stretched and painted into scenery, with scenic artists working from a bridge which they raised or lowered at will."

The opening of the new theatre on 10th June 1887 – presenting *Culeen's Royal Jubilee Circus* – coincided with the day that Queen Victoria celebrated fifty years upon the throne.

In 1903 the theatre changed hands, when it was purchased on behalf of Peter

Oldham Coliseum Theatre: a delightful auditorium which has achieved more than a lifetime of great contributions to the British stage.

Yates, of Yates' Wine Lodges. The decade saw a variety of entertainments – chiefly provided by touring companies in the form of drama, comedy, opera and pantomime. Popular operas doing the rounds at this time included *Cavaleria Rusticana*, *Faust*, *Lohengrin* and *Carmen* and on the comedy side, Charlie Chaplin appeared in 1908 in *Casey's Court Circus*. The decade also brought with it, up and down the country, an increasing favour of the silent film – and eventually, cinemas to house them in. Initially, films were often shown on the bill in theatre shows – interspersed with music hall and comedy acts and called 'cine-variety' – little could the theatre managers of the time have realised that this was the advent of the death-knell over their theatrical empires. The Colosseum went down this very route in 1911.

A notable film in the life of all theatre and cinema then came in 1927 with *The Jazz Singer* starring Al Jolson and this, the first 'talkie', really set the snowball rolling in the massive escalation of theatre conversion or closure generally. In 1931 – after hanging on quite a considerable length of time in comparison with some of the other theatres – the 'Colosseum Super Talkie Theatre' was born, and the theatre went into the full time 'pictures' business. By now the Colosseum had also experienced a couple of changes in ownership. The latest venture, however, lasted only until 1932 when the Colosseum closed its doors, and was to remain 'dark' for the next seven years!

Now a browse through many of the other chapters in this book will tell a similar story. But what is remarkable is that each, uniquely, has its own miraculous turn of fate, and in Oldham the spark of the Colosseum's renaissance was struck by a man called Joe Holdroyd. For while the Colosseum had been heading down its ill-fated slippery slope its local neighbours – with the aforementioned enticing names – had also been heading in a similar direction, with the effect that by just after the middle of the decade there was no live theatre at all left in Oldham! And so this local drama enthusiast who saw the state of affairs as a great shame started the ball rolling via an advert in the local newspaper, which formed the 'Oldham Playgoers Club'.

The purpose of the club was to return live theatre – and repertory – to the town. It started with a handful of people who met where they could, sometimes presenting evenings of a theatrical nature, but fairly quickly (by 1937) it led to them hiring the local Temperance Hall. This they converted into a makeshift theatre (using seats bought from Miss Horniman's Gaiety Theatre in Manchester!), and brought in Roger Williams' company to present the plays. The first hurdle to be cleared was the refusal of the local magistrates to grant a public theatre licence (because of the state of the hall) and this was overcome by creating the 'Oldham Repertory Theatre Club' – which didn't need a licence in respect of presentations to its own members. The first performance, on Saturday January 31st 1938, was George Bernard Shaw's *Arms and the Man*.

This is essentially the story of a uniquely successful repertory company – formed into a club, initially, for the obvious reasons mentioned above. It achieved instant success and eventually required larger premises and this is where, believe it or not, the Colosseum returns to the plot! For the, now, tumbledown ramshackle of a theatre, waiting in the wings for a return to centre stage, begins its grooming for stardom. But despite the hard work put in by the many local people to achieve that stardom, one original fact remained – that it was of wooden construction! And so the earlier problems of licensing requirements were repeated. However, this did not seem to pose any serious threat at the time, for the 'Oldham Repertory Theatre Club' continued to play to its own private membership thus eliminating the necessity for a theatre licence. They opened in July 1939 in the newly refurbished Coliseum (note change of spelling) Theatre!

A glance into the life of the Oldham Repertory Theatre Club will also tell us something about regional theatre between the late nineteen-thirties and today. Its membership in the early Temperance Hall days was around 200 but this quickly increased to 2,000. In its heyday it even achieved 20,000! Like many of its contemporaries in the repertory movement, its popularity was greatly influenced by other forms of entertainment on offer – we have already discussed cinema; the next major competitor, in the 'fifties, was television. The 'forties had been generally very good days – of course punctuated by the Second World War – but even these days supplied an insatiable appetite for entertainment. In Oldham, as a consequence, the locals were cheered by some of Britain's finest theatrical companies evacuated from the capital city, including the Old Vic, Ballet Rambert and Sadler's Wells Opera. There were equally famous names on stage – such touring brought celebs like, for example, Dame Sybil Thorndike. It was the 'fifties – with the growth of television – when the trouble really began, with plummeting ticket sales. For many repertory companies this was to spell sure death, as they were forced to close, but in Oldham they soldiered on!

The club survived until 1977 by which time the original 'wooden' structural problem had been resolved (in the mid-'sixties' renovations) and, of course, times and business methods change. It was at this point that the Metropolitan Borough Council took the building over, with financial help from the Greater Manchester Council and the Arts Council. Financial aid to regional theatre, of course, was not new for subsidies and grants had been used in many parts of the country to assist local theatrical enterprises – from building works to the encouragement of new writing and presentation – since the mid 'forties. Indeed, this was not the first time that the Coliseum had benefited financially – occasionally receiving assistance from as far back as the early 1960s.

An interesting point to note is how, at Oldham, they persevered so long with *weekly* rep. Imagine the effort required to present a new play every week, whilst, at the same time, rehearsing next week's play! They went over to 'fortnightly' rep in 68/69. Other companies throughout the land had been playing 'fortnightly' or even 'three-weekly' or longer for years. But it did provide a good training-ground for new actors, actresses, technical staff etc., and the opportunity to air new works – thus achieving a reputation unsurpassed. And so *it continues to do!* One of the most remarkable features at Oldham has been their long-standing ability to produce quality names – who have gone on to be famous in film, television and theatre – in addition to allowing for premier productions, some of which have eventually found their way onto

London and even Broadway stages! In a complementary way, other famous names have also graced the boards at the Coliseum on many occasions – some of them actually starting out at Oldham in years gone by, and returning to complete the circle!

Perhaps I might select a few who have had the 'honour' of playing the Coliseum – either as members of the company or guests! As far back as the 'forties names such as Marius Goring, Mollie Sugden, Eric Sykes, Dora Bryan, Bernard Cribbins were appearing in the programmes. Ensuing years brought, amongst others, Dame Thora Hird, Ronald Magill, Nova Pilbeam, Claude Hulbert, Jean Alexander, Frank Middlemass, William Roache. The list goes on ... Ian Cullen, Barbara Knox, John Savident, Glyn Worsnip, Julie Goodyear, Roy Barraclough, McDonald Hobley, Adele Leigh, Lynne Carol, Pat Phoenix, David Kossoff, Jessie Matthews. And even more! ... Bernard Latham, Kathy Staff, Toke Townley, Matthew Kelly, Fine-Time Fontayne, Ralph Fiennes, Bill Waddington, Helen Shapiro and Ken Dodd. And towards the centenary ... Nigel Pivaro, Sarah Lancashire, Millicent Martin, Patrick Mower, Hinge and Bracket, Lily Savage and Val Doonican ... to name but a few in this short space. Notable productions which were given their premiers at the Coliseum, going on to fly the nest, were *Saturday Night At The Crown, Fur Coat and No Knickers, The Rocky Horror Show, Having A Ball* and *Spend, Spend, Spend*.

In 1987 the Coliseum celebrated its centenary, and an appeal was launched by Dora Bryan. In addition, the last two decades have seen other appeals, several refurbishment, development and improvement schemes (for example, in 2005 a new studio theatre 'The Where-House') and lots of contributions (financial and otherwise) from friends and colleagues from past and present. Additionally, a continuing reputation for its contributions to the world of theatre has rewarded it with several coveted awards. In short it is as lively as ever! This extremely pleasant theatre, sandwiched between *Coronation Street* country and the beautiful *Last of the Summer Wine* country – and responsible for creating many of their 'stars', plus other favourite TV characters – continues to uphold its traditions, close to the heart of the repertory movement, in true form. Long may it reign!

Coventry Belgrade Theatre

This theatre represents a marker in the British theatrical story, being the first to be built after the Second Word War – opening in March 1958 – and the first Civic Theatre in the country, erected by the local authority and run by a trust. Its features are also highly typical of the time – demonstrating new priorities. With a no-frills, almost cinematic approach its house dispenses with any hint of the frippery of past generations, and places an emphasis on intimacy with the stage and good sightlines, with stalls and one circle only and linking side-boxes (current seating capacity 866). It has an apron stage when the orchestra pit is not in use, and a proscenium almost pretending not to be a proscenium – perhaps hinting towards some of the alternative configurations that would emerge in other venues during the ensuing decades.

The overall effect, even today, is pleasing and vibrant – the warm crimsons of the upholstery working well with the polished plain and clean surfaces of this pristine house! It also has good front of house spaces which, from the start, were utilised for other areas of social activity (exhibitions, concerts, etc.), open in addition to performance times, and ensuring that the building plays an important role within the community. That role was further extended in its early days, when members of the company actually lived in flats belonging to the theatre network! The Belgrade's opening was a royal occasion – before HRH The Duchess of Kent – and its name derives from the Yugoslav city, recording thanks and acknowledgement for a gift of timber provided by them during the rebuilding of Coventry, and used in the fabric of the auditorium. It is an English Heritage Grade II listed building.

The Belgrade has several claims to fame, not least, another first when in 1965 it piloted the very first TIE company – the forerunner of the TIE (Theatre In Education) movement – which was to become national, then even international. Basically this valuable resource takes theatre, sometimes via actor-teachers, into educational establishments to work with students through presentations and workshops. Always at the forefront of the community, the Belgrade is noted for its work beyond the theatre complex, in a range of activities that take theatre out to the people, involving local theatre companies, and encouraging national and international companies into the city.

Back on stage, the Belgrade presents a wide range of shows – from high drama to musicals, comedy to pantomime, interspersed with some one-night concerts and a few weekly tours. It is primarily a producing theatre with most productions running for three weeks (as opposed to the two-weekly 'rep' which was once the norm at this and other venues some years ago). It therefore builds its own sets and makes its own costumes. It has an excellent

Coventry Belgrade Theatre: the first civic theatre to be built in the country combines audience comfort and technical adaptability.

record for 'bums on seats' – the 1990s starting out by achieving the status of fourth best attended theatre funded by the Arts Council – reflecting a regime of presenting popular entertainment with an emphasis on accessibility. Many of the Belgrade's contemporaries in other regions had, by this time, adopted a similar community-focused approach, in some cases replacing former programmes that had attracted only minority interest. It has also always encouraged new writing, greatly aided by its smaller Studio space which has proved an invaluable asset to writers and directors as well as actors, and some of the work has been held to acclaim, and has gone on to national tour, festivals (such as Edinburgh), and even the West End.

A few of the names that the reader will recognise, and who have at one time or another contributed to the Belgrade's success as members of the Company include Trevor Nunn, John Gunter, Joan Plowright, Michael Crawford, Frank Finlay, and Leonard Rossiter.

The Belgrade was a pioneer of post-war British theatre and yet, via its many and varied quality artistic and cultural activities – in and beyond its excellent Coventry venue – remains at the forefront. The latest initiative is a massive new building development project at the theatre, with a grand completion expected in 2006. The major features will include a new 300-seat auditorium in addition to the existing main house, new rehearsal facilities, lifts, loos, etc., and extensive upgrading and refurbishment of existing services and facilities, thus ensuring a continuation of their acclaimed success well into the twenty first century.

A view from the stage showing the stalls, circle and side-boxes.

6 ALTERNATIVE FORMS

The traditional proscenium stage is not the only successful form of theatre and, here and there, exists happily alongside more diverse alternatives…

- *Scarborough, Stephen Joseph Theatre (1936)*
- *Bolton Octagon Theatre (1967)*
- *Sheffield Crucible Theatre (1971)*
- *Northampton, Derngate (1983)*
- *Leeds, West Yorkshire Playhouse (1990)*

Scarborough, Stephen Joseph Theatre

The SJT has earned a place in this book upon two chief counts: firstly it is a perfect example of a theatre which differs from the traditional, for its main auditorium is presented in the 'round'; secondly the present building represents a superb conversion from its former use as a cinema.

Prior to the 1930s the word 'Odeon' would probably have conjured up, in most people's minds, visions of a Grecian hillside; however, as the decade progressed, increasingly that vision would become exchanged for one of the local cinema in the High Street, as countless 'picture palaces' were to emerge all over the country – the product of the golden age of cinema building – and a good proportion of them from the 'Odeon' chain. But the vision would also be clear-cut, for not only did these buildings have a name in common, they also had a definitive trend – the inspiration of their creator, Oscar Deutsch – so that both internally and externally, with their streamlined appearance of curves and straight lines and art deco decoration, their origins would be instantly recognisable. And so prolific was their emergence that the name 'Odeon' even became known as "**O**scar **D**eutsch **E**ntertains **O**ur **N**ation"!

Many, sadly, in the progress of time with its changing whims and new inventions, have been lost or irretrievably altered. Bingo, in umpteen cases, took over from the silver screen and for years has protected a number of remarkable buildings. However a more recent trend has found even bingo to be a precarious saviour as the expectations of its participants, and competition and rivalry between clubs, have spurred entertainment companies to provide purpose-built bingo halls of ever increasing grandeur, capable of accommodating more luxurious and specialised facilities. Thus the formerly converted cinemas and theatres are finding themselves once again compelled to redundancy or other means, their amenities no longer being considered acceptable for present day anticipations, and so the threat of demolition or radical alteration lingers. Others, of course, were long since turned over to a wide variety of alternative uses and even those that have remained as cinemas have, in lots of instances, had their very hearts ripped out to provide for multiple screenings.

The Scarborough Odeon (with seats for 1700 in stalls and circle) survived intact and in use as originally intended longer than many – until 1988 – when it was finally forced to close its doors. When those doors were to reopen in April 1996, it was the result of the happy marriage between theatre-building

Stephen Joseph Theatre: The Round – the main house with 403 seats. A 'trampoline' mesh extends over the whole area upon which technicians can walk to gain easy access to the lighting, etc.

and theatre-company, when the Scarborough Theatre-In-The-Round moved in following extensive conversion and refurbishment. Those adaptations have irrevocably eliminated nearly all traces of the original cinema auditorium, save for a few removable bits and pieces which were carefully salvaged and cleverly incorporated into other areas of the modifications, and parts of the McCarthy (the SJT's second auditorium) where the original film projection holes can still be seen. But the transformations as a whole can be described as none other than jubilant, retaining all of the original features with every possible opportunity.

The story of the Scarborough Odeon began upon its completion in 1936. Cinema was increasingly becoming big business and a number of companies in the country had formed chains and circuits which were rapidly growing to satisfy the demand. No longer being content with the acquisition and refashioning of old theatres and music halls, prominent in the very earliest stages of cinematography, the fierce rivalry of the major circuits impelled the building of new super-cinemas in a quest to be the best! There were also many business deals and take-overs in the power struggle, and the biggest companies obviously fared better with the film suppliers.

Oscar Deutsch formed the Odeon chain in 1933, and it was to become the eighth largest circuit. In 1931 he had had control of six cinemas, but by 1937 he owned more than three hundred, thirty-six being built in that year alone. In 1934, Harry W. Weedon, Architects, joined the Odeon group, and prior to the outbreak of war in 1939, the practice was to design, or act as consultant architect for, over 250 cinemas — Scarborough being one of them, actually being designed by Cecil Clavering, chief assistant to Harry Weedon, and Robert Bullivant.

The Odeon building provides the third home for the Stephen Joseph Theatre (formerly known as the Theatre-In-The-Round). Stephen Joseph had been impressed by theatre in the round in America and was intent upon setting up a company in England. After much searching for satisfactory premises, the first theatre in-the-round (indeed, in England) opened in a small room above Scarborough's public library in 1955. It became extremely successful and remained there until 1976, when it then moved into Scarborough's (former) Boys' High School, before becoming finally established (opening in 1996) in the Odeon. Stephen Joseph was born in 1921, the son of the actress Hermione Gingold and publisher Michael Joseph. Sadly, he died from cancer in 1967, but it is notable that his vision has influenced many of the newer theatre forms which have since developed in different parts of the country, and that his

The lighting rig, the 'trampoline', and below, the stage and 'round' seating.

The McCarthy – the second space – with 165 seats and an end-on stage.

original dream triumphantly lives on. One of those pioneering success stories is featured in part 7 (the Manchester Royal Exchange Theatre).

The SJT Company has an admirable reputation and its policy features new writing alongside conventional works. Its artistic director is Sir Alan Ayckbourn, famed playwright, who has been associated with the theatre, apart from a short break, from the early Stephen Joseph days. Activities extend far beyond the production of shows, encompassing education and outreach programmes featuring talks, training and workshops etc. and covering all aspects of theatre such as writing, acting and directing – and in particular involving young people.

One of the most exiting characteristics of the theatre is the splendid integration of the old and the new. All modern conveniences have been provided for the public and company alike, but in the McCarthy auditorium, as in the bars, corridors and entrance halls and, of course, with the exterior, the 'Odeon' remains delightfully in evidence at every turn!

The main auditorium is, literally, theatre-in-the-round, with five tiered rows of seating along each of the four sides (totalling 403), and providing an extremely intimate centre space with perfect sightlines. The performers' entrances and exits are made via three 'vomitoriums' which are linked by a 'runround' beneath the seating, and a very novel feature is the trampoline mesh – a Canadian idea – not unlike wire netting, which is stretched over the whole space, several feet below the lighting. This allows the technical crew to dispense with ladders when adjusting the lanterns, for they can literally walk around on the mesh (in the absence of the audience) high above the entire auditorium. Another innovation is the stage floor, which can be lowered to the basement and workshops below, allowing a full set to be made up on any one of three palettes, which can then be raised into place in the theatre.

The second auditorium (the McCarthy) has an end-on stage fronted by tiered seating totalling 165, and is formed from the original Odeon circle. Here, in addition to dramatic works, films are also shown on certain days of the week, utilising the original projection room. Even the seats have been saved from the old cinema and, together with the new – but replica – carpet, and art deco panels on the side-walls retrieved from the former auditorium, much of the 'thirties' charm is retained.

Indeed it is this charm – which is carried through nearly all of the public areas – that has made the conversion so remarkable. Careful attention has been paid to detail so as to ensure that the 'ingredients' which gave the Odeons their unanimity – such as light fittings, designs in threes (look at the skirting-boards) and especially the beautifully reproduced carpet are all as they were in Oscar's day. It must also be said that his wife, Lily Deutsch, is known to have had much influence upon the original interiors.

Finally one, very pleasing, innovation that cannot be overlooked is the atrium – a glass shaft inserted into the very centre of the building, which runs from the roof to the basement, letting in natural light to all of the rooms along its course. As the audience passes through the atrium *en route* to the 'Round' it splendidly aids the transition from the 'thirties' era to the present day and *vice versa.*

On a personal note I have to say that whenever I have the chance to visit Scarborough's delightful seaside town I always try to make it coincide with a visit to the Stephen Joseph, and have never been disappointed. I have on several occasions seen productions at the old High School and at the Odeon and, from an audience point of view, it seems to me that there is very little difference between the old and the new 'Rounds'. This is pleasing when one considers that the possibilities afforded by the new building have not been allowed, in the name of advancement, to detract from the original concept and principles which have been meticulously preserved. But the surroundings are so much nicer now which, after all, can only help to make a night out at the theatre (or cinema!) complete.

Bolton Octagon Theatre

This great little modern theatre, with its glass street frontage, attractively beckons the potential customer towards a range of activities from eating, drinking and meeting in its pleasant and vibrant front-of-house spaces to, of course, its main function as a playhouse. Equally at the forefront in 1967, the year of its construction, its auditorium was considered avant-garde because of its unique adaptability, which could offer several vastly differing playing formats and, as a fully professional venue, was noted as being the first of such in the country. It was designed by Geoffrey H. Brooks, won a national Civic Trust award in 1968 and was officially opened by Princess Margaret.

All of the formats are open-stage, with varying seating capacities up to 380, depending on whether a round, thrust, horseshoe or end-on configuration is used, and are housed in an elongated octagon, obviously promoting the name of the theatre which is, itself, hexagonal in shape. The sightlines are excellent and with no seat further than nine rows from the action a wonderful intimacy is achieved, and some quite impressive sets involving differing levels and connecting staircases have been utilised over the years with great success. A studio theatre was added in 1987, now named 'The Bill Naughton Theatre' in honour of the playwright who was brought up in Bolton, famous for *Alfie*,

Spring and Port Wine and *The Family Way* – indeed the Octagon's first production was the world premiere of his *Annie and Fanny*.

The Octagon is obviously a firm favourite with the people of Bolton and the surrounding area and was built for approximately £95,000 from public donation. More recently, in 1992/1993, an appeal brought in further funds, allowing refurbishment and development, and 1997 more refurbishment and major works were enabled following an award of £1.68 million from the Arts Council of England's National Lottery Board. Business sponsorship, the North West Arts Board and the Arts Council of England have also played key roles in supporting the theatre. It was voted Best Entertainment Venue 2005 by listeners of Tower FM.

Truly a regional theatre for the people, the Octagon has many strings to its bow. It is essentially a producing theatre but its own productions are interspersed with some touring from other companies, co-productions, and one-night stands of varying content. It runs many youth, education, outreach and community programmes, often involving other agencies, and makes a huge cultural contribution to the North West.

Bolton Octagon Theatre: this small and delightful auditorium is shown in its "thrust" configuration and is exceptionally intimate.

Sheffield Crucible Theatre

The importance of the Sheffield Crucible is probably not widely appreciated – except to the most theatrically discerning – for not only does it represent one of the finest examples of an open 'thrust' (promontory) stage, its design was greatly influenced by those already renowned in that discipline – notably Sir Tyrone Guthrie with his Festival Theatre at Stratford, Ontario and the Guthrie Theatre, Minneapolis and Tanya Moiseiwitsch, his associate designer. Both were actively involved in the initial concepts in Sheffield although, sadly, Tyrone Guthrie died shortly before the new theatre was to open. In addition to the main house, the Crucible also incorporates a small studio space whose format can be changed as required, which, together with the reopened Victorian proscenium-stage Lyceum Theatre (see part 2) across the way, surely makes Sheffield one of the most theatrically diverse and prosperous cities in the country today.

The present-day Crucible has much to owe to its predecessors, and its 'ancestry' can be traced back as far as 1919. This is a story not just of a wonderful building but one that mirrors closely the developments of regional theatre throughout the country – both from a social-cultural point of view and also in the style of building which housed their activities. As a producing theatre its roots are steeped in the principles of repertory – discussed upon other pages – and may have been prompted by some of the pioneer companies such as those at Manchester (1907), Liverpool (1911 - see part 5), and Birmingham (1913 - see part 5) whose success generated establishments in several parts of the country. Also of note was the growing interest, from the last decades of the 1800s, of amateur entertainments. Improving conditions had given the workers opportunities out of which had developed choirs, bands, orchestras and, not least, amateur dramatics, etc. – often emerging from chapels, Sunday Schools, factories and works' societies, and stimulating, by the turn of the century, an avid fascination in localised music and drama.

In Sheffield, then, it all began in 1919 with an amateur dramatic society run by the YMCA – the St Philip's Settlement Dramatic Society – and they performed their plays at the 'Little Theatre' in Shipton Street. Their work was of a high standard and prolific and by 1921 they renamed themselves the 'Sheffield Repertory Company' and became independent from the YMCA. By 1924 they moved to larger premises (South Street Schoolroom with prices at 8d. and 1/2d. downstairs and 2/4d. and 3/6d. upstairs – the dearest price including a cushion), and by 1928 had moved again to a former temperance hall (Townhead Street) owned by the British Legion, originally erected in 1855. This they converted to become the Sheffield Repertory Theatre, eventually (in 1938) to be renamed the Sheffield Playhouse. A distinguished audience on the opening night included Miss Lilian Bayliss!

As with all other theatres in the country, the outbreak of World War Two in September 1939 meant that the Playhouse had to close. Basically, the Company moved to Southport for the duration of the war years and although another company was eventually set up in Sheffield from the November, business was not great. This led to permanent closure of the Playhouse in June 1940, after which it was used as a store and subsequently sank into a deplorable condition.

After the war it was refurbished, however, and resumed business and then in 1953/4 the Company moved out for a second time (to the Library Theatre) whilst the theatre underwent an extensive reconstruction.

The Playhouse symbolised a typical provincial 'weekly-rep'-type theatre, with seating for 541 on two levels (stalls and circle) and presented a cosy, intimate, modern (in early twentieth century terms) atmosphere, exchanging the opulence and gilt of theatres of an earlier age for a more practical, somewhat pleasingly homely atmosphere. It was exceedingly loved by the people of Sheffield, and had a regular following. Although prior to the war a pattern of weekly-changing productions had been established, once the war was over this altered to two-weekly, amending policy again in 1963 to three-weekly. I suppose I use the term 'weekly rep' generically to describe the type of provincial theatre that had developed all over Britain, making good theatre accessible to ordinary people. Not only was it remarkable in this aspect, it

also provided training opportunities at grass-roots level to many an aspiring young actor, director, stage manager and not least, writer – allowing for the production of new works.

In Sheffield, some of the notable names that graced the Playhouse or trod its boards and went on to national fame, many through television or films, were Donald Wolfit, Bernard Miles, Alec Guinness, Paul Eddington, Patrick McNee, Patrick McGoohan, Keith Barron, Peter Baldwin, John Noakes, Jane Rossington, Anne Stallybrass, Peter Denyer, Nigel Hawthorne, Robin Nedwell and Gordon Kaye, to mention but a few.

By the early 1950s the Playhouse, like most other provincial 'rep' theatres (possibly at their height at this time), was enjoying a high amount of popularity. But let me not create any false impressions for while the Company had had their successes – starting out as amateurs, eventually hiring a number of professionals, and in 1934 becoming totally professional – the problem of finance had never been very far away. We must be grateful for the donations, grants, loans and sheer determination and hard work of the good people that had brought it thus far. It did, in fact, continue to enjoy its success until it closed in 1971, although many establishments in other parts of the country were not so lucky – the 'fifties seeing a gradual decline in them towards the closing of that decade.

The next decade (the 'swinging' 'sixties!) brought changes – in public attitudes and ideas, styles and thinking – and was probably, theatrically, the culmination period of many concepts and theories that had been kicking around since even before the war. Certainly once the war was over there had been an expansion in regional theatre *building* – and this reached its climax in the 'sixties – mostly, up to now, in a similar style to the Playhouse in size, design and policy, with many influenced by the art deco cinema genre. But the new found freedom of the 'fifties and 'sixties promoted, also, the execution of some of the different ideas that had been formulating: not least of these, theatre *forms*, such as the open-stage. The time had arrived to become liberated from pre-war ideals, and to try daring new things!

So in Sheffield, coinciding with the need for a new theatre owing to city redevelopment, came the decision that the replacement Playhouse should have a main-house with an open stage – disregarding the proscenium entirely – indeed: a *thrust* stage. Now what did Sheffielders think to that? Well … in truth, "not very much" was the exclamation from many. The decision, polemical, together with criticisms of the product that was put onto the thrust

Sheffield Crucible Theatre: when smaller audiences are expected several of the back rows are cleverly masked off behind black screens, as shown here, to promote greater intimacy.

stage and a persistent dilemma with the economics, would occupy the pages of local newspapers for some time to come. Suffice it to say that the old Playhouse had been greatly loved; the new Crucible Theatre (for that is what the replacement is called) was a world away from its predecessor – almost returning in style to the days of the Greek and Roman amphitheatres, but with all of the mod-cons! – and would need time to become established.

Nevertheless, the Crucible *is* a remarkable building, and fulfils all the expectations of any (prize-winning) new theatre built in its time (1971). Its name, the result of a competition, was an excellent choice for it represents the heritage of Sheffield – being a large melting pot used in steel making – translating, indeed, into a melting pot of ideas! It comprises a main house where the major productions are mounted, and a smaller studio space for experimental work, concerts, intimate drama, etc. There is also a copious amount of bar and promenade area – useful not only for socialising but also for exhibitions, sale of works, lunch time concerts, etc. in addition to a restaurant, a gift shop, and all of the usual ancillary support such as box office, cloak rooms etc. The whole is pleasingly carried out in concrete, glass, clean lines, and strong colours in a rather low building of pleasant masonry blocks.

Its claim to fame (or, arguably, infamy!) has to be the main house. Its stage *'thrusts'* 28 feet into the auditorium, whose seats, in a steep rake, surround it upon three sides, with none more than 59 feet away from its centre. There are also boxes to the sides on the facing (stage) wall, and the total capacity is 1013. The house certainly achieves one of the prime objectives of the open-stage (thrust, or in-the-round) principle – that of bringing the actors closer the audience – and an intimate performance will usually result.

But its critics may also argue that much is lost due to the lack of scenic potentiality. In their initial quest the 'new school', obviously intent on focusing attention onto the action rather than the scenic element, often incorporated platforms, steps and levels, etc. into their stages as alternatives to traditional scenic settings. Interestingly, at the Crucible, the stage was originally equipped with five moveable triangular towers (*periaktoi*), used to mask the back of the stage, to hang lighting or bits of scenery on for individual productions, and to match the generally anonymous tone of the auditorium. Eventually, however, the periaktoi were dispensed with, and there have been many excellent sets on the Crucible stage over the years – although obviously to a lesser degree than its proscenium neighbours would have demanded. One wonders whether some of the original strong ideals for 'alternative' theatre from the 'angry young' pioneers have been softened over time to fall in with actual public preference, although it has to be said that one of the principal briefs in the design of the building, was that of flexibility.

The stage itself has been likened to a jigsaw puzzle in that it is constructed of sections of birch ply, built upon subterranean metalwork. It is capable of innumerable configurations by the removal of these sections, even to the point of incorporating lifts, revolves, traps, etc. (In one play I attended, the whole was transformed into a lake with real water, upon which floated a boat where much of the action took place!) The area below can also accommodate large orchestras for musicals or opera. Above the stage a further innovation, often referred to as the 'egg box' because that is what it looks like – is the lighting grid. This is very versatile, allowing for a variety of lighting patterns, directional beams, etc. – all the more important owing to the lack of scenery, and closeness of the audience. Four bridges which follow the contours of the thrust stage service the grid, and these are 'underplanted' with the house lights – a myriad of star-lights set into a black surface – supposedly one for every seat in the house! Entrances to the stage are from the back, rear-stage, or from tunnels ('voms' – vomitoriums) which emerge in a gentle slope from below and within the first few rows of seating at each of the downstage (right and left) corners. The voms are equipped with dressing rooms for quick changes and carpeting for quietness of movement. The rear stage is fitted with nine bars upon which can be hung cloths, curtains, lighting etc., and an amount of limited flying is possible over the thrust stage – although there is no fly tower.

Performances in the main house are controlled from three boxes placed above entrance doors at the back of the auditorium. These accommodate the deputy/stage manager for issuing all of the cues and running the show, and sound and lighting facilities. There are excellent views of the stage and all are in direct communication via the usual cuelights and paging facilities, etc.

The studio is a fifty-foot square box, capable of seating up to about 250 people. The seats can even be taken out or, alternatively, may be set out to form an end stage, a theatre completely in the round, seating around three sides, or a diagonal arrangement. There is a similar lighting grid to that in the main house, although less sophisticated. The studio is accessed from the main foyer.

Although the Crucible grew out of the former Playhouse, which was a repertory theatre with its own resident company, today's operations are somewhat different. There is no longer a resident company of actors: groups of actors are now gathered together for each individual 'home' production.

In addition, a season's work will also be augmented by a certain amount of touring, where visiting companies are brought in. There is, however, a production department, comprising workshop staff, electricians, sound personnel, wardrobe and stage management, and much good work goes on here, so that it is still, predominantly, a producing theatre. To support all of this, the 'building' provides all of the required facilities – workshop space, rehearsal room, eighteen dressing rooms, green room, stage door facilities and the usual office accommodation.

A year's fare will include a selection of plays, a little opera, some dance, children's shows, youth theatre, one-night concerts, a musical or two and a Christmas show – not forgetting that for a number of years now the main house has also hosted the World Snooker Championships!

Although the Crucible is comparatively 'young' in terms of theatre buildings, consideration is now being given towards its being granted listed status – after all, it does attract a special and historical interest representative of its own period – besides being a house of national importance. Moves are also afoot for an extensive upgrading and refurbishment scheme, the likes of which will ensure that present day requirements are fully met, while simultaneously paving the way for a fabulous and exciting future.

A large bar area serves both the main house and the studio, in addition to daytime activities and catering, etc.

Northampton Derngate

Not only is Northampton one of England's biggest market towns, it also boasts one of the largest market squares, and with a myriad of fine buildings and a heritage to be traced well into the past, is abundant in colourful history. One of its historic buildings is the charming Royal Theatre, and this is examined in detail in part 1. However, it is the building to be found right next door that is for discussion here – the Derngate (theatre) – standing in total contrast to the Royal and, as a state-of-the-art multi-purpose venue, it has

attracted world-wide attention for its avant-garde design and technology.

And the story gets better – for these very special features are now to be built upon and enhanced – in a massive refurbishment and development programme which began in April 2005 when the theatre, and its neighbour, closed for a proposed period of 14 months. Firstly, taking advantage of the ideal strategic positions of each venue, and the fact that they are also, since 1999, managed by the same organisation (Northampton Theatres Trust Ltd.), the refurbishment will physically interconnect the two buildings via a superb new foyer. There will also be a new 'creativity centre' which will provide additional space for rehearsal, education and outreach activities. Secondly, the theatres themselves will be extensively upgraded.

At the Derngate it all started with a bus station and an old leather warehouse and concluded with a touch of the space-age! Indeed the elevation to Guildhall Road retains the original warehouse frontage erected in 1876, but the delights within spring from a much later period. Since the 4th April 1983 they have provided the town, community and surrounding area with one of the most advanced auditoriums in the world, capable of a metamorphosis that makes possible every theatrical, concert, conference, business presentation, and social event, imaginable – all to the highest standards of quality. There have been classical performances, pop concerts and plays; bands of all types; ballet and boxing; ice shows, gang shows, fashion shows, Christmas shows; circuses and opera and conferences and seminars; dinner-dances and election counts, antique fairs, art exhibitions, snooker, civic functions and wrestling; comedy and all that jazz! To name but only a few of the possibilities!

So how is this achieved? Because the auditorium can be transformed into several differing formats, each tailored perfectly to the particular requirement. I say perfectly because a theatre format is a theatre, and a concert hall format is a concert hall and so on, and not just an attempt to be these things. Not only can the physical shape be altered, but also so can the ambience! The four chief styles are described below:

The Lyric ... has a proscenium stage (with full flying facilities, lighting etc.) for theatre productions such as opera, ballet, drama and musicals. Seating for 1,198.

The Concert Hall ... is a traditional concert hall layout with no proscenium and seating to the front, rear and sides of the stage; for classical presentations – it is a favourite with some of the leading orchestras of the world, and also with popular artists. Seating for 1,464.

The Arena ... you may have seen snooker on television from here; also used as an ice rink, and for wrestling, theatre-in-the-round and even a full performing circus. Seating for 1,500.

The Flat Floor ... is used mainly for exhibitions and dinner-dance-type entertainment and can be combined with raked seating. Further space is also available in the foyers.

The transformations can usually be completed in the space of three to five hours depending upon the complexity, by a team of six. This is because within the auditorium 'room' are a number of wagons and towers – which carry the stalls seating and boxes – all, naturally, tremendously heavy. These are moved into position to form the various layouts required, by a system of screw-jack elevators and components worked on the hovercraft principle – initially developed by Boeing for the United States space program to enable heavy gear to be transported around the hangars. Thus, what on the face of it might seem

Northampton Derngate Theatre: it is difficult to imagine that this marvellous, permanent-looking, auditorium is so flexible.

a massive operation, can be performed comparatively quickly and easily.

Much interest has been shown in the technology and philosophy of the building from many leading countries of the world, and the Derngate has been pleased to respond by showing off its versatility and virtuosity. I can also think of many a town in Britain where, perhaps not being as strategically well placed as Northampton, has struggled to keep theatre alive. The Derngate's example, in many of these cases, could provide the perfect solution – by presenting the opportunity of multi-purpose use, linked to quality, when a variety of activities could then be accommodated in a complementary and mutual environment, with shared economic objectives.

The Derngate has attracted a wide range of leading performers and companies such as the London City Ballet, Simon Rattle and the Birmingham Symphony Orchestra, the re-formed D'Oyly Carte, Glyndebourne Touring Opera, Sadler's Wells Ballet, Vladimir Ashkenazy, and the resident orchestra is the Royal Philharmonic. Additionally, the Derngate has been rated in the top three best acoustic spaces in the country for classical music. Popular names such as Petula Clark, Des O'Connor, Van Morrison, Russ Abbot, Englebert Humperdink, Tom Jones, Howard Keel, John Dankworth, Brian Ferry and Dame Kiri Te Kanawa abound. During the Derngate's existence many performances have been patronised by members of the Royal Family.

To complete the spectrum, the Derngate has also been extremely popular with local organisations: providing quality technical support to local operatic societies, orchestras and choirs; ideal facilities for craft and antique fairs; several spaces for the exhibition and sale of photography, paintings, sculpture etc., and guided tours of the building – not to mention the huge conference, business and catering side – the space was kept continuously alive from morning until night. Having therefore already admirably satisfied the requirements of a successful cultural, entertainment and business centre, the completion of the latest grand refurbishment, eagerly awaited, will doubtlessly bring with it even more opportunities and exciting possibilities for the future reflecting their mission statement: "The best in live performance".

Leeds, West Yorkshire Playhouse

This splendid modern theatre turns our story full circle on two counts. Firstly its main house returns us almost to the times of the Greek amphitheatres, set up on their hillsides as they so often were, with seating in a steep semicircular arrangement around a semi-promontory stage (in this case, with all mod-cons, of course!). Secondly, as a regional producing theatre it epitomises some of the early repertory principles – for example, that which favours its artistic activity over profit. And for good measure the building itself enables all of the most important characteristics that, traditionally, have become synonymous with quality regional funded theatre. These are via its main house (the Quarry Theatre) and a second house (the Courtyard Theatre), rehearsal rooms, technical workshops, recording studio, costume hire, excellent foyer spaces, conference facilities, meeting rooms, function rooms, café, restaurant and bar, coffee shop, art gallery, etc. all of which now play a vital part in the artistic, cultural and social life of the city.

The seeds of the Playhouse were sown as far back as 1964 when a group of active campaigners, recognising that their city did not possess what many of their contemporaries had acquired – a theatre for the community: subsidised and accessible and with artistic freedom – fought relentlessly for a goal which culminated in 1970 with the opening of the original Leeds Playhouse. This was, basically, a sports hall converted into a theatre erected upon a site on the campus of the University and, as it turns out, the forerunner of the present prestigious, purpose-built venue opened in 1990, so additionally important as a trend-setter. Of equal note is the fact that the design of the main house of the present building is, in fact, a replica of the auditorium of the first building – its twenty years' success providing ample evidence for duplication.

The Quarry Theatre takes its name from the Quarry Hill area upon which the theatre now stands, following city centre redevelopment. It seats 750 in a broad curving single sweep surrounding a thrust stage (adaptable for orchestra pit, etc.) The main stage has full flying facilities, and it is in this house that all of the largest productions are mounted. Perfectly complementary to the house is a smaller space, the Courtyard Theatre, which has seating for 350 most of which is on bleachers, with some on surrounding galleries, and therefore adaptable to a number of formats. Although the Quarry is intimate enough for its size, the Courtyard is even more so: perfect for the smaller production – straight plays and the like – and I have seen some absolutely fabulous sets on its stage!

And so, conceived at a time when regional theatre was taking a close look at itself, the final result benefits not only from the original concepts of its pioneering forefathers, but also from the newer wave of thinking and financing. Some of these themes are shown below. 'Weekly rep' – once the staple diet of the provinces – long since replaced by longer productions, with more rehearsal time and increased quality, and cast per production; subsidised ticket prices – leading to accessibility for all; the content of productions aimed at a broader

The Quarry Theatre: the proscenium stage, which is equipped with full height flying facilities, can be fronted with a 'thrust' or forestage around which the seating is arranged in a single-tier fan.

audience, thus increasing audience numbers (a good thing financially too) whilst at the same time allowing for new works and experimentation; and community orientated – buildings open from morning until night offering a range of activities and community events in an atmosphere comfortable to all walks of life.

The West Yorkshire Playhouse benefits from all of these things: at the time of writing staging, annually, more than 1,000 performances and events to more than 250,000 people, and claiming the distinction, outside London and Stratford, of being the largest regional repertory company in the UK. Its main productions – of which there are usually around sixteen or seventeen in a year – vary greatly in content, including world premieres and transfers to London and other important outlets, and there is a great commitment to many types of artistic activity and youth and educational promotion.

The Courtyard Theatre: it is an adaptable space capable of a number of formats.

During its life, the West Yorkshire Playhouse has been presented with many prestigious awards, and the present building – modern and trendy, with bright colours and a unique vibrancy – provides the absolute as a launch pad for all of these quality events.

A spacious foyer not only supplies access to both theatres, but provides spaces for catering, entertaining, exhibition and retail opportunities, etc.

7 UNUSUAL HOUSES

Successful theatres can originate from the most unlikely situations…

- *Manchester, Royal Exchange Theatre (1874/1976)*

Manchester Royal Exchange Theatre

Now for something completely different! Not just a theatre, but a unique experience! And one which combines so many diverse, yet compatible, features that I have already heard the words 'spaceship', 'module' and 'Victorian' all comfortably mentioned within the same description. And an experience that will continue our story in the pioneering decades after the Second World War in the search of some for an alternative form of theatre – yet in this case one which can hark back as far as 1729. Now they don't come much more 'alternative' than that!

As in all stories, unconnected facts which just happen to coincide can sometimes lead to the most improbable conclusions – and in this story they did! Here was a theatre company that was looking for a home where it could operate along the principles upon which it had been founded – while simultaneously, looking for a purpose, lay a redundant monumental and majestic tribute to Victorian architectural accomplishment waiting to be reunited with its bygone glories: the former Manchester Royal Exchange.

The time was the early 1970s and a theatre company that had been formed in 1968 – the 69 Theatre Company – was presenting significant work at the Manchester University Theatre. The group included some of the members from a former company – the 59 Theatre Company – which, at the Lyric, Hammersmith a decade earlier had likewise presented meaningful works, and their overwhelming stimulus was a desire to create theatre away from what had become the traditional in post-war Britain. In particular they were anxious to provide, possibly courageously for the time, an alternative form of staging designed to bring audiences and actors together; one which would, in any event, remove the proscenium arch from the equation. And with a policy that would allow for new works and experimentation, and in the regions. It became clear that if the group were to achieve their ambitions to develop a theatre of provincial importance they needed a more prominent position in the city, minus the constraints of the existing accommodation.

When hope seemed to be quickly fading, following unsuccessful attempts to rouse interest in the City Council for a site and funding of a new theatre, the group became aware of the Royal Exchange Building – right in the centre of town – which had lain empty since it ceased to operate on the 31st December 1968. Could this provide a cheaper alternative to a completely new-build project and therefore be more easily obtainable? Could the two work successfully together? – On the one hand a modern theatre company striving to implement new and modern ideals; on the other the overwhelming space of a Victorian cotton exchange! We now know that answer is yes, and that the result is stunning. Encompassing the very best of both worlds the coalition achieves so much: the epitome of regeneration; the ideals of the theatre company; the return of entertainment to the Exchange; the life of past centuries 'reborn'; a present centre for a miscellany of artistic and social activity.

Now the Exchange had begun life in 1729 when Manchester was a small country weaving town. But a few years later the Industrial Revolution was to change all that – big time – with an amazing explosion of infrastructure: engineering, factories, mills, machinery, canals, belching chimneys, (eventually) railways, and slums. And affluence – depending upon which side of the factory smoke you lived! Manchester goods – the product of great indigenous talent – began to make a name in the world, and consequent trading became increasingly important: so much so that by the time Victoria came to the throne, were springing up an abundance of warehouses and trading spaces. The grandest trading space of them all of course – indeed, eventually to be bestowed its present name by Queen Victoria herself, following a visit with the Prince Consort in 1851 – was the Manchester Royal Exchange. Responding to the climate this was by now a second, superior, building from 1809 and by 1874 the third, present, structure was erected representing Manchester's immense commercial standing, and has been described as 'the biggest room in the world'.

Originating as a meeting and market place, and its principal occupation associated with the cotton industry (though not exclusively so), the Exchange has experienced real life – in a range of events and activities. It has seen great fortunes made, rampage from down-trodden workers, pioneers of the textile industry such as Richard Arkwright, John Kay and Samuel Crompton displaying their new ideas and machinery and, on occasions, hosted entertainments. In 1743 the first record of a performance; in 1760 a grand ball celebrating the coronation of George III; opera in 1773; a call for Shakespeare, although the authorities seemingly frowning upon drama but not music – perhaps mindful of the Theatre Licensing Act of 1737!

Another royal visit occurred in October 1921 when, following extensive additions to the Hall, King George V and Queen Mary performed an opening ceremony – on the 'Floor' – with no less than 15,000 people in attendance, all seated! What a thrilling sight! But in a changing world there were changing fortunes (a bit like with theatres, really!) and the next royal visit was to be in November 1953 when Princess Margaret came to reopen the hall after World War II bomb damage. Now half the size, this was sadly quite adequate to cope with the vastly reduced business – the exports of the cotton industry having substantially declined.

A period of success followed, but by the 1960s due to changes in working practices and in the cotton industry itself the end was nigh. And although the purchase of the Exchange Company by Jack Cotton and Charles Clore (whose interest was the value of the land and rents rather than the going concern) may have brought a stay of execution, the bubble burst on the 31st December 1968, and the Hall was thrust into darkness. By now the building, incorporating offices and shops in addition to the great empty Hall, passed into the hands of the Prudential Assurance Company. But the Hall had not yet had its day…

…Although the few intervening years of disuse deposited layers of dirt and grime over the vastness, once seen, the 69 Company immediately realised its potential as a theatre. By constructing an auditorium as a separate domain (which was to become known as the 'module'), and placing it *inside* the Hall, the artistic world was their oyster, while the remaining space adjacent to the new theatre would provide the perfect spot for the supporting (e.g. foyer, cloaks, box-office, shop, café-bar etc.) facilities. These facts worked well – an attraction of opposites – satisfying many of the objectives on both sides of the 'footlights' (though, of course, without the footlights!). The Hall scrubbed up beautifully to reveal oceans of pristine coloured marbles; and gleaming towering pillars supporting the high ceiling with its three huge glass

Manchester Royal Exchange Theatre: the old and the new – the exterior of the module within the great hall, glorious in vibrant materials and colour.

domes (the centre of which still bearing it's original inscription *"who seek to find eternal treasure must use no guile in weight or measure"*). And shafts of sunlight now poured onto the clean and modern lines of the glass and steel theatre module which, placed in the centre of the three-quarters-of-an-acre parquet flooring, provided the jewel in the crown!

Work on the Royal Exchange Theatre began 14th April 1975 and the official opening was performed on the 15th September 1976 by Lord Olivier. This followed the usual period of negotiations – kicked off in November 1972 – a lease from the Prudential, financial guarantees and promises from various bodies such as Manchester City Council, the Arts Council, etc., the formation of a Trust, an Appeal Committee, and many, many fund-raising events involving many, many people and so on. In May 1973 the 69 Theatre Company set up a temporary stage – a tent – in the Exchange building as part of a festival to mark the formation of 'Greater Manchester', from which much experience was gained towards their proposed future activities. Indeed, an offer made by the City to build a free-standing theatre on a green field site was rejected in favour of the Hall, as the Company now knew that it would easily provide the most suitable solution. In 1976 the 69 Theatre Company changed its name to the present Royal Exchange Theatre Company.

The theatre module, to the designs of Richard Negri – himself a director of the 69 Company – incorporated all of their ideals and it has to be said, is a remarkable contraption that must be seen to be believed! It is truly theatre-in-the-round, with seating for 750 on three levels, each of the galleries surrounding the stage and accessible via staircases and gantries. Fully enclosed, it has its own heating, air conditioning, acoustics, stage lighting system, opportunity for only minimalist scenery, and not much else. And it puts the actors amongst the audience and vice versa, and in that sense removes the traditional proscenium barrier concept, thus satisfying the Company's original ideals.

Before leaving the building, it is impossible not to mention Saturday 15th June 1996, upon which day at 11.15 in the morning an IRA bomb went off outside the theatre. Literally shattering the whole area, which earlier had been evacuated, the miracle is that there were no deaths or serious injury, but such was the destruction that even large buildings had subsequently to be demolished. As for the Royal Exchange, it fortunately survived demolition, but still had suffered extensive damage to its structure and, obviously, glassware. Is it not typical, however, that in times of disaster – wars and suchlike – the end result, of people pulling together for the common good, and the opportunity

A view which shows the interior of the module from the stage to the lighting rig, with the three levels of seating around.

for refreshed thinking, can often achieve great things? Here, coupled with an existing lottery application, now ratified, it became possible to refurbish the old building on a grand scale – retaining the best and reworking where necessary – so that today's rendition is quite dazzling.

Bright and cheerful, with coloured glasses casting a warm glow everywhere, the entire space has been used to maximum advantage, incorporating a new studio theatre with 120 seats, rehearsal room, dressing rooms, offices etc., a café/restaurant, bar, craft shop, book shop, box-office, raised walk-ways, lift to all levels, and comfortable seating, enticing the public to 'pop in' throughout non-playing times. Of course the 'jewel-in-the-crown' – the 'space-ship' of a module – was given a complete make-over and, fitted out with the latest technology, also ensures the very best in performance. So the 'whole' can truly be said to belong to the community – one of the fundamental goals – admirably providing it with the facilities for a range of activities from drama, concerts of every description, exhibitions, shows, entertaining, eating, drinking, to simply meeting.

The lighting rig.

The 'boards' at the Royal Exchange have been trodden by an illustrious array of actors, in an equally impressive line-up of productions. It is impossible to do justice to the numbers, but I pick out at random a few of the most famous players simply because, having heard of them they may be of more immediate interest to the reader: Tom Courtenay, Patricia Routledge, Richard Wilson, Eleanor Bron, Robert Lindsay, Irene Handl, Max Wall, Vanessa Redgrave, Charlie Drake, Julie Walters, John Thaw, Pam Ferris and Maureen Lipman, and stress that there have been many more, including those whose names may not so easily spring to mind, but whose work has also been exceptional. The productions ... well, feature such diversity – from high drama to farce, musicals to pantomime, and the writers, again where do I begin? Of course, all of the classical greats – Shakespeare, Sheridan, Chekhov, Moliere, to Rodgers and Hammerstein ... again a diversity ... Thornton Wilder, Noel Coward, Joe Orton, Arthur Miller ... to those from a little nearer home such as Walter Greenwood who used to try out some of his plays at Oldham Coliseum (see part 5).

Which brings me to the excellent writing tradition at the Exchange. During 30 years there have been over 70 world premiers here, clearly a result of a policy which encourages new writing by the provision of opportunity, and since the arrival of the Studio this possibility has further increased. Also there is clearly a strong and caring commitment to the successful future of British theatre generally – covering every aspect from design and technical to acting and directing – via a positive spectrum of events, starting with the youngest individuals upwards. There are workshops and talks, partnerships and links to other organisations, work experience, experiments, tasters, play readings, presentations, sessions, groups, and an absolute abundance of information, education, encouragement and guidance just for the asking...

...For a company whose original objectives were to break down the barriers of post-war theatre by putting the very stage amongst the people, it must be said that those objectives have been achieved ... but far beyond the confines of even such a glamorous and vibrant setting as is the Royal Exchange. Certainly there is no lack of weight or measure in the standards and aspirations seen here today, and those who enter are sure to find treasure, whether eternal or not...

8 AND WHAT OF TODAY?

Here are some examples of the latest houses ...

- *Llandudno, North Wales Theatre (1994)*
- *Salford, Lowry Centre (2000)*

Llandudno, North Wales Theatre

With clean modern lines this gleaming theatre occupies a prominent position on the sea-front promenade, its two corner towers projecting a somewhat jaunty image of the delights that might be found within.

To the left of it, and as part of the same complex, is a splendid conference centre equipped to provide the finest accommodation and facilities that any function could ever require and it is here, perhaps, that the story begins. It was officially opened on 27th October 1981 by HRH Prince of Wales and was initially conceived as a conference/leisure facility, consequently having three squash courts (converted to meeting rooms in a 1998 re-modelling) and a main hall which hosted indoor bowls and dancing alongside conference events.

Then during the 1980s, perhaps partly due to the diminishing theatrical accommodation in the town, the availability of adjacent land and an anticipated conference role, came the idea to build a theatre alongside. Original projections forecast its conference activity as being up to six months in a year but in reality – due to its incredible success as a theatre in its own right – this has been nearer to only one month! And so the state-of-the-art theatre that we have today, capable of staging all of the great West End productions in addition to major opera (the Welsh National Opera Company were in on the original consultation) and ballet, was duly built at a cost of £4.75 million, and officially opened by Prince Charles on the 3rd July 1994. The first show was a pro-am production of *Jesus Christ Superstar*.

The theatre was designed by the Ellis Williams Partnership from Liverpool, with a design and build contract with Mowlem Construction Ltd. (also from Merseyside) being the main contractor. Its association with the conference side of things means that, in addition to its 'normal' theatrical provision (which is excellent), it is also very adaptable, and the auditorium can be quickly transformed into a variety of formats, both for conference and theatrical use. The bleacher seating is electronically retractable and the very front stalls can be manually removed. Thus a fully flat floor is achievable which can be used for exhibitions, cabaret-style performance, promenade concerts and rock shows whose requirement might be a mixed standing/seating arrangement, etc. In its theatrical format it can seat 1505 in an impressive modern configuration of stalls, circle and balcony with the predominant colour being a pleasant cool blue. Complementary to the house are equally impressive front-of-house facilities, which include a first-class box office, suites, promenades, bars, breakout rooms, media gallery, and café-bars (a 40-seat café bar adjacent to the auditorium can be utilised for lunchtime readings, exhibitions and trade-fairs, etc.).

Behind the 14 metre wide x 8 metre high proscenium is equally as impressive with a stage of 13.7 metres' working depth – one of the biggest in Britain, a

Llandudno North Wales Theatre: one of the largest stages in Britain ensures that even the biggest of productions can be played here

20 metre high grid which has 58 single-purchase counterweight fly-line sets, band and dressing room accommodation for 80 (including 2 'star'), wardrobe, laundry, wig room, and offices for technical and visiting staff.

A theatre of such high standing has attracted only the best from the world of entertainment, and its large stage has presented opera and ballet, pantomime, classical music, drama, popular music, variety and comedy – all in spectacular fashion. To recite a few: the City of Birmingham Symphony Orchestra, London City Ballet, D'Oyly Carte, the Royal Liverpool Philharmonic, Carl Rosa Opera Company, Russian National Ballet. Its individual artistes are also wide ranging – Dame Kiri Te Kanawa, Joe Pasquale, Sarah Brightman, Ken Dodd, Jim Davidson, Tommy Steele, Su Pollard, The Hollies, etc. Premier shows have included *Blood Brothers*, *Five Guys Named Mo*, *Return to the Forbidden Planet*, *Whistle Down The Wind*, *Me and My Girl*, *Grease*, *Run For Your Wife* and many more. The North Wales Theatre presents spectacular shows to a wide catchment area – as far as Merseyside and Manchester – and, occupying the perfect spot on Llandudno's gently curving promenade, the town is especially fortunate in being able to provide the visiting holidaymaker with the ultimate in lavish entertainment.

The clean, modern, lines of the house guarantees a good view from every seat

Salford, The Lowry
(The Lyric Theatre and the Quays Theatre)

With roots firmly planted in the past, and a head clearly looking to the future, both aspects completely touching the lives of countless people, this fantastic visionary complex provides the perfect conclusion to my story, on a note of great optimism. Situated in the old 'Port of Manchester' – the docklands of a previous life and up to a few years ago the most unlikely place for such a venture – the Lowry and its upbeat neighbours have rejuvenated an area of immense decline, redundant from former glories.

On the banks of the Manchester Ship Canal, the artery which connected the city to the sea and which, opened by Queen Victoria in 1894, was to place Manchester firmly on the world map of trade, industry and commerce, has arisen a futuristic centre for the arts. Opening on the 28th April 2000, it includes galleries (notably devoted to the works of L. S. Lowry alongside other exhibitions), cafes, restaurants, bars, shops, and two theatres – the *Lyric* and the *Quays*. Additionally, the project at Salford Quays comprises the Plaza, an outdoor space fronting the Lowry which can accommodate performances and up to 7,000 spectators; the Digital World Centre; the Lowry lifting Footbridge; access and car-parking facilities. And the surrounding area is equally progressive – actually starting the ball rolling, and gradually replacing the once industrial landscape with modern waterfront developments, encompassing the main elements of housing, business and leisure, in an ongoing transmogrification.

Externally the architectural award-winning Lowry, designed by Michael Wilford and Partners, presents itself chiefly in steel and glass which, upon entering, tend to give way to the extremely vibrant colours of the foyers, promenades, terraces, decks, balconies and staircases. The theatres, which form the central portion of the building, continue the theme of the dominant

Salford Lowry: The Lyric Theatre – even in such a large house an intimacy is maintained via its impressive sweep, presented in a colour scheme of sheer vibrancy.

The Lyric Theatre – a stage which boasts to be the largest in England outside London.

and striking colours with the purple *Lyric* and the red *Quays*. Between them they are able to cater admirably for the entire theatrical vocabulary of plays, musicals, opera, ballet, dance, children's shows and popular and chamber music etc., as they offer a great diversity of format.

The *Lyric Theatre* is the large one, with seats for 1,730 on the traditional stalls / dress circle / balcony configuration, which remain quite intimate with the proscenium stage for such a large house in view of its natural roundness and comparatively shallow balconies. The stage boasts to be the largest in England outside London – its area has been compared to the London Coliseum, and has 79 fly lines, over

The Quays Theatre – another vibrant colour scheme, here shown with an end-stage which can be transformed also into thrust, round, promenade and traverse, capable of staging a wide variety of works.

75 miles of ropes, can hang 40 tons of scenery, and affords good wing-space. The orchestra pit comes in three different sizes and so can appropriately house small ensembles, to a total of 125 players. The stage of the *Quays Theatre* is positioned adjacent to that of the Lyric's (they form the centre of the theatre complex, back-to-back) and, separated by a shared scene-dock and loading bay, provide ideal get-in/out for the visiting companies. The Quays is the small space, with seats for 466 and a highly flexible format, which can offer end-stage, thrust, round, promenade and traverse configurations.

The theatres are both receiving houses and their diversities and quality facilities are reflected in the interest shown from the best in the entertainment world, including some of the most prestigious national and international companies. Names already appearing on the bills of these theatres – still in comparative infancy and with a constantly increasing reputation – have included The Paris Opera Ballet, St Petersburg Ballet Theatre, Rambert Dance Company, The Birmingham Royal Ballet, The Halle Orchestra, Opera North, Scottish Opera, The Royal Shakespeare Company, Northern Stage Ensemble and English Touring Theatre. Many productions are billed as "straight from the West End" or "direct from Broadway" and, of course, there are solo artistes, comedy performers, singers, singer-songwriters and a range of bands etc. – even a *Sing-a-long-a-Sound of Music* and a *Sing-a-long-a-Joseph And The Amazing Technicolor Dreamcoat*! Similarly, nearer to home, the facilities meet the region's important community and educational requirements, resulting in many performing arts ventures, workshops, summer schools, talks and even holiday activities.

Capital Funding for the Lowry Project came from a variety of sources including The National Lottery - The Arts Council of England, The Millennium Commission, and Heritage Lottery Fund, and The European Regional Development Fund, English Partnerships, Salford City Council, Trafford Park Development Corporation, North West Development Agency, and private sector support.

This book is about theatres, and therefore not the place to examine all of the other major and breathtaking features and events offered by the Lowry and its environs. Suffice it to say that these can be sampled by visiting the Lowry, perhaps for a full day or more, when a tour of the theatres might also be a possibility subject to their working-accessibility. Or take in a performance; have dinner, or a drink, and absorb the wonderful ambience; see it at night, beautifully lit – see its reflections in the Ship Canal! Reflections that will repeatedly conjure links with the past, but unfailingly ensure that there will always be a stage for the arts of tomorrow.

ACT I CURTAIN

This final chapter could so easily have been called 'Final Curtain' – but that, I felt, would have been a mistake for although *my* particular story has concluded, it is a story that will, nevertheless, continue endlessly. There will most certainly be a second Act as the present theatres continue to play out their roles and new ones are born – their fates influenced, just as in the old days, just as now, by public demand or lack of it, finances and economics, new technologies and new preoccupations – life!

My story has taken the reader on a journey of nearly two-hundred-and-fifty years – from 1766 to the present day – and has travelled many miles to present the delights of just forty theatres: a mere handful in the scale of things! But a special handful, all of which I have personally sampled and, like picking up sweets in a shop, have enjoyed tremendously. They represent a diversity of richness and beauty which clearly shines out today, illustrative of our present great theatrical wealth while many, additionally, remain symbolic of a marvellous heritage. The Act I curtain cannot fall, therefore, without mentioning some of their creators – the craftsmen and artisans without whom these achievements would not exist.

As with the theatres themselves, in dealing with the skilled workforce I have aimed at being selective and representative, to provide merely a flavour and a background in an attempt to elucidate the complete story. Therefore in my choice of architects, for example, I have featured just a handful of those most prolific in *theatre* projects – the specialists, shall we say – while there are also others whose theatres, perhaps of equal calibre, represent a much smaller proportion, if not the only example, of their work.

To begin with I choose Charles John Phipps (1835-1897) whom I see as the bridge between the Georgian and Victorian periods. His work on view in this book can be seen in Bath Theatre Royal, Northampton Royal Theatre & Opera House, Nottingham Theatre Royal (of especial note is the entrance portico) and Wolverhampton Grand Theatre, and he also did the 1867 interior at Newcastle Theatre Royal prior to it being replaced by the present Matcham one. Other venues of note not included here but which can still be seen include the Edinburgh Lyceum, the Glasgow Theatre Royal and in London the Garrick, the Lyric and the important Her Majesty's.

His style has been described as 'classical' and is elegant and his work was obviously superb; however a major setback occurred in 1887 when his Exeter Theatre Royal burned down killing no less than 160 for which his design was severely criticised*. There were, of course, other venues, many now demolished, and makeovers to buildings that already existed. He is considered to be a leading and outstanding architect of the period in the annals of the theatre.

Frank Matcham (1854-1920), it has been said, built more than a hundred music halls and theatres and possibly designed a hundred more. Those on view here show the interior of Newcastle-upon-Tyne Theatre Royal, Nottingham Theatre Royal's auditorium reconstruction of Phipps' original, Wakefield Theatre Royal & Opera House, Bristol Hippodrome, Buxton Opera House and Blackpool Grand. He also built the first Blackpool Opera House, since replaced by two later versions. Additionally there were countless makeover jobs.

He was born in Newton Abbot, Devon, afterwards moving to Torquay. In the mid-1870s he began working for J. T. Robinson, the London architect who was, importantly, also the surveyor to the Lord Chamberlain; married his daughter in 1877, and took over the firm in 1878 upon the death of his father-in-law.

His particular claims to fame were a high regard for safety, and his iron cantilever designs, which permitted theatre balconies to be constructed without the need for visible supporting pillars. His early style especially is unrestrained, going in for an absolute *furore* of ornamentation like no other – in his houses the entertainment begins *before* the curtain rises! His work was prodigious and he was soon building for the big theatre magnates, in particular the Moss' Empires chain.

Other notable examples of his theatres which can still be seen include the Aberdeen His Majesty's, the Belfast Grand Opera House, the Cheltenham Everyman and the Glasgow King's and in London the Hackney Empire, the Victoria Palace, the London Coliseum and the London Palladium. In more recent times he appears to have become somewhat of a 'cult' figure among theatricalists as his flamboyant auditoriums have at last been appreciated as exceptional, some of his houses actually dedicating specific areas of their operations to his honour, e.g. 'Matcham Court' and 'Matcham's Bar' at Blackpool Grand.

Of his seven years' training, W. G. R. Sprague (1865-1933) received the first four of them while articled to Frank Matcham. He went on to build many theatres of distinction of which the Lincoln Theatre Royal (with Bertie Crewe) and Sheffield Lyceum are featured within these pages. His style is generally elegant as many of his remaining London houses will demonstrate, but he was not beyond the frivolous either as his proscenium arch at Sheffield reveals, as do old photographs of some of his now-demolished music halls. Other notable examples of his work are all, sadly, confined to London: they include the Albery, the Aldwych, the New Ambassador's, the Gielgud, the St Martin's, the Strand (Novello) and Wyndham's. He was born in Australia, arriving in England prior to his professional training.

Lastly I mention Sunderland's W. & T. R. Milburn which, starting with the two brothers, was to become a very sizeable firm of architects. Their work displayed in this book includes the Empires at Sunderland and at Liverpool – two venues that, although quite different, typify the mighty houses they put up in various parts of the country. Their later buildings, born in the emerging cinema age, reflect the influences of that period – the advent of the super-cinema era – and other important venues not included here are the Southampton Mayflower and the London Dominion. More recently I feel that some of their works have been unfairly criticised as theatres.

But the story does not even end with the architects, for the theatre and music hall business also spawned a whole workforce of associated trades. Naturally the quantity of business put by firms whose purpose was not solely confined to the theatre, e.g. the builders, plumbers and joiners etc. was boosted, but in addition grew a whole army of establishments aimed at satisfying requirements specifically generated by the entertainment profession. A flip through newspaper reports of the day, which in the absence of modern TV coverage, often went to town when reporting the opening of a new theatre or music hall, by listing the entire artisan entourage, will confirm.

Here, an amalgam of reports dated Friday 12 July 1878, Tuesday 19 November 1878, Friday 7 June 1889, Tuesday 24 July 1894 and even Monday 9 March 1925 and Saturday 15 July 1939 gives us clues of the shopping lists of the entrepreneurs of the day: brickwork, masonry, iron foundry, plastering, zinc work, tiles, fountains, stained glass, slating, heating, terra cotta, bar fittings, plaster figures, decorations, gas fittings, ornamental brass and marble works, bronze statues, upholstering, the iron curtain, stage gas fittings, limelight tanks and other stage apparatus, new scenery, plaster decorations, chairs and seating, fireproof curtain and stage apparatus, art decorations, fibrous and solid plasterwork, tip-up chairs, swing doors, patent spring hinges, all the draperies, marble, alabaster and Venetian Terrazzo decoration.

Of particular note I highlight just a handful of firms who were involved in creating the wonderful art work – paintings and plasterwork – that is so ubiquitous within these pages – again these 'decorators' worked prolifically – Jonas Binns of Halifax (Wakefield Theatre Royal & Opera House, Buxton Opera House, Blackpool Grand Theatre); Felix de Jong & Company (Newcastle Theatre Royal, Bradford Alhambra Theatre, Buxton Opera House); The Plastic Decoration Company, Strand, London (Blackpool Grand Theatre).

And to conclude I give the last word to the twenty-first century – but carefully and appropriately enveloping those immediately preceding. The latest technologies have allowed a number of very fine modern buildings to arise in recent times to great effect, as these pages will demonstrate; a new age which also, however, inevitably now exposes the inadequacies of some of our predecessors by comparison. To remedy this we have seen that many of these have introduced schemes of improvement ranging from the modest to major multi-million-pound makeovers. With tremendous results, the general theme appears to have been to preserve the 'heritage' fabric and to re-work the utilities to modern day standards. Several firms have been responsible for these metamorphoses but again I wish to be representative and so confine my example towards the prolific, therefore mentioning just one specific organisation, that of the Renton Howard Wood Levin Partnership whose talents within these pages include the following examples: Newcastle Theatre Royal, Northampton

Royal Theatre, Nottingham Theatre Royal, Wolverhampton Grand Theatre, Sheffield Lyceum Theatre, Bradford Alhambra Theatre, Sheffield Crucible Theatre (new build) and Northampton Derngate Theatre.

So now take all of these observations and with them let the heavy, extravagant, luxurious, resplendent and richly ornate house curtain very slowly descend, to rise again only upon another good fortune, another era.

---

*The story of the Exeter Theatre Fire is fully described in David Anderson's book, also published by Entertainment Technology Press, see page 294.

BIBLIOGRAPHY

Information for this book has been drawn from, cross-matched and corroborated by, many sources: substantially from material provided by the relevant individual theatre managements themselves such as 'potted' histories and technical details, from additional articles, from theatre programmes and posters, from newspaper reports, from websites, from many libraries' local-studies and archives departments, from theatre tours, and with reference to the following publications, all of which I have enjoyed reading tremendously.

Ackroyd, Harold, *The Liverpool Stage* (Amber Valley Print Centre, 1996); Adamson, Simon H., *Seaside Piers* (B. T. Batsford Ltd., 1977); *An Illustrated History of the Tyne Theatre and Opera House, Newcastle upon Tyne* (booklet, 1987); Allen, Tony, ed., *Britain – Library of Nations* (Time Life Books); Atwell, David, *Cathedrals of the Movies* (The Architectural Press Ltd., 1980); Aylett, J. F., *In Search of History 1714-1900* (London: Edward Arnold, 1985); Bainbridge, Cyril, *Pavilions on the Sea* (Robert Hale Ltd.,1986); Bamford, Phil., 1995 project co-ordinator, *Manchester 50 Years of Change* (London HMSO, 1995); Band, Barry, *Blackpool Grand Theatre - 1894-1930* (1993); Band, Barry, *Blackpool Grand Theatre - 1930-1994* (1994); Band, Barry, *Blackpool Grand Theatre - the early years* (1986); Band, Barry, *Blackpool Opera House 1939-89* (1989); Barker, Kathleen, *The Theatre Royal Bristol 1766-1966* (The Society for Theatre Research, 1974); Begg, Jonathon and researched by Prescott, Cyril, *Scarborough's Renewed Splendour* (Scarborough Borough Council Tourist & Amenities Dept., 1981); Beynon, Robin, ed., including contributions from Ashton, Geoffrey; Mackintosh, Iain and Thompson, Nicholas, *The Theatre Royal Nottingham 1865-1978*; Booth, Michael R., *Theatre in the Victorian Age* (Cambridge University Press, 1995); *British Theatre Directory* (Richmond House Publishing Company Ltd., 1995); Broadbent, R. J., *Annals of the Liverpool Stage* (Edward Howell, 1908); *Buxton Opera House* (brochure produced by theatre, undated); Carter, James, *Oldham Coliseum Theatre - The First Hundred Years* (Oldham Leisure Services, 1986); Cinnamond, Martin, ed., *The Theatre Royal, Newcastle upon Tyne* (Proscenium Publications, 1988); Clementson, Diana W., *The Theatre Royal at Lincoln* (a Drama Study, the Training College Lincoln, c1960 unpublished, held at Lincoln Central Library); Cook, Philip, *How To Enjoy Theatre* (Judy Piatkus Ltd., 1983); Critchlow, Cyril, *The North Pier Story, Blackpool* (2002); Culpin,

Christopher with Turner, Brian, *Making Modern Britain* (Collins Educational, 1987); Cunningham, Hugh, *Leisure in the Industrial Revolution c.1780-c.1880* (Croom Helm, London, 1980); Dunn, Kate, *Exit Through the Fireplace* (John Murray, 1998); Earl, John and Sell, Michael, ed., *The Theatres Trust Guide to British Theatres 1750-1950* (A. & C. Black (Publishers) Ltd., 2000); Eyles, Allen, *ABC The First Name in Entertainment* (Cinema Theatre Association, 1993); Eyles, Allen, *Old Cinemas* (Shire Publications Ltd., 2001); Foulkes, Richard, *Teach Yourself Theatre* (Hodder Headline plc., 1999); Fraser, M. F. K., *Alexandra Theatre, the story of a popular playhouse* (Cornish Brothers Ltd., 1948); Friends of the WTR&OH, *A Guide to the Theatre Royal & Opera House*; *The Georgian Theatre Royal and Theatre Museum, Richmond,* (Theatre Publication); Glasstone, Victor, *Victorian and Edwardian Theatres* (Thames & Hudson Ltd., 1975); *Grand Theatre & Opera House Leeds 1878-1978 - The First Hundred Years, The,* (Theatre Souvenir Publication, 1978); Grant, Neil, *History of Theatre* (Hamlyn, 2002); Haill, Catherine, *Fun Without Vulgarity* (The Stationery Office, London, 1996); Hardy, Clive, *Manchester since 1900* (Archive Publications, 1988); Hartnoll, Phyllis, ed., *The Oxford Companion to the Theatre* (Oxford University Press, 1983); Hartnoll, Phyllis, *The Theatre - A Concise History* (Thames & Hudson Ltd., 1998); Hewett, Hilda, *A Week at the Seaside* (Robert Hale, London, 1955); Hocking, Joseph, *A Brief History of the (Wolverhampton) Grand* (Internet article, 1998); Holdsworth, Peter, *Domes of Delight, the history of the Bradford Alhambra* (Bradford Libraries & Information Service, 1989); Holland, Phil and Smith, Mark, *Memories of Blackpool* (True North Books, 1997); Law, Jonathon; Wright, John; Salad, Mark; Isaacs, Alan; Pickering, David; Fergusson, Rosalind; Alexander, Fran; Isaacs, Amanda; Roberts, Jenny; Thompson, Lynn; Lewis, Peter; *Brewer's Theatre* (Cassell, 1994); Leacroft, Richard and Helen, *Theatre and Playhouse* (Methuen, 1984); Leacroft, Richard, *The Development of the English Playhouse* (Methuen, 1973); Leitch, Michael, ed., *Your Day at the Lowry* (The Lowry Press, 2002); Lindley, Kenneth *Seaside Architecture* (Hugh Evelyn, London 1973); Llewellin, Mark, *They Started Here* (P. & D. Riley, 2000); Loudon, Andrew, *The Amazing Story of the Famous City Varieties Music Hall, Leeds* (pamphlet, undated); Lowndes, William, *The Theatre Royal at Bath* (Redcliffe Press Ltd., Bristol, 1982); *Lyceum Theatre Appeal Book* (Sheffield Libraries and Information Services, 1990); Mackintosh, Iain and Sell, Michael, ed., *Curtains, or a New Life for Old Theatres* (John Offord (Publications) Ltd., 1982); McCoola, Ros., *Theatre In The Hills* (Caron Publications, 1984);

McMahon, Pelham and Brooks, Pam *An Actor's Place* (The Bluecoat Press, 2000); Mellor, G. J., recalled, *A Hundred Years of the City Varieties* (article, undated); Mellor, G. J., *The Northern Music Hall* (Frank Graham, 1970); Newlyn, Doreen, *Theatre Connections, a very personal story* (Walter Newlyn, 1995); Nicoll, Allardyce, *The English Theatre: a short history* (Thomas Nelson & Sons Ltd., 1936); Norris, Fred, *Birmingham Hippodrome 1899-1999* (Birmingham Hippodrome Theatre Trust Ltd., 1999); Norwich, John Julius, *Britain's Heritage* (Granada Publishing Ltd., 1983); O'Brien, P. J., *A People's Culture* (George Alen & Unwin Ltd., 1975); Oswald, Harold, *History of the Theatres Royal in Newcastle upon Tyne* (Northumberland Press Ltd., 1936); Palmer, Steve, *Blackpool: Centuries of Progress* (1999); Percy, Richard J., compiled, *Scarborough in the 50's and 60s* (Stroud: Chalford, 1994); Pertwee, Bill, *Beside the Seaside* (Collins & Brown, 1999); Pertwee, Bill, *Pertwee's Promenades and Pierrots, One hundred years of seaside entertainment* (Westbridge Books, 1979); Price, Victor J., *Birmingham Theatres, Concert and Music Halls* (K. A. F. Brewin Books, 1988); Read, Jack, *Empires, Hippodromes and Palaces* (Alderman Press, 1985); Reid, Francis, *Designing for the Theatre* (A. & C. Black (Publishers) Ltd., 1989); Reynolds, Ernest, *Northampton Repertory Theatre* (1976); Rix, Brian, *Tour de Farce* (Hodder & Stroughton, 1992); Robinson, Alistair, *Sunderland Empire: A History of the Theatre and its Stars* (TUPS Books, 2000); Robinson, Christopher, *A History of the Bristol Hippodrome 1912-1982* (ed., Martin Cinnamond, Proscenium Publications, 1982); Robinson, Ken, *Newcastle upon Tyne's Theatres Royal 1788-1870* (reprinted from an article in Archaeologia Aeliana, 5th series, volume 15, 1987); Rowell, George and Jackson, Anthony, *The Repertory Movement, a History of Regional Theatre in Britain* (Cambridge University Press, 1984); Royal Exchange Theatre Company, The, *Words & Pictures 1976-1998,* including an adaptation of *The Biggest Room in the World* by Robert Scott (The Royal Exchange Theatre Company, 1998); Salberg, Derek, *A Mixed Bag* (Cortney Publications, Luton, 1993); Salberg, Derek, *My Love Affair with the Theatre* (Cortney Publications. Luton, 1978); Salberg, Derek, *Ring Down the Curtain* (Cortney Publications, Luton, 1980); Seed, T. Alec, *The Sheffield Repertory Theatre: A History* (The Sheffield Repertory Co., 1959); Senior, William, *The Old Wakefield Theatre* (Radcliffe Press, 1894); Sheffield Year Book and Record (various); Slinn, Bill, *The History of the Birmingham Hippodrome* (The Wensum Press, 1983); Southern, Richard, *The Victorian Theatre - A Pictorial Survey* (David & Charles, 1970); Stanton,

Sarah and Banham, Martin, *Cambridge Paperback Guide to Theatre* (Cambridge University Press, 1996); *The Story of the Theatre Royal, Bristol,* (The Trustees, 1981); Talbot, Richard, *The Regent Story* (1999); Taylor, C. M. P., *Right Royal Wakefield Theatre 1776-1994* (Wakefield Historical Publications, 1995); Todd, Barry, compiled, *Wakefield Theatre Royal & Opera House 1894-1994* (1994); Trussler, Simon, *Cambridge Illustrated History of British Theatre* (Cambridge University Press, 1994); Turner, Brian and Palmer, Steve, *The Blackpool Story* (1976); Walker, Brian Mercer, ed., *Frank Matcham: Theatre Architect* (Blackstaff Press, 1980); Weightman, Gavin, *Bright Lights, Big City* (Collins & Brown, 1992); Whittaker, Meredith, *The Book of Scarbrough Spaw* (Barracuda Books Ltd., 1984); Wickham, Glynne, *A History of the Theatre* (Phaidon Press Ltd., 1992); Williams, Ned, *Wolverhampton's Theatres - Beyond the World of the Grand* (Internet article); Wilmut, Roger, *Kindly Leave the Stage!* (Methuen London Ltd., 1985); *York Theatre Royal, 1744-1994, 250 Years at the Heart of York* (Theatre Souvenir Publication, 1994); Young, John N., *A Century of Service* (NODA Ltd., 1999).

INDEX

Little Theatre, Sheffield 237
Liverpool and Merseyside Theatres Trust
    208
Liverpool Repertory Company
    208, 210, 212
Liverpool Repertory Theatre 211, 212, 214
Lloyd, Marie 90, 119, 158
Lloyd George, David 103
Lloyd Webber, Andrew 118
Lockwood, Margaret 110, 119
London City Ballet 247, 264
London Coliseum Theatre 14, 81, 92, 160,
    163, 166, 268, 273
London Criterian Farce Company 175
London Festival Ballet 90, 127, 132, 166
London Hippodrome 162
London Palladium 126, 273
Longthorne, Joe 184
Loss, Joe 119, 127, 136, 151, 165
Lowry, L. S. 265
Lumley, Joanna 146
Lune, Ted 184
Lupino, Stanley 133
Lyceum Theatre, Birmingham 141
Lyceum Theatre, Edinburgh 272
Lyceum Theatre, Sheffield 9, 22, 105, 273
Lyndhurst, Nicholas 43
Lynn, Vera 119, 136, 197
Lyric Theatre, Hammersmith 252
Lyric Theatre, London 272
Lyric Theatre (Lowry) 265
Lytton, Henry 184

MacKeith, C. H. 196
Mackintosh, Cameron 119
Macklin, Larry 184
Macready, William Charles
    25, 35, 42, 49, 73
Magill, Ronald 223
Mangnall & Littlewood (Manchester) 193
Margaret, Countess of Snowdon, Princess
    44, 234, 254
Marie, Rose 184
Martin, Millicent 146, 223
Martin-Harvey, Sir John 127

Marvin, Hank 90
Mary, Queen 254
Matcham, Frank 9, 10, 14, 58, 60, 62,
    69, 72, 81, 89, 94-96, 105, 110,
    131, 154, 157, 159-162, 169, 170,
    172, 176, 192, 193, 198, 199,
    201, 206, 272, 273
Matthews, Jessie 90, 127, 196, 223
Mayall, Rik 43
Mayflower Theatre, Southampton 129, 273
Maynard, Bill 119
McCarthy Auditorium 230, 232
McGoohan, Patrick 239
McKenzie, Julia 50
McNee, Patrick 239
Melba, Paul 184
Melville, Frederick 95
Metropolis Management & Building Acts
    Amendment Act (1878) 13, 85
Middlemass, Frank 43, 223
Midlands Theatre Company 55
Mike and Bernie Winters 138, 166, 184
Milburn, W. & T. R. 115, 129, 273
Miles, Bernard 213, 239
Millar, Gertie 90
Millennium Commission 269
Miller, Arthur 259
Miller, Max 165
Mills, Hayley 146, 213
Mills, John 110, 146, 166
Milner, Edward 170
Miracle play 37
Mirren, Helen 119
Miss Saigon 73
Mitchell, Thomas 185
Mitchell, Warren 56, 213
Modley, Albert 127, 184
Moiseiwitsch, Tanya 236
Moliere 259
Monkhouse, Bob 190
Moore, Dudley 127
Moore, Kenneth 103
Morality play 11
Morecambe and Wise 132, 146
Morris, Dave 184

ENTERTAINMENT TECHNOLOGY PRESS

FREE SUBSCRIPTION SERVICE

Keeping Up To Date with

Theatres of Achievement

Entertainment Technology titles are continually up-dated, and all major changes and additions are listed in date order in the relevant dedicated area of the publisher's website. Simply go to the front page of www.etnow.com and click on the BOOKS button. From there you can locate the title and be connected through to the latest information and services related to the publication.

The author of the title welcomes comments and suggestions about the book and can be contacted by email at: joncar@gawber5.freeserve.co.uk

Titles Published by Entertainment Technology Press

ABC of Theatre Jargon *Francis Reid* **£9.95** ISBN 1904031099
This glossary of theatrical terminology explains the common words and phrases that are used in normal conversation between actors, directors, designers, technicians and managers.

Aluminium Structures in the Entertainment Industry *Peter Hind* **£24.95**
ISBN 1904031064
Aluminium Structures in the Entertainment Industry aims to educate the reader in all aspects of the design and safe usage of temporary and permanent aluminium structures specific to the entertainment industry – such as roof structures, PA towers, temporary staging, etc.

AutoCAD – A Handbook for Theatre Users *David Ripley* **£24.95** ISBN 1904031315
From 'Setting Up' to 'Drawing in Three Dimensions' via 'Drawings Within Drawings', this compact and fully illustrated guide to AutoCAD covers everything from the basics to full colour rendering and remote plotting.

Basics – A Beginner's Guide to Special Effects *Peter Coleman* **£9.95** ISBN 1904031331
This title introduces newcomers to the world of special effects. It describes all types of special effects including pyrotechnic, smoke and lighting effects, projections, noise machines, etc. It places emphasis on the safe storage, handling and use of pyrotechnics.

Basics – A Beginner's Guide to Stage Lighting *Peter Coleman* **£9.95** ISBN 190403120X
This title does what it says: it introduces newcomers to the world of stage lighting. It will not teach the reader the art of lighting design, but will teach beginners much about the 'nuts and bolts' of stage lighting.

Basics – A Beginner's Guide to Stage Sound *Peter Coleman* **£9.95** ISBN 1904031277
This title does what it says: it introduces newcomers to the world of stage sound. It will not teach the reader the art of sound design, but will teach beginners much about the background to sound reproduction in a theatrical environment.

A Comparative Study of Crowd Behaviour at Two Major Music Events
Chris Kemp, Iain Hill, Mick Upton **£7.95** ISBN 1904031250
A compilation of the findings of reports made at two major live music concerts, and in particular crowd behaviour, which is followed from ingress to egress.

Electrical Safety for Live Events *Marco van Beek* **£16.95** ISBN 1904031285
This title covers electrical safety regulations and good pracitise pertinent to the entertainment industries and includes some basic electrical theory as well as clarifying the "do's and don't's" of working with electricity.

The Exeter Theatre Fire *David Anderson* **£24.95** ISBN 1904031137
This title is a fascinating insight into the events that led up to the disaster at the Theatre Royal, Exeter, on the night of September 5th 1887. The book details what went wrong, and the lessons that were learned from the event.

Fading Light – A Year in Retirement *Francis Reid* **£14.95** ISBN 1904031358
Francis Reid, the lighting industry's favourite author, describes a full year in retirement. "Old age is much more fun than I expected," he says. Fading Light describes visits and experiences to the author's favourite theatres and opera houses, places of relaxation and re-visits to scholarly intitutions.

Focus on Lighting Technology *Richard Cadena* **£17.95** ISBN 1904031145
This concise work unravels the mechanics behind modern performance lighting and appeals to designers and technicians alike. Packed with clear, easy-to-read diagrams, the book provides excellent explanations behind the technology of performance lighting.

Health and Safety Aspects in the Live Music Industry *Chris Kemp, Iain Hill* **£30.00** ISBN 1904031226
This title includes chapters on various safety aspects of live event production and is written by specialists in their particular areas of expertise.

Health and Safety Management in the Live Music and Events Industry *Chris Hannam* **£25.95** ISBN 1904031307
This title covers the health and safety regulations and their application regarding all aspects of staging live entertainment events, and is an invaluable manual for production managers and event organisers.

Hearing the Light – 50 Years Backstage *Francis Reid* **£24.95** ISBN 1904031188
This highly enjoyable memoir delves deeply into the theatricality of the industry. The author's almost fanatical interest in opera, his formative period as lighting designer at Glyndebourne and his experiences as a theatre administrator, writer and teacher make for a broad and unique background.

An Introduction to Rigging in the Entertainment Industry *Chris Higgs* **£24.95** ISBN 1904031129
This book is a practical guide to rigging techniques and practices and also thoroughly covers safety issues and discusses the implications of working within recommended guidelines and regulations.

Let There be Light – Entertainment Lighting Software Pioneers in Interview *Robert Bell* **£32.00** ISBN 1904031242
Robert Bell interviews a distinguished group of software engineers working on entertainment lighting ideas and products.

Lighting for Roméo and Juliette *John Offord* **£26.95** ISBN 1904031161
John Offord describes the making of the Vienna State Opera production from the lighting designer's viewpoint – from the point where director Jürgen Flimm made his decision not to use scenery or sets and simply employ the expertise of LD Patrick Woodroffe.

Lighting Systems for TV Studios *Nick Mobsby* **£45.00** ISBN 1904031005
Lighting Systems for TV Studios is the first book written specifically on the subject and is now the 'standard' resource work for the sector as it covers all elements of system design – rigging, ventilation and electrical as well as the more obvious controls, dimmers and luminaires.

Lighting Techniques for Theatre-in-the-Round *Jackie Staines* **£24.95** ISBN 1904031013
Lighting Techniques for Theatre-in-the-Round is a unique reference source for those working on lighting design for theatre-in-the-round for the first time. It is the first title to be published specifically on the subject, it also provides some anecdotes and ideas for more challenging shows, and attempts to blow away some of the myths surrounding lighting in this format.

Lighting the Stage *Francis Reid* **£14.95** ISBN 1904031080
Lighting the Stage discusses the human relationships involved in lighting design – both between people, and between these people and technology. The book is written from a highly personal viewpoint and its 'thinking aloud' approach is one that Francis Reid has used in his writings over the past 30 years.

Model National Standard Conditions *ABTT/DSA/LGLA* **£20.00** ISBN 1904031110
These *Model National Standard Conditions* covers operational matters and complement *The Technical Standards for Places of Entertainment*, which describes the physical requirements for building and maintaining entertainment premises.

Mr Phipps' Theatre *Mark Jones, John Pick* **£17.95** ISBN: 1904031382
Mark Jones and John Pick describe "The Sensational Story of Eastbourne's Royal Hippodrome" – formerly Eastbourne Theatre Royal. An intriguing narrative, the books sets the story against a unique social history of the town. Peter Longman, director of The Theatres Trust, provides the Foreword.

Pages From Stages *Anthony Field* **£17.95** ISBN 1904031269
Anthony Field explores the changing style of theatres including interior design, exterior design, ticket and seat prices, and levels of service, while questioning whether the theatre still exists as a place of entertainment for regular theatre-goers.

Practical DMX *Nick Mobsby* **£16.95** ISBN 19040313668
In this highly topical and important title, the author discusses DMX Networks and Installations and the equipment involved. Analogue networks are also covered and there is an introduction to Ethernet networks and cabling systems.

Practical Guide to Health and Safety in the Entertainment Industry
Marco van Beek **£14.95** ISBN 1904031048
This book is designed to provide a practical approach to Health and Safety within the Live Entertainment and Event industry. It gives industry-pertinent examples, and seeks to break down the myths surrounding Health and Safety.

Production Management *Joe Aveline* **£17.95** ISBN 1904031102
Joe Aveline's book is an in-depth guide to the role of the Production Manager, and includes real-life practical examples and 'Aveline's Fables' – anecdotes of his experiences with real messages behind them.

Rigging for Entertainment: Regulations and Practice *Chris Higgs* **£19.95** ISBN 1904031218
Continuing where he left off with his highly successful *An Introduction to Rigging in the Entertainment Industry*, Chris Higgs' second title covers the regulations and use of equipment in greater detail.

Rock Solid Ethernet *Wayne Howell* **£24.95** ISBN 1904031293
Although aimed specifically at specifiers, installers and users of entertainment industry systems, this book will give the reader a thorough grounding in all aspects of computer networks, whatever industry they may work in. The inclusion of historical and technical 'sidebars' make for an enjoyable as well as informative read.

Sixty Years of Light Work *Fred Bentham* **£26.95** ISBN 1904031072
This title is an autobiography of one of the great names behind the development of modern stage lighting equipment and techniques.

Sound for the Stage *Patrick Finelli* **£24.95** ISBN 1904031153
Patrick Finelli's thorough manual covering all aspects of live and recorded sound for performance is a complete training course for anyone interested in working in the field of stage sound, and is a must for any student of sound.

Stage Lighting Design in Britain: The Emergence of the Lighting Designer, 1881-1950 *Nigel Morgan* **£17.95** ISBN 190403134X
This book sets out to ascertain the main course of events and the controlling factors that determined the emergence of the theatre lighting designer in Britain, starting with the introduction of incandescent electric light to the stage, and ending at the time of the first public lighting design credits around 1950. The book explores the practitioners, equipment, installations and techniques of lighting design.

Stage Lighting for Theatre Designers *Nigel Morgan* **£17.95** ISBN 1904031196
This is an updated second edition of Nigel Morgan's popular book for students of theatre design – outlining all the techniques of stage lighting design.

Technical Marketing Techniques *David Brooks, Andy Collier, Steve Norman* **£24.95** ISBN 190403103X
Technical Marketing is a novel concept, recently defined and elaborated by the authors of this book, with business-to-business companies competing in fast developing technical product sectors.

Technical Standards for Places of Entertainment *ABTT/DSA* **£30.00** ISBN 1904031056
Technical Standards for Places of Entertainment details the necessary physical standards required for entertainment venues.

Theatre Engineering and Stage Machinery *Toshiro Ogawa* **£30.00** ISBN 1904031021
Theatre Engineering and Stage Machinery is a unique reference work covering every aspect of theatrical machinery and stage technology in global terms, and across the complete historical spectrum.

Theatre Lighting in the Age of Gas *Terence Rees* **£24.95** ISBN 190403117X
Entertainment Technology Press has republished this valuable historic work previously produced by the Society for Theatre Research in 1978. *Theatre Lighting in the Age of Gas* investigates the technological and artistic achievements of theatre lighting engineers from the 1700s to the late Victorian period.

Theatres of Achievement *John Higgins* **£29.95** ISBN: 1904031374
John Higgins affectionately describes the history of 40 distinguished UK theatres in a personal tribute, each uniquely illustrated by the author. Completing each profile is colour photography by Adrian Eggleston.

Walt Disney Concert Hall – The Backstage Story *Patricia MacKay & Richard Pilbrow* **£28.95** ISBN 1904031234
Spanning the 16-year history of the design and construction of the Walt Disney Concert Hall, this book provides a fresh and detailed behind the scenes story of the design and technology from a variety of viewpoints. This is the first book to reveal the "process" of the design of a concert hall.

Yesterday's Lights – A Revolution Reported *Francis Reid* **£26.95** ISBN 1904031323
Set to help new generations to be aware of where the art and science of theatre lighting is
coming from – and stimulate a nostalgia trip for those who lived through the period, Francis
Reid's latest book has over 350 pages dedicated to the task, covering the 'revolution' from
the fifties through to the present day. Although this is a highly personal account of the
development of lighting design and technology and he admits that there are 'gaps', you'd be
hard put to find anything of significance missing.

Go to www.etbooks.co.uk for full details of above titles and secure online ordering facilities.